To Daddy —
Happy Anniversary
From —
Alice Pat & Peter
September 2, 1976

John D Mahoney
4240 Lafayette Rd
Jamesville NY 13079

A Treasury of American Clocks

Benjamin Willard, Roxbury, Massachusetts; dial, numbered 209
and engraved, "Ab Hoc Momento Pendet Æternitas."

A
TREASURY
OF
AMERICAN
CLOCKS

BROOKS PALMER

Macmillan Publishing Co., Inc.

NEW YORK

Collier Macmillan Publishers

LONDON

EIGHTH PRINTING 1975

Macmillan Publishing Co., Inc.
866 Third Avenue, New York, N.Y. 10022
Collier Macmillan Canada, Ltd.

Printed in the United States of America

TO

DYNA

MY BELOVED WIFE

WITHOUT HER INSPIRATION AND HELP

THIS BOOK NEVER WOULD

HAVE BEEN

ACKNOWLEDGMENTS

MANY good people have been of great assistance in the preparation of this book. As large a project as this is, it is beyond the abilities of any one person. Among many, the author is especially indebted to the following:

James W. Gibbs and *Charles Sumner Parsons* for specially photographing extensively the treasures of their personal collections for this book.
Edwin B. Burt for making available illustrations of the masterpieces shown at the NAWCC 1959 convention.
Irving Cooperman for many pictures of his clock collection, taken by his son Stephan.
Frederick Fried for his excellent advice, and pictures from his unique collection.
Dr. Donald Shelley, Director, and *William Distin*, Curator, of the Ford Museum, Dearborn, Michigan, for special photography of clocks of the museum and permission for their use.
Jesse Coleman for distinguished long-time research and practical information, which he so willingly shares.
Edward and *Victoria Ingraham* for sharing, over the years, a vast knowledge of Connecticut clocks and their making.
Charles O. Terwilliger for ingeniously making available certain desirable timekeepers of an earlier day.
Earl T. Strickler for his excellent *Bulletin* editing, including a column, and for the Museum Columbia, which he established.
Howard G. Sloane for knowledge and examples from his personal collection, which he gladly shared.
Dr. Charles A. Currier for his guidance and helpful research.

Others who were both generous and gracious are:

Howard Alcorn
George H. Amidon
Willard I. Andrews
Nelson O. Argueso
Lee J. Atwood
Amos and Betty Avery

Seward J. Baker
A. P. Balaban
Mr. and Mrs. Barny
Lockwood Barr
E. A. Battison
The Frank Beavens
The Ivan Belknaps
Dr. Anthony Benis
William O. Bennett
James Biddle
The George Bizlewiczs
Russell V. Bleeker
Nelson Booth

Bernie and Rose Brandt
M. H. Brightman
Dr. Warner D. Bundens
Mrs. Yves Buhler
C. W. Burnham

William Ely Chambers
David Chapman
Frank Church
Dr. Howard Coates
George Coggill
Cyril Cogswell
Ben Cohen
Robert and Camille Condon
Dr. Alfred G. Cossidente
E. A. Cramer
G. B. Cutten

Paul W. Dann
Carl Dauterman

The R. B. Davisons
Paul de Magnin
Robert Dickey
Earl S. Dowd
Elisha Durfee

Dallas H. Edwards

John G. Flautt
George F. Ford
Fraser R. Forgie
Kenneth Fox
Robert Franks
The Albert Freys
Henry B. Fried

D. F. I. Galer
John Graham
Charles F. Graf
Bernard A. Grassie
Efroim Greenberg

Samuel Greenglass
Robert J. Gunder

F. Earl Hackett
Curator Orville and Jo Hagans
Curator C. Wesley Hallett
Robert and Charlotte
    Hamilton
Lee S. Hamm
S. V. Harlow
Westley B. Hauptman
Robert Hodgson
Rev. Paul Hollingshead
Evers Hushman

Jerome Paul Jackson
Mrs. Thomas Jarman
Samuel Jennings
James A. Jensen
Earl W. Jones

Dr. Charles Kennedy
The Howard Klocks
Joe D. Kordsmeier
The Samuel Kutners

Dr. S. P. Lehv
Ira W. Leonard

Johnston V. McCall
John R. McGinley
Roy MacKinney
Leroy Makepeace
James E. Merrill

The Willis Micheals
The Willis I. Milhams
John A. Miner
George E. Missbach
Edward Mitchell
William C. Moodie
John E. Moore
Reginald and Shirley Morrell
Walter Mutz
John Myers

Cyrus H. Nathan
James Niehaus
Olin S. Nye
C. J. O'Neil

Donald K. Packard
The Ned Parkhursts
Albert L. Partridge
Edwin C. Pease
The Louis W. Petersens
Charles E. Poore
David Proper
David Protas
Edwin Pugsley

Herbert S. Rand
Bernie Ratzer
Dr. Robert L. Ravel
John L. Rawlings
Bayard L. Renniger
Walter Roberts
S. C. Robinson
The Jean Louis Roehrichs

E. E. Runnells

The Anthony J. Sakowichs
The George Scammons
John Scharp
John Schenk
Frederick Mudge Selchow
Dr. Douglas A. Shaffer
J. R. Shawn
Charles E. Smart
Gordon Kroll Smith
George Stearns
Harold E. Smith
Elmer O. Stennes
The Warren Stumpfs

Frank A. Taylor
Edward Thomas
Floyd Thoms
Samuel Thorne
Urban Thielman
Haskell Titchell

David Urquhart

Vincent Versage

John S. Walton
Ray Walker
The Arthur Warshauers
Theodore Waterbury
Janos Weinberger
Clyde and Myrtle Welch
Alice Winchester

Dr. E. L. Zalinski

And for pictures and help given most freely from members of the National Association of Watch & Clock Collectors, the author's thanks are due. This organization is a rapidly growing group of now about 10,000 clock and watch enthusiasts. Headquarters is at Columbia, Pennsylvania, with some sixty local chapters spread around the country and abroad. If some names, through error, have not been included on this list, it is hoped the author will be forgiven.

B. P.

CONTENTS

FOREWORD

Brooks Palmer's *A Treasury of American Clocks*, which complements his *The Book of American Clocks*, published in 1950, represents a landmark in the pictorial history of American craftsmanship. The interval of nearly twenty years between the publication of the two books has been dictated by the author's continuing research and his insistence on reproducing the most outstanding examples of the clockmaker's art.

The illustrations in this book, with their accompanying captions, show the development through more than two centuries of the American clock and timepiece, from the early grandfather clock through windup alarms and electric timepieces. For the reader a sentence in explanation may be helpful. In the strictest sense a timepiece merely keeps time—as, for example, the ordinary watch. A clock, in addition to being a timepiece, strikes the hours, or even half hours or quarter hours—sometimes with chimes. Another interesting point is the mistaken modern use of IV rather than IIII, which was the original Roman form. The effect is to make the dial seem to tilt to the left, because of the imbalance between the VIII and IV opposite each other. Use of the IV rather than IIII clearly marks the clock as modern.

Through the illustrations which follow, the reader will become familiar with examples of historic and modern types of both clocks and timepieces, many of them things of particular beauty, such as the Banjo and the Steeple. But the clocks and timepieces illustrated here show something perhaps more important than beauty—namely, the resilience, the ingenuity, and the imagination of the makers of one of the great industries of America.

Grandfather Clocks

The name grandfather clock is now in general use, replacing "Tall," "Hall," "Floor," or "Long Case." The first grandfather clocks were made in Europe around 1680 by individual craftsmen, working by hand.

Grandfathers were the first type of clocks to be made in the Colonies. They became the world's first mass-produced product, when they were manufactured by Thomas Harland in 1791.

American grandfather clocks have the following types of movements:

Brass—eight day, two weights
      one day, one weight
      eight day, spring powered—in later years.

Wood movement—one day, pull wind
      one day, dial wind
      eight day, two weight (rare)

Wood cases were made of various but beautiful designs.

1. Samuel Mulliken (1720–1756) Bradford, Massachusetts—later at Newbury Port. Here, he learned clockmaking with his brother, Nathaniel. Eighty-six inches high; *ca.* 1745.

CHARLES E. POORE COLLECTION

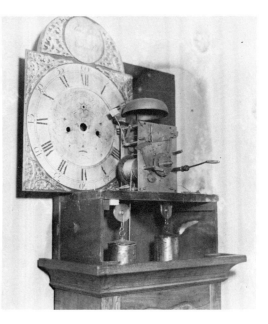

2. Samuel Mulliken, Newbury Port, Massachusetts. Grandfather clock with engraved brass dial and spandrels; eighty-four inches high; *ca.* 1752.

HENRY FORD MUSEUM

3. Samuel Mulliken, Newbury Port, Massachusetts. With hood removed, and dial placed in rear, showing the brass eight day, two weight movement, with the weights and winding key on time wind post.

BILLINGS COLLECTION,
DR. CHARLES CURRIER

4. Nathaniel Mulliken, Lexington, Massachusetts. Grandfather clock with flat top hood, maple case, eighty-eight inches high, *ca.* 1745.

WELLS COLLECTION,
OLD STURBRIDGE VILLAGE

5. Brass dial with spandrels, silvered chapter ring, engraving in boss of No. 5.

6. Nathaniel Mulliken, Lexington, Massachusetts. Grandfather clock, ninety inches high.

7. The dial of No. 6.

4

8. Benjamin Willard (1743–1803), Grafton, Massachusetts. Grandfather clock with "105" on dial. Eighty-eight inches high.

FREDERICK MUDGE SELCHOW COLLECTION

9. The dial, no spandrels of No. 8.

10. The brass eight-day, two-weight movement, with dead beat escapement of No. 8.

11. Benjamin Willard, Roxbury, Massachusetts; dial, Numbered 209 and engraved, "Ab Hoc Momento Pendet Æternitas."

ELMER STENNES
COLLECTION OF PICTURES

12. Simon Willard. Grandfather clock with white iron dial plus moon and calendar. No place name on dial. 92″x20″

HENRY FORD MUSEUM

13. The 30-hour movement; the cast brass support plates are reduced to save brass, but to provide sufficient support.

14. Preserved Clapp, Amherst, Massachusetts. Pine-cased grandfather 30-hour clock. Dial is of wood with brass spandrels, chapter ring of pewter, 80 inches high; *ca.* 1755.

AMOS AVERY COLLECTION

15. Gawin Brown, Boston, Massachusetts. Pine case is japanned and grained; 89"x21"; 11" dial; *ca.* 1766.

16. Paine Wingate, Haverhill, Massachusetts. White dialed grandfather clock; *ca.* 1817.

RAY L. WALKER COLLECTION

17. The eight-day brass movement.

18. Isaac Doolittle, New Haven, Connecticut. Engraved brass 10¾ inch dial with spandrels and boss dated "1745." 90½"x20½"

HENRY FORD MUSEUM

19. Thomas Harland, Norwich, Connecticut. Grandfather clock dial, dated "1776."

Housed in a typical Harland whales tails hooded case.

The names of the six tunes are not familiar today.

FREDERICK L. HANKS COLLECTION

20. Thomas Harland, Norwich, Connecticut, a great American clockmaker, the first to use interchangeable parts and mass production principles from 1791 on.

A fine, typical Harland grandfather clock with whales tails on hood and silvered dial with moon phase. 89½"x20½"; dial 10¼." ca. 1780.

HENRY FORD MUSEUM

21. Thomas Jackson, Preston, Connecticut. Hood with whales tails and three pineapple finials, after the manner of a Thomas Harland case. 89¼"x18¼"

HENRY FORD MUSEUM

22. Isaac Blaisdell (1738–91), Chester, New Hampshire. Grandfather clock with flat top hood; engraved brass dial with spandrels and calendar. Endless rope drive one-day metal movement using a single weight; *ca.* 1762.

WELLS COLLECTION
OLD STURBRIDGE VILLAGE

23. Richard Blaisdell (1762–90), Chester, New Hampshire, son of Isaac. The front of the movement of brass and iron; metal for plates kept at a minimum of endless rope drive one-day single weight clock movement.

C. S. PARSONS COLLECTION

24. Timothy Chandler (1764–1846), Concord, New Hampshire. Grandfather clock in maple case made by David Young. "Joiner" 90"x19"; 10" dial; *ca.* early 1800's.

25. The movement of No. 24, with rack and snail strike.

26. Christian Forrer, Lampeter, Pennsylvania. Flat top hood grandfather; 1-day brass movement with one weight, endless chain drive; 84"x20"; 10¾" dial; *ca.* 1748.

27. Jacob Eby, Manheim, Pennsylvania. Eight-day grandfather clock with center mounted sweep second and calendar hands; 100"x19"; *ca.* 1835.

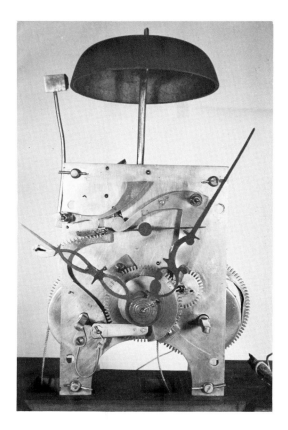

28. "Effingham Embree, New York" on moon dial of grandfather clock, with calendar slot; 90"x19½"; ten inch dial; *ca.* 1790.

HENRY FORD MUSEUM

29. Early Connecticut 30-hour, two-weight wood movement for a hang up or grandfather case. The wood dial had pewter chapter ring and spandrel; *ca.* 1765.

1959 SWAMPSCOTT CONVENTION

30. A typical Connecticut one-day pull up, two-weight (canisters filled with sand) wood dial, pendulum ball, and label; *ca.* 1810.

JOHN L. RAWLINGS COLLECTION

31. The back of the wood movement and dial.

32. Exploded train gear placement of 30-hour wood movement. Arranged on clear plastic racks and photographed by John L. Rawlings.

33. A. (Abraham) & C. (Calvin) Edwards, Ashby, Massachusetts. One-day wood weight movement in pine case. 87"x20"; 10¼" dial; *ca.* 1795.

C. S. PARSONS COLLECTION

34. The wood dial; the house is the home of the Edwards.

35. A. Edwards dial of clock similar to No. 33; no calendar dial; *ca.* 1795.

36. The one-day two-weight pull up wood weight movement used by the Edwards, a distinctively different Ashby-Ashburnham type.

37. Silas Hoadley, (1786–1870). Eight-day grandfather, pull up weights of seven lbs.; escape wheel and pendulum shown at the back of the movement.

GEORGE F. FORD COLLECTION

Grandmother Clocks

Grandmother clocks are diminutive editions of grandfather clocks, standing four feet or less in height.

There came to be a demand for these beautiful, smaller clocks from 1800 to 1830, and they were primarily made by a group of Boston clockmakers which included among others the Willards, Samuel Mulliken and Levi Hutchins.

The Massachusetts Shelf Clocks, also called "Half Clocks" or "Box on Box" are not too easily distinguishable from the grandmothers. They were made from 1780 to 1820.

38. B. Youngs, Schenectady, New York. Grandmother timepiece, winds at 6. 36"x11"; seven inch dial; pre-revolution.
HENRY FORD MUSEUM

39. B. S. Youngs, Watervleit, New York. Grandmother clock with name on both sides of dial; 36¼"x10"; 4½ inch dial; *ca.* 1770.

HENRY FORD MUSEUM

40. Samuel Mulliken, Newbury Port, Massachusetts. Grandmother clock with engraved brass dial; *ca.* 1780.

41. The movement.

42. Joshua Wilder, Hingham, Massachusetts. Grandmother clock, 43″x11¼″; six inch dial; *ca.* 1810.

HENRY FORD MUSEUM

43. The movement.

44. Noah Ranlet, Gilmanton, New Hampshire. Grandmother clock; *ca.* 1810.

EDWARD MITCHELL COLLECTION

45. Nathaniel Hamlin, Augusta, Maine. Grandmother clock, flat top case 43″x11″; seven inch dial; *ca.* 1815.

HENRY FORD MUSEUM

46. David Studley, Hanover, Massachusetts. Grandmother clock; 45"x14"; 6½ inch dial; *ca.* 1815.

HENRY FORD MUSEUM

Massachusetts Shelf

47. Aaron Willard, Boston, Massachusetts. Shelf alarm timepiece with quarter hour repeater; broken arch top with single finial; mirror in lower panel; 30¾"x13¼"; six inch dial; *ca.* 1800.

E. H. PARKHURST COLLECTION

48. The movement, with unusual rack and snail.

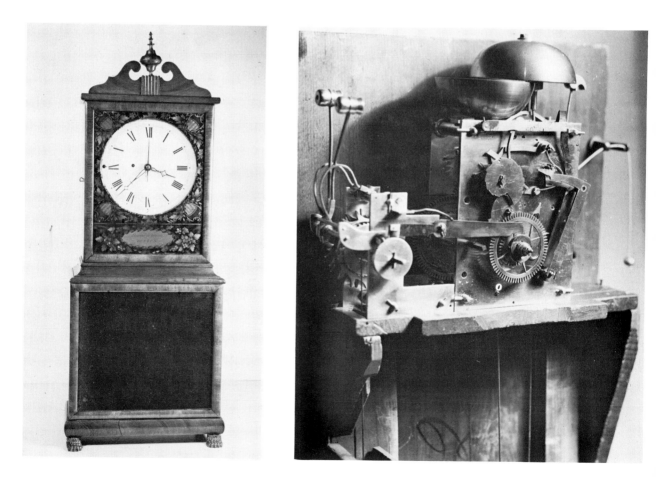

49. Levi Hutchins, Concord, New Hampshire. Massachusetts shelf time-piece; tablet over tablet; case mahogany veneer over pine; eight-day weight movement; winds at 2:20; 45"x12"; six inch dial; *ca.* 1800.

MR. AND MRS. PAUL C. SARGENT

50. The movement.

51. David Wood, Newbury Port, Massachusetts. Hood surmounted with fret work and three pillars with finials; mahogany paneled door in base; winds at 2. 39″x13½″; six inch dial; *ca.* early 1800's.
HENRY FORD MUSEUM

52. David Wood. Massachusetts shelf timepiece; hood with three finials, door in base. Rests on feet, winds at 10. 37½"x12½"; six inch dial; *ca.* 1810.

53. The movement.

54. Silas Parsons, Swansey, New Hampshire. Massachusetts shelf timepiece; eight-day weight with fret work on flat top. Kidney dial opening. Winds at 2. 36½"x13½"; 6½ inch dial; *ca.* 1815.

C. S. PARSONS COLLECTION

55. John Sawin, Boston, Massachusetts. Massachusetts shelf alarm timepiece; tablet over mirror, flat top hood. Winds at 2, alarm winds at 8:50. 30″x13½″; six inch dial; *ca.* 1830.

HENRY FORD MUSEUM

56. Nathan Hale, Chelsea, Vermont. Massachusetts shelf timepiece; hood with splat and three small finials. Purple tablets in exquisite color. 34″x13″; 5½ inch dial; *ca.* 1815.

HENRY FORD MUSEUM

Banjo

Simon Willard patented in 1802 his
unique and beautiful wall timepiece. The
case is shaped like a banjo, though the
inventor referred to these clocks as "Improved Timepieces." Typically American, the shape persists even to today.

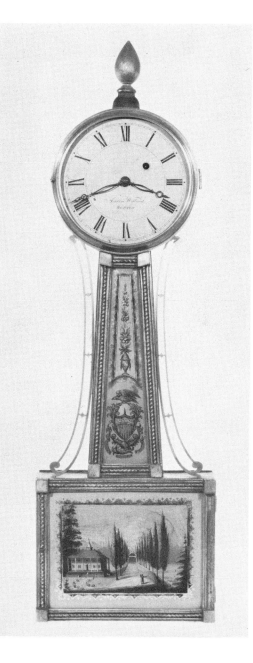

57. Aaron Willard, Boston, Massachusetts. Banjo, with acorn finial. 33"x10"; *ca.*
1808.

HENRY FORD MUSEUM

35

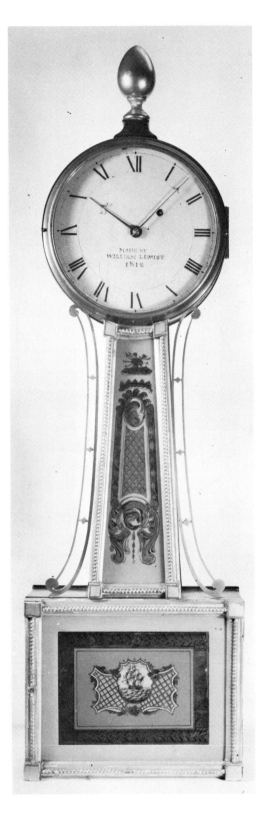

58. William King Lemist, Boston, Massachusetts. "Made . . . 1812" on dial. Acorn finial, mahogany case, finely shaped barbed arrow hands. 33″x10″

1959 SWAMPSCOTT CONVENTION

59. The eight-day movement.

60. "S. Willard's Patent" on lower tablet. Eagle finial with ball, short bracket. 40¾ inches high.

HENRY FORD MUSEUM

61. William Cummens, Roxbury, Massachusetts. Dial has five minute markers; ca. 1818.

CHARLES POORE COLLECTION

62. Sawin & Dyar, Boston, Massachusetts.
Banjo, with eagle finial; *ca.* 1822.

CHARLES POORE COLLECTION

63. Aaron Willard, Boston, Massachusetts. Striking banjo clock with two weights. Bracket 47 inches high; four inch dial.

HENRY FORD MUSEUM

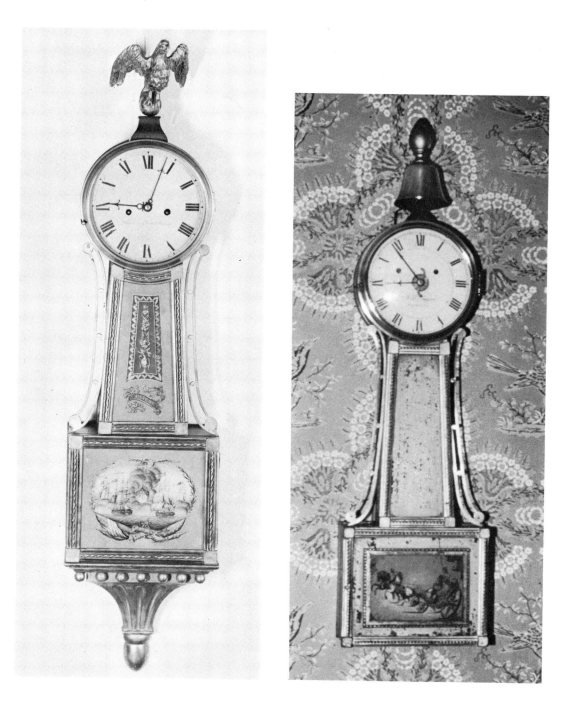

64. Curtis & Dunning, Concord, Massachusetts. Striking banjo clock. 51″x11½″; *ca.* 1815.

HENRY FORD MUSEUM

65. J. F. Tappan, Manchester, Massachusetts. Alarm banjo with bell on top, acorn finial.

ROLAND HAMMOND COLLECTION
DR. CHARLES CURRIER

66. John Sawin, Boston, Massachusetts. Alarm banjo with wood panels, side arms, and bezel.

IRVING COOPERMAN COLLECTION

67. With dial and upper tablet removed. The T-shaped alarm hammer strikes the left side of the case. The weight to operate this is in the narrow slot on left.

68. The New Haven Clock Company. "Willard" eight-day weight powered timepiece with bracket.

69. The movement.

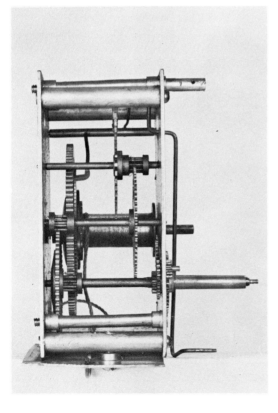

70. The E. Ingraham Company. "Treasure," a very popular banjo clock with two rod strike, mahogany case, brass side arms. 39 inches high; eight inch dial.

EDWARD INGRAHAM COLLECTION

71. Seth Thomas banjo clock; *ca.* 1940.

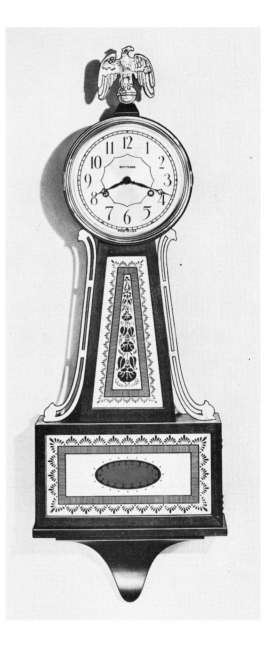

INGRAHAM
TREASURE BANJO
SPECIAL
For a Limited Time Only

Eight-Day Pendulum Movement
Furnished with 2 Rod Strike Only
Height 39 inches
Made of Genuine Mahogany
Hand Rubbed Finish
8 inch Etched Brass Silver Plated Dial
Solid Brass Side Rails

$6.50 each

THE E. INGRAHAM COMPANY
Bristol, Conn., U. S. A.
ESTABLISHED 1831

72. Seth Thomas. Banjo "Homestead" designed by Paul Gaston Darrot.

JACK WARREN COLLECTION

73. Maker unknown. Round banjo box wall timepiece, with solidly constructed eight-day weight movement. 33 inches high; hood diameter, 14 inches; box, 10½ inches.

IRVING COOPERMAN COLLECTION

74. Sessions Clock Company. Eight-day spring banjo clock with pendulum, large dial, short case of mahogany. 27″x9½″x5″

L. W. PETERSON COLLECTION

75. Sessions banjo, mahogany case. 34″x10½″x5″

L. W. PETERSON COLLECTION

76. Wm. L. Gilbert Clock Company. Banjo clock, eight-day spring pendulum, mahogany case, and side arms. 27″x9½″x5″

L. W. PETERSEN COLLECTION

77. Seth Thomas eight-day balance wheel movement timepiece. 23″x6½″x3″.

L. W. PETERSEN COLLECTION

Girandole

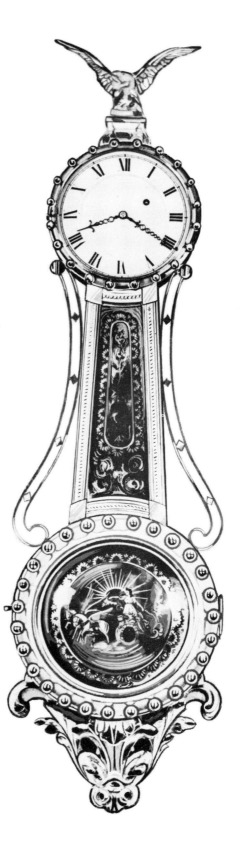

Lemuel Curtis, Concord, Massachusetts, originated this beautiful American Clock of the banjo family. Some few, perhaps twenty-five in all, were made from 1815–1818.

78. Lemuel Curtis, Concord, Massachusetts. This fine reproduction of the original clock is by Elmer Stennes.

79. J. L. Dunning, formerly of Concord, Massachusetts. "Girandole" after the form of the standard but all dark wood panels, bezel, and side arms. Spread winged gold leafed eagle finial; *ca.* 1818.

DR. A. G. COSSIDENTE COLLECTION

Lyre

This is a more ornate form of banjo; the fronts of the cases have some type of a carved leaf motif.

80. Sawin & Dyar, Boston. Lyre time-piece; spread-eagle finial; *ca.* 1822.
HENRY FORD MUSEUM

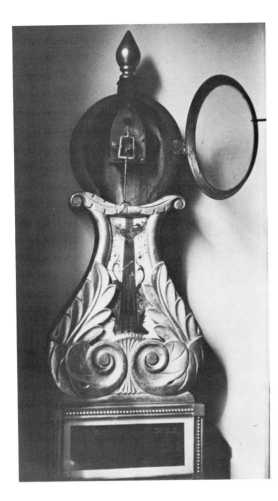

81. David Wood, Newburyport. Lyre timepiece; believed to be the only one of his extant.

HISTORICAL SOCIETY OF OLD NEWBURY

DR. CHARLES CURRIER

82. William Grant, Boston, Massachusetts. Lyre timepiece all of wood with carved front. 38 inches high; *ca.* 1825.

1959 SWAMPSCOTT CONVENTION

83. The movement and interior of the case.

84. John Sawin, Boston, Massachusetts. Lyre timepiece with alarm, mahogany case. 39″x11½″; 4¼ inch dial.

85. The movement and the two weights, the small one on left for the alarm.

86. Albert Phipps. Lyre clock, "fecit 1829" on dial. Case is white with gilt front. Height 40 inches.

1959 SWAMPSCOTT CONVENTION

87. The striking eight-day movement with rack and snail, and unusual pendulum suspension. Two weights.

88. Lemuel Curtis, Concord, Massachusetts. Shelf lyre timepiece. 30″x12½″; six inch dial.

Lighthouse

The Lighthouse was invented and made first by Simon Willard, then of Roxbury, who patented it in 1822. Later others adopted the style, which at first neglected, later became popular. See Willard's 1822 advertisement.

89. Simon Willard. Lighthouse alarum timepiece. This is believed to be one of the first he made; the movement bears the number "8." Mahogany case with octagonal base, tapered circular trunk, and glass dome covering the eight-day alarm movement, and an engraved brass dial with typical Willard arrow hands.

90. The engraved brass dial and arrow hands.

91. "Simon Willard & Sons, Boston; Patent" are shown on dial of this mahogany octagonal base, tapered round trunk, glass dome with white porcelain dial. Eight-day brass weight time only movement, no alarm. 28½ inches high; *ca.* 1830.

1959 SWAMPSCOTT CONVENTION

92. The brass eight-day time only weight movement with T-bridge and dead beat escape.

TO THE PUBLIC.

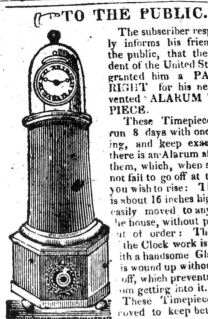

The subscriber respectfully informs his friends and the public, that the President of the United States has granted him a PATENT RIGHT for his newly invented ALARUM TIMEPIECE.

These Timepieces will run 8 days with once winding, and keep exact time; there is an Alarum affixed to them, which, when set, will not fail to go off at the hour you wish to rise: The *Case* is about 16 inches high, and easily moved to any part of he house, without putting it ut of order: The whole the Clock work is inclosed ith a handsome Glass, and is wound up without taking off, which prevents the dirt om getting into it.

These Timepieces have roved to keep better time .... and have a decided preference .... *former* Patent, in point of *elegance* and *usefulness*. The demand for these have already exceeded his expectations.

Those wishing to ornament their parlors with these clocks, *may rest assured that they are made under his immediate inspection, and can rely on their being genuine*

The gentlemen authorized to sell them are Mr. THO'S RICHARDS, New-York, and Mr. J. B. JONES, of Boston—No. 57, Market-street, where they are now to be seen.

The subscriber continues to make at his Factory, on the most improved plans, warranted STEEPLE, CHURCH and BANK CLOCKS; he has also just constructed a Clock, which will run 9 days, with once winding—the weight descends but 8 inches—they come cheap, and answer an excellent purpose for an office.

Dstant orders will be promptly and faithfully executed.   SIMON WILLARD.

Roxbury, Aug. 10, 1822.

CAUTION.

I believe the public are not *generally* aware, that my former Patent Right expired 6 years ago; which induces me to *caution* them against the frequent impositions practiced, in vending *spurious Timepieces.* It is true, they have " Patent" printed on them, and some with my *name*, and their *outward* appearance resembles those *formerly* made by me : *Thus they are palm'd upon the public.*

Several of them have lately been brought to me for repairs, that would certainly put the greatest bungler to the blush. Such is the country inundated with, and such, I consider prejudicial to my reputation ; I therefore *disclaim* being the *manufacturer* of such vile performances.   S. WILLARD.

aug 10   2is6os

93. The advertisement of Simon Willard introducing his patented "newly invented Alarum Timepiece" from Roxbury, August 10, 1822.

New Hampshire Mirror

New Hampshire developed its own distinctive form of wall clock. The movements were mostly all eight-day and of metal, weight-powered. Mostly time only; many of the most amazing construction. The case door ran the full length of the clock (tp), divided to show time on the dial, and below, a mirror in tastefully proportioned oblong design.

94. Benjamin Morrill, Boscawen, New Hampshire. Mirror timepiece, label inside case. Winds at 10. 39¾″x17″; five inch dial; *ca.* 1830.

HENRY FORD MUSEUM

95. Maker not known. New Hampshire mirror eight-day timepiece. Dish dial surrounded by black panel, typical case. Winds at 10. 33½ inches high; *ca.* 1830.

CHARLES POORE COLLECTION

96. Door open, showing arrangement of movement, pendulum to the right of center, and single compounded weight on left.

97. Maker not known. New Hampshire mirror eight-day clock. Flower design tablet around dial. Winds at 10 and 2. 33 inches high; *ca.* 1830.

1959 SWAMPSCOTT CONVENTION

98. Unusual eight-day two-weight brass striking movement of the "rat-trap" type. One wheel on strike side.

99. James Collins (1802–1844), Goffs-town, New Hampshire. New Hampshire mirror eight-day brass clock movement, weight driven. Economy in use of brass is typical of New Hampshire clocks. This is from a full striking clock with rack and snail control.

C. S. PARSONS COLLECTION

100. James Collins, New Hampshire. Mirror timepiece with weight driven eight-day brass movement.

C. S. PARSONS COLLECTION

Edward Howard

Edward Howard (1813–1904) after apprenticeship at 16 years old to Aaron Willard, Jr., became a prominent and successful maker of clocks. With Aaron L. Dennison, he created the world's first mass-produced watch (*ca.* 1850), another American first in time keeping. The clocks he made, which included banjos, figure 8's, regulators, grandfathers, wall and tower clocks, and timepieces, were of his own design. The Howard type banjo, first manufactured in 1842 under the name of Howard & Davis, had a bezel of wood, no side arms, and a curved sided lower box. Some of these continued to be made well into the twentieth century. Howard's figure 8's were created about the same time, and enjoyed a long run of popularity.

101. Howard eight-day weight banjo and figure 8 timepieces. Sizes from (L.) 29 inches to (R.) 56 inches.

RAY WALKER COLLECTION

102. Howard & Davis. Eight-day banjo timepiece, winding at 2:20. Typical rounded curved box ends, rosewood case, 14 pound pendulum. 50"x19½"; 5¾ inch dial. Manufactured, 1842–49 in Boston.

C. S. PARSONS COLLECTION

103. The movement.

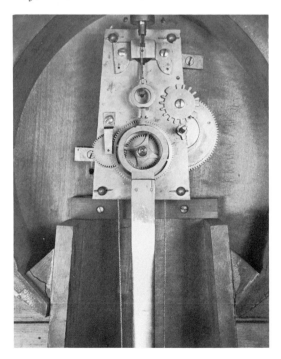

104. Three Howards; all eight day. (L.) 24-hour dial. Numbers change from roman to arabic. Weight regulator. (C.) Gallery timepiece. (R.) Square box Howard banjo.

RAY WALKER COLLECTION

105. Howard figure 8 timepiece. The movement is stamped "1872." 34 inches high.

KENNETH FOX COLLECTION

106. Dial of Howard Astro Regulator.
KENNETH FOX COLLECTION

107. Howard #70 eight-day wall time-piece.

108. "E. Howard & Co.; Boston." Eight-day weight brass movement regulator. Case has rounded bottom.

109. "E. Howard & Co.; Boston." Long pendulum eight-day Vienna regulator. Single glass door. 38"x12"

IRVING COOPERMAN COLLECTION

Tower

These were installed in towers or steeples of public buildings for the use of the general public.

110. Seth Thomas tower clock movement; built in 1905 and installed in the tower of the Elgin National Watch Company, Elgin, Illinois. The weights that run the time and strike are electrically wound. This was a first "self winding" tower clock and had the electric motors built into the original construction.

The Dennison double three-legged gravity escape is used. The pendulum, weighing 360 pounds, is 14 feet long and has a two-second beat.

When the Elgin Tower was dismantled, the clock was moved to and is now a part of the Hagans Clock Manor Museum at Bergen Park, Colorado.

ORVILLE R. HAGANS COLLECTION

111. The eight-day weight driven three-dialed clock in the White Church Tower on the Green at Sturbridge Village. The fans slow the strike action. The center vertical rod runs a contrite gear wheel at top that simultaneously moves the hands on all the dials. The rods connecting the dials and the movement are of wood, as a protection against lightning damage.

Benjamin Franklin's "Clock"

112. "A timepiece Showing the Hours, Minutes, and Seconds; having only three Wheels and two Pinions. Invented by Dr. Benjamin Franklin of Philadelphia."—from a 1773 description by James Ferguson. This example made by Percy Breakwell, Philadelphia.

GEORGE K. ECKHARDT COLLECTION

Pillar & Scroll

This was America's first mass produced shelf clock. It was pleasant appearing, with nice proportions; the cases were of pine with mahogany veneer. The thirty-hour wood movement was two-weight driven. After 1816 some eight-day brass movements which were weight driven became available. The original design was attributed to Eli Terry.

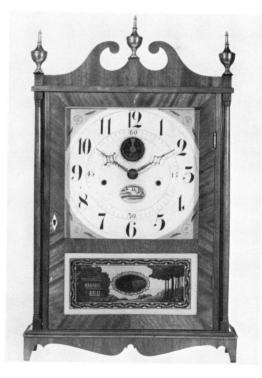

113. Eli Terry, Plymouth, Connecticut. Outside Scape Pillar & Scroll (II) 1817-18. 29¼ inches high.

HENRY FORD MUSEUM

114. Eli Terry, Plymouth, Connecticut. Inside–Outside Scape Pillar & Scroll (III). 27 inches high; *ca.* 1818.

HENRY FORD MUSEUM

116. Strap type #2 wood movement with count wheel, patented by Eli Terry in 1816.

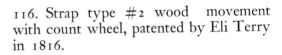

115. Seth Thomas, Plymouth, Connecticut. Off-center Pillar & Scroll. As can be seen, the pendulum does not hang in the exact center. 30 inches high; *ca.* 1818.
E. B. BURT COLLECTION

117. Ephraim Down(e)s. Bristol, Connecticut. This is his standard Pillar & Scroll. 31½ inches high; *ca.* 1820.

HENRY FORD MUSEUM

118. "E. Terry & Sons," Plymouth, Connecticut. Label of a standard thirty-hour Pillar & Scroll.

CHARLES GRAF COLLECTION

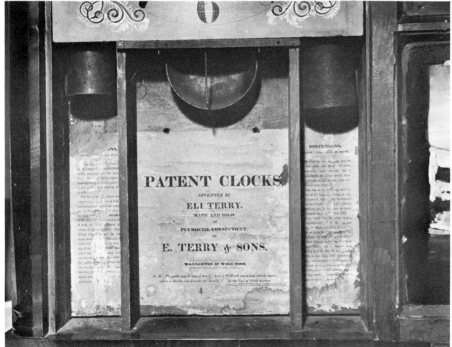

119. Riley Whiting, Winchester, Connecticut. Pillar & Scroll, *ca.* 1819. He was one of the first makers of clocks in volume.

120. Riley Whiting. Front plate wood movement in his Pillar & Scroll.

121. Side view of
    Whiting movement.

122. Wood thirty-hour movement, Terry type, in operation. The front plate is of clear plastic to show the complete action. Designed, made, and photographed by Mr. Barny, New York City.

123. Samuel Terry (brother of Eli), Bristol, Connecticut. Standard Pillar & Scroll; *ca.* 1829.

C. S. PARSONS COLLECTION

124. With door off showing standard Terry type wood one-day movement, the weights, and label.

125. Ansel Merrell, Vienna, Ohio. Pillar & Scroll; *ca.* 1828.

JAMES W. GIBBS COLLECTION

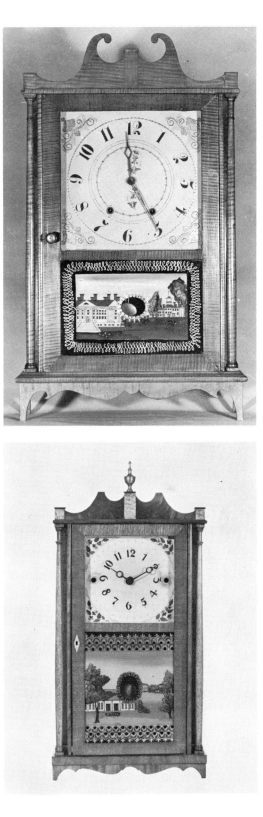

126. Erastus Hodges, Torrington, Connecticut. Torrington type Pillar & Scroll. Horizontal wood movement, one-day, winds at 9 & 3. Finials missing, dial refinished. 28 inches high; *ca.* 1820.

HENRY FORD MUSEUM

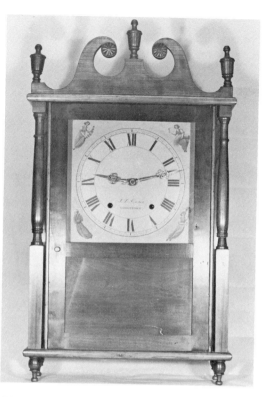

127. Ethel North (brother of Norris), Torrington, Connecticut. Torrington Pillar & Scroll. 35 inches high.

E. B. BURT COLLECTION

128. With door off, showing horizontal one-day wood movement with weights descending directly down, not over pulleys at case top.

E. B. BURT COLLECTION

129. Lucius B. Bradley, Watertown, Connecticut. Pillar & Scroll. Eight-day weight brass movement, seconds hand on dial; painted iron dial; 33 inches high. Made prior to 1830 when "factory burnt."

E. B. BURT COLLECTION

130. Inside view, with rack & snail strike.

131. Jacob D. Custer (1805–72), Norristown, Pennsylvania. Penna. Pillar & Scroll one-day brass movement, time & strike; 30½ inches high; *ca.* 1840.

JAMES W. GIBBS COLLECTION

132. Jacob D. Custer, Norristown, Pennsylvania. A more traditional Penna. Pillar & Scroll type. Dial reads "Norristown, Patent." Brass eight-day movement; 38 inches high.

HENRY FORD MUSEUM

133. Seth Thomas. Pillar & Scroll. Eight-
day brass movement; *ca.* 1895.

Looking Glass
& Transition

Just before 1825, when the Pillar & Scroll was at the height of its popularity, Chauncey Jerome produced and sold his Looking Glass clock (L.G.). Another type of Connecticut shelf clock of the later 1820's was called a Transition clock. The Transition followed the Pillar & Scroll and was more economical to manufacture. Squatter than the L.G. and often with a splat and side columns, this type was either stenciled or carved, and with feet. Following this style came the Double and Triple Deckers.

Movements, then all weight driven, were mostly one-day wood. Cast brass, since brass was still a scarce commodity, was available for an occasional eight-day movement. Rolled brass was available in increasing quantities after 1830 for eight-day movements, but some eight-day wood movements were still made.

134. Label reads, "Invented by Eli Terry, made & sold by Eli Terry Junior." Transition clock, single door stenciled with tablet. Side columns heavily stenciled; unusual broken arch splat with eagle insert; flower decorated dial, 30-hour standard wood movement; only 25 inches high; *ca.* late 1820's.

JAMES W. GIBBS COLLECTION

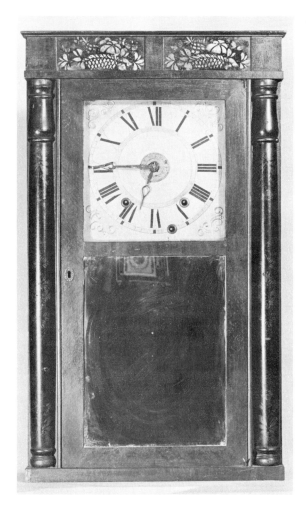

135. Henry Terry & Company, Plymouth, Connecticut. Looking Glass shelf clock. Single door with mirror; unusual flat top splat with two inserted small tablets, stenciled columns. 30-hour wood, three weight movement; alarm at 5:30; *ca.* 1828.

JAMES W. GIBBS COLLECTION

136. Maker unknown. Transition clock. Single door with tablet; stenciled splat and quarter columns, paw feet. 30-hour standard wood weight movement; *ca.* late 1820's.

C. E. GRAF, JR. COLLECTION

137. Rodney Brace, North Bridgewater, Massachusetts. Miniature 23 inch Looking Glass shelf clock. Mirror in single door; *ca.* late 1820's.

JAMES W. GIBBS COLLECTION

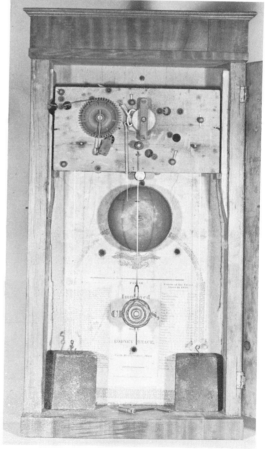

138. With door open and dial off. The 30-hour wood movement is of the Torrington type.

139. E. & G. Bartholomew, Bristol, Connecticut. Transition clock, single door with tablet, stenciled splat and half side columns on door. Pineapple finials, paw feet; 30-hour standard weight wood movement; *ca.* 1828.

HENRY FORD MUSEUM

140. Bassett & Gibbs, Litchfield, Connecticut. Miniature 23 inch L.G. clock; mirror in single door. Split half columns on case sides; stenciled splat; *ca.* 1830.

JAMES W. GIBBS COLLECTION

141. Munger & Benedict, Auburn, New York. Mirror Empire type. Flat top, spiraled, side-columned. Eight-day weight timepiece dish dial, winds at 2. 31¼″x-14″x5¼″; *ca.* late 1820's.

IRVING COOPERMAN COLLECTION

142. Movement with heavy brass plates, cut out sections. Pendulum on back of movement.

143. Munger & Pratt, Ithaca, New York. Mirror on single door; half carved side columns on door, carved splat. 30-hour wood movement, eagle hands. 35½"x-16¼"; six inch dial; *ca.* 1830.

C. S. PARSONS COLLECTION

144. Ephraim Downs, Bristol, Connecticut. Transition shelf clock. Half column stenciled sides, and stenciled splat; claw feet, pineapple finials. Standard 30-hour movement; *ca.* 1825.

JOHN BUELL COLLECTION

145. Eli Terry, Jr., & Company, Terrysville, Connecticut. Two decker Transition clock, tablet in lower door; carved side columns and splat with eagle; paw feet. Eight-day wood weight movement; 38½″x18½″; 4½ inch dial; *ca.* 1833.

HENRY FORD MUSEUM

146. Burr & Chittenden, Lexington, Massachusetts. L.G. with door open, dial removed, showing 30-hour "groaner" wood weight movement. Probably made by Chauncey Boardman, of Bristol; *ca.* 1834.

AUTHOR'S COLLECTION

147. E. K. Jones, Bristol, Connecticut for O. Hart, Waterloo, New York. L.G. clock; half columned case with tablet of "Emily" in single door. 34"x16½"; five inch dial; *ca.* 1834.

C. S. PARSONS COLLECTION

148. 30-hour standard wood weight Terry type movement; and the label.

149. Daniel Pratt, Jr., Reading, Massachusetts. Wood movement 30-hour "groaner" type wood weight movement in an L.G. case. Hour bell on top of case. 33"x16"; *ca.* 1836.

AUTHOR'S COLLECTION

150. C. & L. C. Ives, Bristol, Connecticut. Triple decker, solid dial with roman chapters; flower decoration, carved splat. Side columns in three parts with gold capitals; unusual finials; *ca.* early 1830's.

HOWARD G. SLOANE COLLECTION

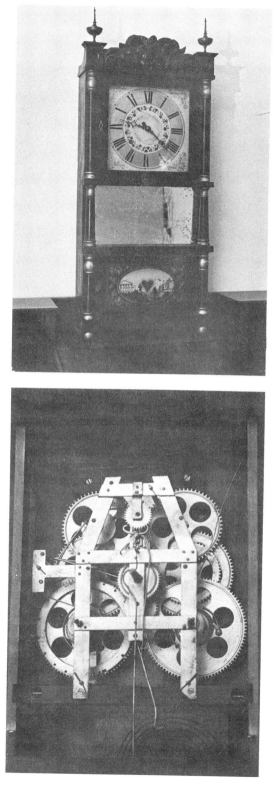

151. J. Ives brass strap movement, large gears; eight-day weight driven.

152. R. & J. B. Terry, Bristol, Connecticut. Triple decker Transition. Gold leaved crested capitals on three sectioned side columns; plain splat; gold leafed ball feet. Note the duplicated tablets except for bob opening in the lower one. Arabic dial with adjustment opening; unusual finials; *ca.* 1835.

HOWARD G. SLOANE COLLECTION

153. Eight-day brass strap movement with rolling pinions.

154. Spencer, Hotchkiss & Co. Triple decker with side columns in three sections, center in gold leaf, gold leaved carved splat. Eight-day brass weight movement; 31″x17″x5½″; *ca.* early 1830's.

IRVING COOPERMAN COLLECTION

155. Eight-day "Salem Bridge" type brass weight movement, with rack and snail strike.

156. C. & N. Jerome, Bristol, Connecticut. Transition clock with dial door; center tablet actually an advertisement; lower door with tablet. Larger side columns with capitals; flat, empire splat top with small longitudinal mirror, paw feet. Dial opening for adjustment; *ca.* 1835.

JAMES W. GIBBS COLLECTION

157. Dyer, Wadsworth & Company, Augusta, Georgia. Triple decker Transition clock with gold carved eagle splat; dial with black chapter ring, white roman chapters. Label: "Patent Brass Eight Day Clocks." Probably made by Birge, Mallory & Company; *ca.* 1838.

HENRY FORD MUSEUM

158. Barnes, Bartholemew Company, Bristol, Connecticut. Triple decker, Transition clock, tablet marked "View near Natchez." 36 inches high; *ca.* 1835.

159. Eight-day brass weight movement with rolling pinions and large gears; the Ives side arm not used.

160. Birge, Mallory, & Company, Bristol, Connecticut. Rare miniature three decker; gold leaf carved splat, 30-hour weight brass movement with rolling pinions. 25 inches high; *ca.* 1840.

Silas Hoadley

The famous Connecticut clockmaker was born in 1786; he died in Plymouth, Connecticut, in 1870, at the age of 84. As a boy he was apprenticed to his Uncle Samuel; he successfully engaged in clock-making from 1808 to 1849, starting as a worker with Eli Terry in Terry's first mass production of wood hang-up movements at Greystone, later in Hoadleyville, Connecticut. The firm name "Terry, Thomas, and Hoadley" is a myth. Hoadley and Seth Thomas bought out Terry's interests about 1810 and continued making one-day wood hang-ups in grandfather cases. In 1813, Hoadley purchased Seth Thomas's share in the business and continued on his own. When shelf clocks came into vogue, he made those, mostly with his own distinctively different wood movements, as shown in this section. Successful, always at the one location of the factory, he retired in 1849 with a fortune. Here are eight pictures of his shelf clocks. His eight-day pull-up weight movement, made in the early 1830's is shown in illustration No. 37.

161. Silas Hoadley. Pillar & Scroll with "upside-down" wood movement, including ivory bushings. Wind holes at 10 & 2. 30½ inches high; ca. 1825.

1959 SWAMPSCOTT CONVENTION

162. The ingenious Hoadley rearrangement may have been to avoid any conflict with Terry patents. His label shows a picture of Ben Franklin and his proverb: "Time is Money."

163. Hoadley shelf clock with half-seconds pendulum. Tablet in door. Carved splat and side columns, solid mahogany case. Paw front feet. 30-hour upside-down movement. 23 inches high.
GEORGE F. FORD COLLECTION

164. Hoadley Alarm timepiece. Case with single mirrored door—the door catch not original. Stenciled splat with unusual cylindrical side columns and top posts. Label: "by Silas Hoadley, Plymouth, Connecticut, Cased and sold by L. Smith."
HENRY FORD MUSEUM

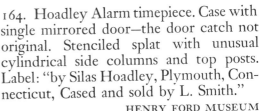

165. Hoadley alarm timepiece. Single mirrored door, plain splat with conventional corner posts, stenciled side columns. Winds at 12; alarm winds at 8:30. 25¾ inches high.

GEORGE F. FORD COLLECTION

166. The unusual Hoadley timepiece alarm, and label.

167. Hoadley shelf clock with "upside-down" 30-hour wood weight movement, long pendulum. Case has single door with large mirror. The small bottom tablet is inscribed "Time Is Money" (Ben Franklin); stenciled splat and half columns, paw feet. 37¼"x17"; 4¾ inch dial.

HENRY FORD MUSEUM

168. Door and dial off, showing the long pendulum 30-hour weight "upside-down" movement, and label: "With the Improvement of bushing the pivots with Ivory." Carved eagle splat.

GEORGE F. FORD COLLECTION

Wagon Spring

The Wagon Spring clock was Joseph Ives' invention. It utilized flat leaved springs to power the clock movement. Ives made his eight-day clocks from 1825–30 in Brooklyn, New York. Later clocks with the same type of movement were made by Birge & Fuller, Bristol, Connecticut. These are the steeple on steeple cases. The one-month clocks in shelf and wall cases were made by Atkins (1850–56); the dates of the one-day Hour Glass clocks are uncertain.

169. Joseph Ives. Wagon spring clock— "Duncan Phyfe" or "Brooklyn" type. The dial is decorated with a vase of flowers, and has a painted picture tablet.

Eight-day strap brass movement. 29 inches high; *ca.* 1830.

E. B. BURT COLLECTION

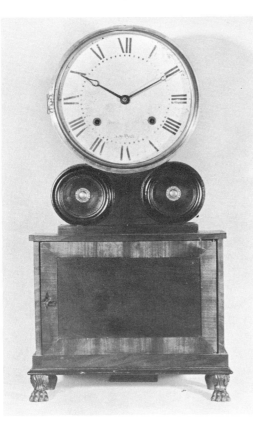

170. Ives wagon spring clock with wood
paneled door; *ca.* 1825–30.

171. Movement of Ives wagon spring.

172. Birge & Fuller, Bristol, Connecticut (1844–48). A standard steeple on steeple eight-day wagon spring shelf clock. 27¼ inches high; *ca.* 1844–48.

HENRY FORD MUSEUM

173. Birge & Fuller. Eight-day wagon spring; case with four candles; *ca.* 1844–48.

BEN COHEN COLLECTION

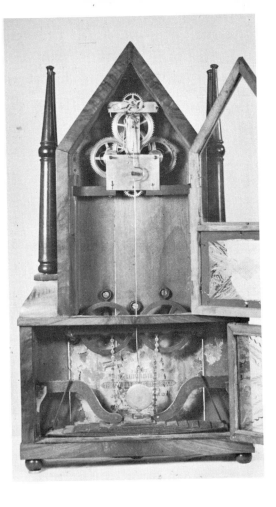

174. Ives wagon spring one-month timepiece; winds at 10 and 2. Dual time power, no strike. 26 inches high; *ca.* 1850.

1959 SWAMPSCOTT CONVENTION

The unusual movement on No. 174.

175. Birge & Fuller. Eight-day wagon spring clock with side candles ⅔ the usual height.

BEN COHEN COLLECTION

176. Wagon spring clock with rounded top. Four usual candles.

EDWARD MITCHELL COLLECTION

177. Ives one-month "pony shoe" wagon spring movement and squirrel case escapement.

JAMES W. GIBBS COLLECTION

178. Birge & Fuller. Eight-day wagon spring clock in an unusual case with side columns. 26 inches high.

HENRY FORD MUSEUM

179. Joseph Ives. Hour glass one-day wagon spring clock. Label: "Plainville, Conn." 23 inches high; *ca.* 1850.

E. B. BURT COLLECTION

180. Movement, showing the single leaf spring inverted down at top of case.

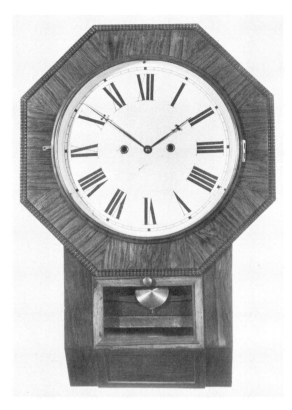

181. Drop Octagon wall-case wagon spring. No label extant but possibly Atkins, Whiting & Co., Bristol; 29¾"x-17"x4"; *ca.* 1850.

HENRY FORD MUSEUM

182. Pony shoe movement with winding wagon spring.

183. Joseph Ives, Bristol, Connecticut. "Connecticut Lyre" eight-day wall clock. Gold leafed front decoration; 34½ inches high; *ca.* 1830.

E. B. BURT COLLECTION

184. With door open: showing brass strap eight-day weight driven movement with Ives rolling pinions.

185. Chauncey Jerome, New Haven, Connecticut. Drop octagon wall case with pie crust trim; eight-day fuzee movement.

IRVING COOPERMAN COLLECTION

186. Movement, showing fuzees, barrel springs and heavier than usual plates.

187. Ives 30-day wagon spring in drop Octagon pie crust case.

IRVING COOPERMAN COLLECTION

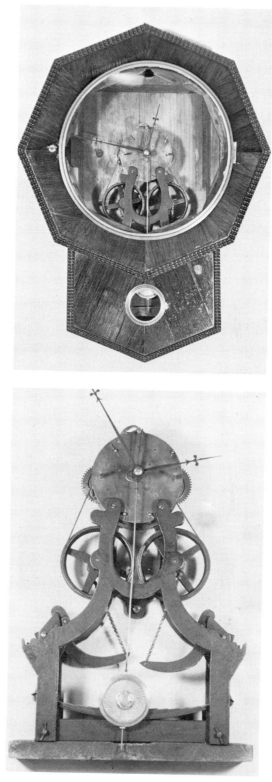

188. Pony shoe wagon spring movement with squirrel cage escapement.

OG

The OG shelf clock was manufactured in great quantities in America from 1825 to 1918. The name is derived from the S-like curved molding on the door.

(The OOG is reported to have meant that the S-curve was repeated on the outer side of the front of case.)

This was the clock type selected by Chauncey Jerome in 1838 to become his famous "clocks for everyone."

The first of these OG's carried the label: JEROMES (C. & Noble), GILBERT (Wm. L.), GRANT (Zelotes) & CO.; Bristol, Conn., as shown on the tax rolls of 1839–40.

Jerome was also famous for his exploitation of the English Market.

The principle sizes are: one-day weight standard, wood and brass movements, *ca.* 26 inches high. Eight-day brass weight movement, 34 inches high. One- and eight-day brass spring movement, 18 inches high. One-day brass weight clock, *ca.* 19 inches high. The smaller spring one-day miniature, 15½-16" high. The "flat OG" with no S-curve on the door—so-called for lack of a better name.

189. Three sizes of OG alarm clocks:

1. Seth Thomas—16 inches, 30-hour spring movement.

2. Waterbury Clock Company—19 inches spring movement.

3. Terry & Andrews (1842–50), Bristol, Connecticut—one-day weight movement.

IRVING COOPERMAN COLLECTION

190. OG on OG. Two-door double OG with eight-day brass weight movement displaying original Forestville Mfg. label; *ca.* 1836.

AMERICAN MUSEUM OF TIME, BRISTOL

191. Manross, Pritchard & Co., Bristol, Connecticut. OG standard; tablet reads "View in Boston." 26″x15½″x4¼″; *ca.* 1841–42.

C. S. PARSONS COLLECTION

192. Movement and label.

193. Jerome & Company, New Haven, Connecticut. This is one of the OG clocks Jerome sold in England in the late 1840's.

WILLIAM JOHNSTONE COLLECTION
PHOTO BY DAVID URQUHART

194. Brewster & Ingrahams, Bristol, Connecticut. Standard OG; etched glass tablet.

JOHN STURDEVANT COLLECTION

195. J. C. Brown. Forestville Mfg. Company. OG standard 30-hour brass weight movement. Note there is a separate wind hole in the dial at 6 for unusual alarm. 26″x15½″x4½″; *ca.* 1850.

196. Movement, showing unusual alarm which is between the plates, not separately mounted below.

197. Ansonia Clock Company, Ansonia, Connecticut. OG standard 30-hour brass weight movement. 26″x15½″x4″; *ca.* 1855.

C. S. PARSONS COLLECTION

198. Movement and label. The unusual label shows a picture of the factory.

199. Seth Thomas. OG 30-hour brass movement.

200. Riley Whiting, Winchester, Connecticut. Flat OG with a 30-hour wood weight movement. 29½"x18"; *ca.* early 1800's.

DAVID URQUHART COLLECTION

201. Boardman & Wells, Bristol, Connecticut. Flat OG with 30-hour weight movement. Name is repeated on bottom of tablet. 26"x15½"x4½"

C. S. PARSONS COLLECTION

202. Wood movement and label.

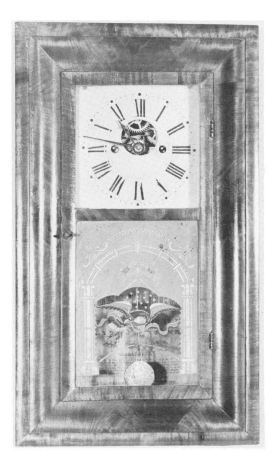

203. Henry Terry, Plymouth, Connecticut. Small weight-driven OG with a 30-hour brass movement. 19½ inches high.

This may be one of those mysteriously made, possibly *ca.* 1859, long after Terry's reported retirement.

JAMES W. GIBBS COLLECTION

204. Jason R. Rawson, Saxton's River, Vermont. Flat OG with 30-hour wood movement; *ca.* 1839.

JAMES W. GIBBS COLLECTION

205. Smith & Brothers, New York City. Flat OG with alarm. 30-hour wood weight movement. Extra wind hole for alarm at 5:30. Tablet may or may not be original. 26″x16″x4¾″

206. 30-hour weight wood alarm movement, and label showing New York Factory of Smith & Brothers. Building stood until recently, the 3rd Ave El passed on the left, the 2nd Ave El on the right.

207. C. (Chauncey) Jerome, Bristol, Connecticut. This pleasant variant of the OG with a 30-hour brass weight movement was made before 1845. 28″x13″

BERNARD BRANDT COLLECTION

208. Smith & Goodrich, Bristol, Connecticut. 16 inch OG with 30-hour fuzee spring movement.

JAMES W. GIBBS COLLECTION

209. Seth Thomas, Plymouth Hollow, Connecticut. 30-hour spring brass movement alarm clock. 16½ inches high; *ca.* 1860's.

C. S. PARSONS COLLECTION

210. 30-hour spring movement with separate alarm.

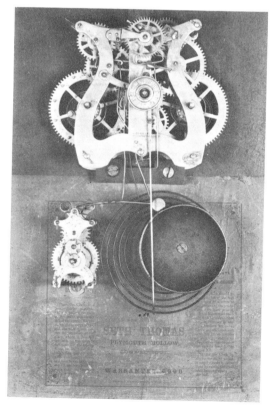

211. Ansonia Clock Company, Ansonia, Connecticut. An OG clock with a 30-hour alarm spring movement. 18½"x-10½"; four inch dial.

C. S. PARSONS COLLECTION

212. Showing movement with separate alarm.

213. Seth Thomas, Thomaston, Connecticut. 16½ inches OG alarm with ST hands and dog's head on green tablet.

AUTHOR'S COLLECTION

214. A ST "lyre" eight-day alarm spring movement similar to No. 213.

C. S. PARSONS COLLECTION

215. E. N. Welch Manufacturing Company, Forestville, Connecticut. An OG clock with a 4¾ inch dial, eight-day spring movement. Building on tablet not identified. 18¾"x12"

HENRY FORD MUSEUM

216. Waterbury Clock Company, Waterbury, Connecticut. 30-hour spring alarm OG. 18½"x12"; 3¾ inch dial.

HENRY FORD MUSEUM

217. E. N. Welch Manufacturing Company, Forestville, Connecticut. Eight-day OG, 18½ inches high.

JAMES W. GIBBS COLLECTION

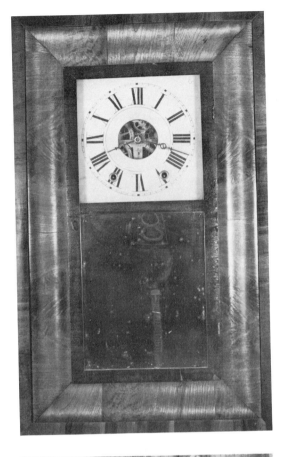

218. New Haven Clock Company. Eight-day OG clock with brass weight movement. 33″x14″; 4¼ inch dial.

219. Eight-day OG movement.

Steeple

These are clocks "topped with spires," an enduring American clock form. Elias Ingraham of Bristol is credited with the design. These clocks were manufactured after American coiled springs came into use, *ca.* 1843. The first of these springs were actually made of brass; many of them still function satisfactorily after almost a century and a quarter. (J. E. Coleman has called them the "first unbreakable springs.") Heights ran from 10½ to 24 inches. Examples are still being made in the 1960's.

220. Four sizes of Steeple clocks. (L. to R.)

1. Sub-miniature, Ansonia, 10½ inches high.

2. Minature, Waterbury Clock Company, 14¾ inches high.

3. Standard Seth Thomas, 20 inches high.

4. Steeple on steeple, Elisha Manross, 24 inches high.

PAUL DE MAGNIN COLLECTION

221. 14 Steeple clocks in the Paul de
Magnin Collection, Larchmont, New
York. Photographs by Maurice Andre.

222. Five shelf clocks of distinction. (L. to R.)

1. Round Gothic twin steeple, with overpasted label "Daniel Pratt & Sons, Boston," Brewster & Ingrahams, eight-day brass springs; *ca.* 1848.

2. Standard steeple, Terry & Andrews, eight-day brass springs in iron barrels.

3. Bee Hive, Terry & Andrews, eight-day spring movement with lantern pinions.

4. Sharp Gothic twin steeple with alarm; Brewster & Ingrahams, eight-day brass springs in iron barrels; rack & snail strike with repeater; rolling pinions.

5. Round Gothic rippled twin steeple, Forestville Manufacturing Company, eight-day spring movement with alarm.

JAMES W. GIBBS COLLECTION

223. (L.) Sharp Gothic twin steeple Brewster & Ingraham eight-day clock, a design of Elias Ingraham; *ca.* 1845.

(R.) Door open to show the eight-day movement and the label.

RAY WALKER COLLECTION

224. Forestville Manufacturing Company. Round Gothic twin steeple with a rippled finish, designed by Elias Ingraham, eight-day spring movement; tablet shows early view of the White House and Potomac River; *ca.* late 1840's.

HENRY FORD MUSEUM

225. Movement of Brewster & Ingrahams eight-day brass spring standard steeple; *ca.* 1848.

226. Pond & Barnes, Boston, Massachusetts. Steeple with alarm, 3 fuzees, over-pasted label; *ca.* 1848.

227. Elisha Manross, Bristol, Connecticut. Movement of eight-day steeple on steeple, fuzees with cones of wood; *ca.* 1848.

PAUL DE MAGNIN COLLECTION

228. Chauncey Jerome, New Haven, Connecticut. Movement of standard steeple; fuzee movement.

PAUL DE MAGNIN COLLECTION

229. Wm. L. Gilbert Company, Winsted, Connecticut. Miniature steeple, 30-hour ladder movement alarm timepiece, winds at 6. Curley maple sides; top and front, mahogany; 14½ inches high, *ca.* 1850–60.
JAMES W. GIBBS COLLECTION

230. S. B. Terry designed the movement.
PAUL DE MAGNIN COLLECTION

231. Forestville Hardware & Clock Company, Bristol, Connecticut. Sub-miniature steeple; 30-hour timepiece; winds at 3. 12½ inches high; *ca.* 1853–55.

JAMES W. GIBBS COLLECTION

232. Ansonia Clock Company, Ansonia, Connecticut. Steeple movement with alarm; 30-hour.

PAUL DE MAGNIN COLLECTION

233. Standard steeple, "Daniel Pratt Sons, Reading, Mass." overpasted label. Eight-day movement. Tablet shows view of Potomac River and the White House.

PAUL DE MAGNIN COLLECTION

234. Waterbury Clock Company, Waterbury, Connecticut. Miniature steeple; 30-hour spring movement. 15 inches high; *ca.* 1875.

JAMES W. GIBBS COLLECTION

235. Waterbury Clock Company. Miniature steeple. Winds at 11; 30-hour timepiece. Label on back reads "Small Gothic, One Day Time." 14¾"x8¼"; 3¾ inch dial; *ca.* 1880.

HENRY FORD MUSEUM

236. Seth Thomas "Sharon" steeple. After 1938 this style was made either as an eight-day wind-up or an A/C TP, but was not in such good proportions as Ingraham's Originals.

AUTHOR'S COLLECTION

237. Elmer Stennes, Massachusetts. Modern steeple shelf clock.

Bee Hive

A Bee Hive clock is a Connecticut shelf clock cased in the shape of a rounded gothic arch, or "the hull of a ship, inverted." These clocks were made in the late 1840's, using coiled springs for power. Many of them were manufactured into the early twentieth century. The average dimensions were: 18½ inches high; 11 inches wide; four inches deep. Most of the more important clock manufacturers made them.

238. Brewster & Ingrahams, Bristol, Connecticut. Bee Hive, etched glass tablet, *ca.* 1847, a very early example.

C. S. PARSONS COLLECTION

239. Movement and label.

240. E. & A. Ingraham, Bristol, Connecticut. Bee Hive with alarm, *ca.* 1852–55.

C. S. PARSONS COLLECTION

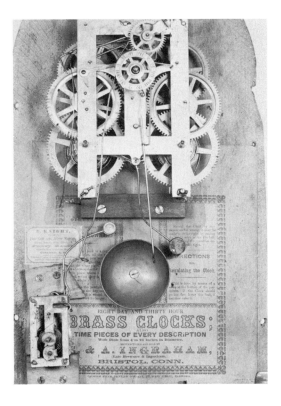

241. Movement and label.

242. Chauncey Jerome, New Haven, Connecticut. Bee Hive with mirror tablet. 19 inches high.

IRVING COOPERMAN COLLECTION

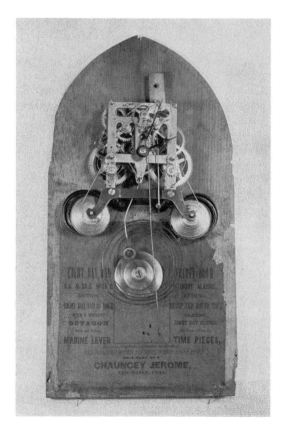

243. Back board, label, and movement, showing fuzees.

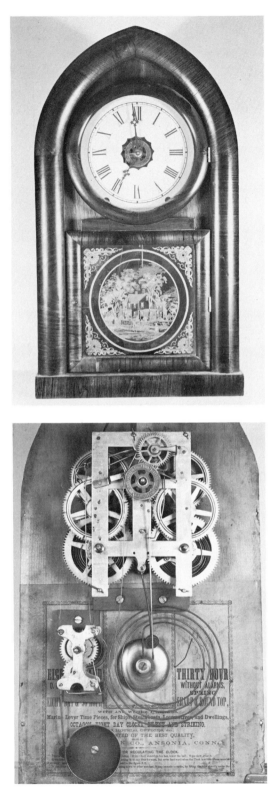

244. Ansonia Clock Company, Ansonia, Connecticut. Bee Hive with alarm. Gold leafed decal tablet.

C. S. PARSONS COLLECTION

245. Back board, alarm mechanism, and movement.

246. E. C. Brewster & Son (Noah), Bristol, Connecticut.

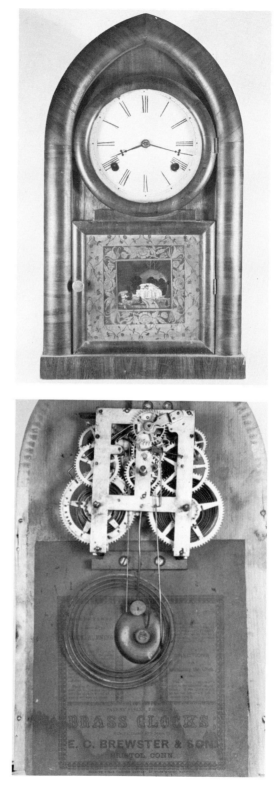

247. Movement and label.

Acorn

This graceful form of shelf clock was manufactured, probably exclusively, by the designer, J. C. Brown of Forestville Manufacturing Company, Bristol, Connecticut in the years 1847–50. No original catalogue or prices are known today. The shape of the clock was made possible by the use of the coiled spring. The earliest are about 25 inches in height with fuzees in wood cones at the bottom of the case. Later examples were made either with fuzees attached to the movement or regular coiled springs.

248. E. N. Welch, Forestville, Connecticut. Miniature Bee Hive. One-day etched glass tablet. 15½ inches high.

JAMES W. GIBBS COLLECTION

249. Original model Acorn. The house on the tablet is that of J. C. Brown, in Bristol, which is still standing.

HENRY FORD MUSEUM

250. Standard Acorn with "State House, Hartford" on tablet.

EDWARD MITCHELL COLLECTION

251. Dark background surrounding dial. Tablet shows Merchants' Exchange, Philadelphia.

HENRY FORD MUSEUM

252. Standard Acorn with dial off and door open showing movement and the wood fuzees. Stamped "Forestville Mfg. Co."

E. B. BURT COLLECTION

253. One type of J. C. Brown labels used with Acorn clocks. The side arms are replaced by acorns on the base board.

AMERICAN MUSEUM OF TIME

254. Intermediate model acorn with
fuzees attached to base of movement.
Etched glass tablet. 23 inches high.
WESLEY HALLET MUSEUM,
NEWPORT, NEW HAMPSHIRE

255. Acorn-type, three feet high, but
with side arms gone.
F. M. SELCHOW COLLECTION

256. Acorn, the final type, and probably the last. No legs or side arms.

F. M. SELCHOW COLLECTION

257. Acorn; last type, showing fuzees attached to base of movement and pendulum ball removed to display the label.

FREDERICK MUDGE SELCHOW COLLECTION

Silas Burnham Terry

This son of Eli, a creative Connecticut inventor in his own right, has never been given adequate recognition for his contributions to American clockmaking. He started work with his father at Plymouth with the Pillar & Scroll and was one of the Eli Terry & Sons on the labels. He soon learned to prepare brass for movements, many of which were unique. He also contributed to the development of the American coiled clock spring, receiving a patent dated Nov. 3, 1830, for "Combined spiral spring for Clocks." His tempering process was sold to Butler Dunbar after 1840.

For time control, Terry used the pendulum, the balance wheel—both vertically or horizontally mounted—and later the "marine" which was used in the alarm timepiece.

His torsion bar control was unique. He designed machinery, as well as Seth Thomas Regulators #1 & 2. He was at Bristol by 1831; later at Terryville, Waterbury, and Winsted. He was also in business with his sons at Winsted after 1852.

258. Silas B. Terry, Terryville, Connecticut. Miniature reverse OG cased clock, 13 inches high.

JAMES W. GIBBS COLLECTION

259. Door open showing label and 30-hour pendulum movement.

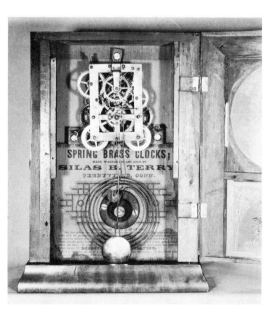

260. Silas B. Terry, Terryville, Connecticut. Shelf clock with small solid case, not veneered, dial opening, and 30-hour spring pendulum movement. 12½ inches high.

JAMES W. GIBBS COLLECTION

261. Silas B. Terry, Terryville, Connecticut. Shelf steeple clock with eight-day spring balance wheel (marine) control. The upper dial opening is for the seconds hand, the lower to allow oscillations of the balance wheel to be seen. 24½ inches high; *ca.* 1848.

1959 SWAMPSCOTT CONVENTION

262. SBT's eight-day fuzee movement with rack lever driven vertical balance wheel. Label reads "Invented by Eli Terry, Aug. 9, 1845."

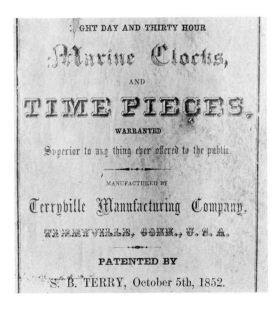

263. Silas B. Terry, Plymouth, Connecticut. Label of the late 1840's.

J. E. COLEMAN COLLECTION

264. The label of No. 265.

265. Terryville Manufacturing Company, Terryville, Connecticut. Small shelf steeple 30-hour timepiece with horizontally mounted large balance wheel. 13 inches high; *ca.* 1852.

C. W. BURNHAM COLLECTION

266. Marine movement with horizontally mounted balance wheel.

267. Terryville Manufacturing Company. Small square-cased shelf timepiece; torsion bar controlled. 10 inches high; *ca.* 1852.

1959 SWAMPSCOTT CONVENTION

268. 30-hour brass movement with two-ball torsion bar below.

269. S. B. Terry's torsion bar controlled 30-hour brass spring movement clock in Octagonal wall case. Movement is stamped "Pat. Oct. 5, 1852."

270. Terryville Manufacturing Company. Candle stand timepiece with metal dial, white, milk glass base, and glass dome. 30-hour torsion bar control. Time is controlled by torsion twist of flat steel rod on which are fastened two hemispheres 1½ inches apart. 8¼ inches high; *ca.* 1852.

271. Terryville Manufacturing Company. Candle stand timepiece with white paper dial and horizontal balance wheel control for the 30-hour movement. The glass dome is removed. 8¼ inches high; *ca.* 1852.

272. S. B. Terry wall regulator; rose-wood case; eight-day timepieces; winds at 2. 33″x9½″x3¾″

IRVING COOPERMAN COLLECTION

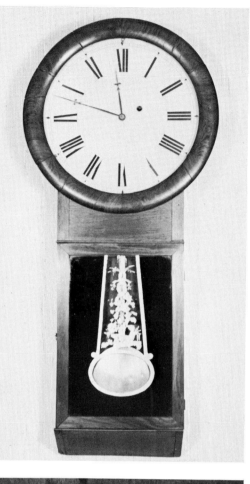

273. SBT's solid plate eight-day timepiece movement with maintaining power; inverted T-suspension holds pendulum; odd crutch wire fits into a slot at base of keystone.

274. The Terry Clock Company, Waterbury, Connecticut. "Patent Dec. 1, 1855." Wall timepiece with eight-day movement, winds at 5.

JAMES W. GIBBS COLLECTION

275. S. B. Terry & Co. Terryville, Connecticut. Plain wood cottage type case;
one-day brass ladder movement timepiece;
winds at 6. 10¼ inches high.

JAMES W. GIBBS COLLECTION

276. SBT's "ladder movement." Two
brass strips, ¾ inches-wide hold, all the
gears in line. Pendulum control. On label:
"Patent. Caveat filed, A.D. 1851"—this
was a warning, not a patent.

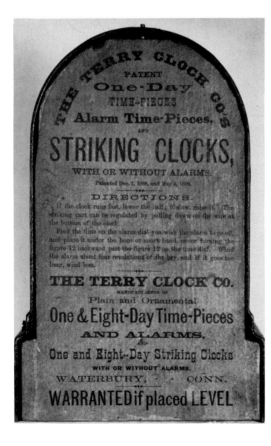

277. The Terry Clock Company, Waterbury, Connecticut. Round top black iron cased one-day spring clock. 8⅛ inches high; *ca.* 1868.

C. S. PARSONS COLLECTION

278. The movement mounted on back board.

279. The back label.

280. The Terry Clock Company. (L.)
eight-day timepiece; (R.) one-day timepiece. Both pendulum controlled, black
iron cases.

JAMES W. GIBBS COLLECTION

281. (L.) S. B. Terry timepiece; metal case with mother of pearl inlay and stenciling. 30-hour brass spring movement with torsion bar control. 8½ inches high; *ca.* 1852.

(R.) J. C. Brown, Bristol, Connecticut. 30-hour balance spring marine movement, time only. Possibly an S. B. Terry movement used by Brown; *ca.* 1852.

JAMES W. GIBBS COLLECTION

Labels & Advertisements

With the development of the American clock, paper was applied inside the case to act as a block against dust—enemy #1 of timepieces. Obviously a fine medium for advertising, makers were quick to take advantage. The history and development of clock labels is a story by itself. The wonder continues that now after some have been affixed for 120 or more years, whatever adhesive was used, they continue to stick!

282. Label of Eli Terry, Jr.; Plymouth, Connecticut; *ca.* 1834.

J. E. COLEMAN COLLECTION

283. A "local" label, possibly to minimize
some Southern State tax laws. "Made &
Sold by Couch, Stowe & Co.; Rock-
springs, Tennessee." No exact date.

J. E. COLEMAN COLLECTION

284. Brewster & Ingrahams, Bristol, Connecticut; *ca.* 1851.

EDWARD INGRAHAM COLLECTION

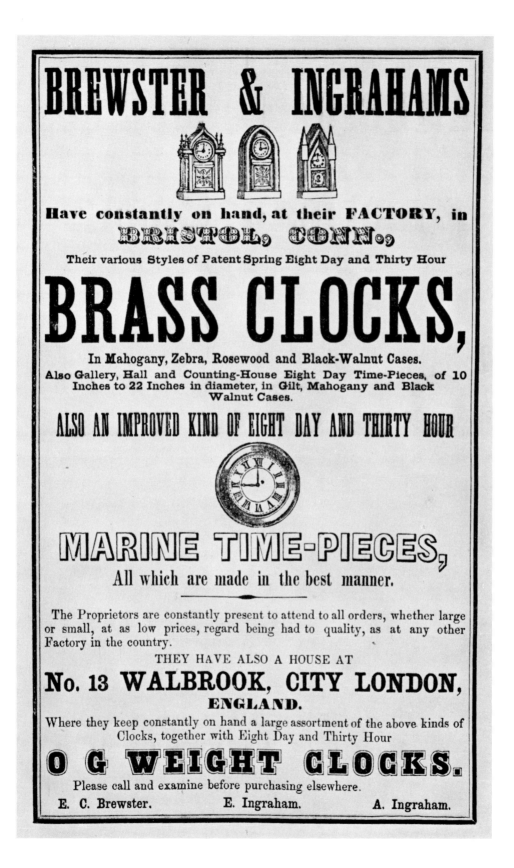

PATENT CLOCKS,

MADE AND SOLD

AT

CINCINNATI, OHIO,

BY

H. BLAKESLEE.

WARRANTED IF WELL USED.

DIRECTIONS FOR REGULATING THIS CLOCK.

If the Clock goes too fast, lengthen the Pendulum; but if too slow, shorten it—by means of a screw at the bottom.

The public may rest assured that Clocks made at this Factory, are equal, if not superior, to any made in this Country.

PRINTED AT THE OFFICE OF THE EVANGELIST.

285. "H." Blakeslee, Cincinnati, Ohio; label of uncertain date. ("H." not previously listed.)

J. E. COLEMAN COLLECTION

286. American Clock Company, New York City; advertisement showing names of associated companies; ca. 1851.

EDWARD INGRAHAM COLLECTION

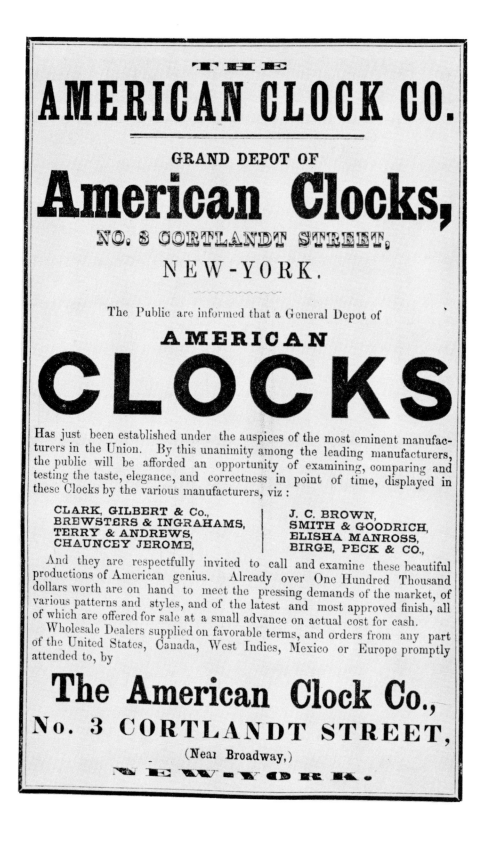

THE AMERICAN CLOCK CO.

GRAND DEPOT OF

American Clocks,

NO. 3 CORTLANDT STREET,

NEW-YORK.

The Public are informed that a General Depot of

AMERICAN CLOCKS

Has just been established under the auspices of the most eminent manufacturers in the Union. By this unanimity among the leading manufacturers, the public will be afforded an opportunity of examining, comparing and testing the taste, elegance, and correctness in point of time, displayed in these Clocks by the various manufacturers, viz:

CLARK, GILBERT & Co.,	J. C. BROWN,
BREWSTERS & INGRAHAMS,	SMITH & GOODRICH,
TERRY & ANDREWS,	ELISHA MANROSS,
CHAUNCEY JEROME,	BIRGE, PECK & CO.,

And they are respectfully invited to call and examine these beautiful productions of American genius. Already over One Hundred Thousand dollars worth are on hand to meet the pressing demands of the market, of various patterns and styles, and of the latest and most approved finish, all of which are offered for sale at a small advance on actual cost for cash.

Wholesale Dealers supplied on favorable terms, and orders from any part of the United States, Canada, West Indies, Mexico or Europe promptly attended to, by

The American Clock Co.,

No. 3 CORTLANDT STREET,

(Near Broadway,)

NEW-YORK.

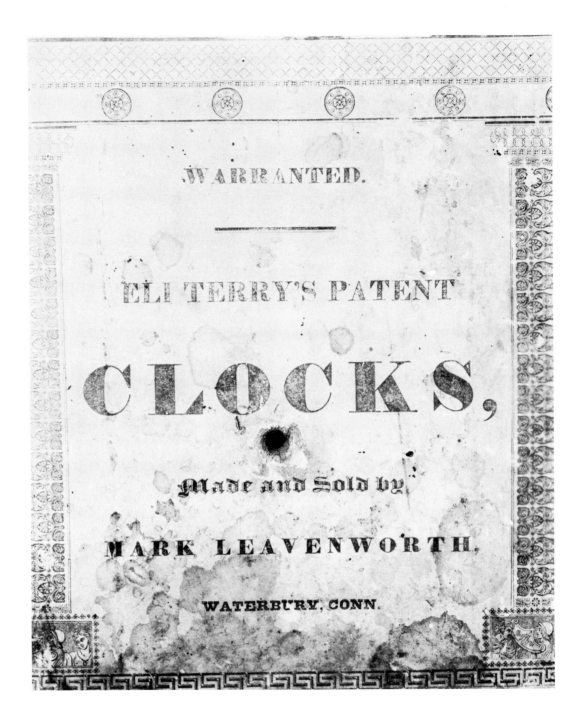

287. Mark Leavenworth, Waterbury, Connecticut; label of the early 1830's.

J. E. COLEMAN COLLECTION

288. "Forestville Clock Manufactory, J. C. Brown, Proprietor," 1851 advertisement. Some of the clock types mentioned are not too well known today.

EDWARD INGRAHAM COLLECTION

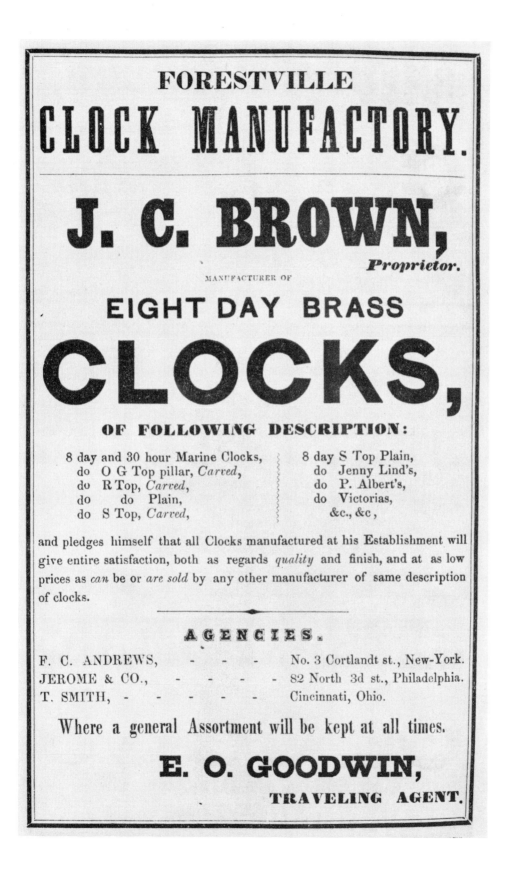

FORESTVILLE
CLOCK MANUFACTORY.

J. C. BROWN,

Proprietor.

MANUFACTURER OF

EIGHT DAY BRASS
CLOCKS,

OF FOLLOWING DESCRIPTION:

8 day and 30 hour Marine Clocks,
  do O G Top pillar, *Carved*,
  do R Top, *Carved*,
  do   do Plain,
  do S Top, *Carved*,

8 day S Top Plain,
  do Jenny Lind's,
  do P. Albert's,
  do Victorias,
  &c., &c,

and pledges himself that all Clocks manufactured at his Establishment will give entire satisfaction, both as regards *quality* and finish, and at as low prices as *can* be or *are sold* by any other manufacturer of same description of clocks.

AGENCIES.

F. C. ANDREWS,	No. 3 Cortlandt st., New-York.
JEROME & CO.,	82 North 3d st., Philadelphia.
T. SMITH,	Cincinnati, Ohio.

Where a general Assortment will be kept at all times.

E. O. GOODWIN,

TRAVELING AGENT.

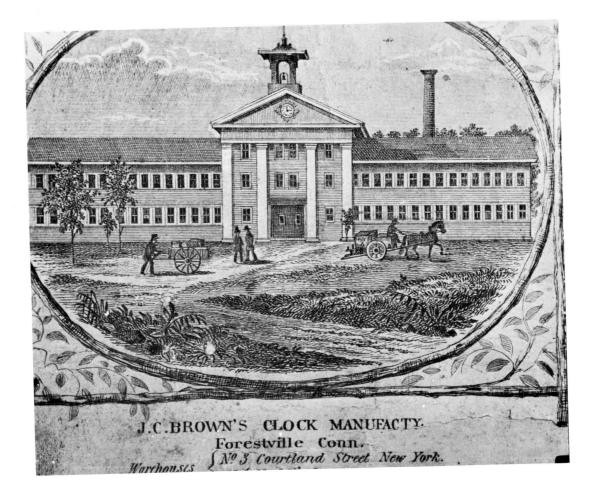

J.C.BROWN'S CLOCK MANUFACTY.
Forestville Conn.
{ Nº 3 Courtland Street New York.
Warehouses

289. J. C. Brown's Clock Manufactory,
Forestville, Connecticut; later destroyed
by fire; *ca.* 1850.

J. E. COLEMAN COLLECTION

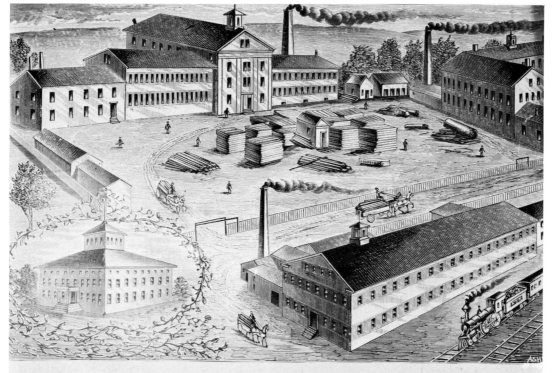

Works of the E. N. Welch Manufacturing Co., Forestville, Connecticut. U. S.

NUFACTURING CO.   and all clocks manufactured and sold by these Companies, are warranted to   manufacturers o

290. The factories of E. N. Welch Manufacturing Company, Forestville, Connecticut; *ca.* 1870.

J. E. COLEMAN COLLECTION

NEW BRASS and WOOD CLOCKS,
TIMEPIECES, WATCHES,
and SHOE KITT.

NOTICE THE PRICES!

EIGHT day Brass Clocks, $16 ; one day do. $6 ; one day do., of Wood, $3 ; eight day Brass Timepieces $10 ; Alarm Clocks, Timepieces, and Alarm Watches, at various prices ; all warranted to perform well. The above articles, and Watches of various kinds and prices, for sale at the subscriber's shop, near Wilder's Bridge, South-Hingham ; where they continue to repair all kinds of Clocks and Watches, that may be left with them, or at the office of Benjamin Wilder, or Mr. Henry Ripley, near Hingham Harbor.

N. B. Clocks of all descriptions, repaired or cleansed, at the Dwellings of those who may wish it, and at as low prices as can be afforded, and warranted to perform well.

JOSHUA WILDER,
EZRA WILDER.

South-Hingham, Nov. 17, 1843.   tf

291. Joshua and Ezra Wilder advertisement from South Hingham, Massachusetts; November 17, 1843.
ELMER STENNES COLLECTION

292. J. J. & W. Beals, Boston, Massachu-
setts; clock label of the late 1840's.
AUTHOR'S COLLECTION
PHOTO BY WILLIAM OSGOOD BLANEY

PRATT'S

CLOCK DEPOT,

No. 2, UNION BLOCK, Up Stairs,

Corner of Union & Marshall Streets, BOSTON.

The Subscribers would respectfully inform the citizens of Boston and vicinity, and the public generally, that they continue the Manufacture of their

CELEBRATED CLOCKS,

at READING, MASS., and have on hand at their Sales Room in Boston, as above, Clocks of every description—suitable in style and finish for Churches, Banks, Counting Houses, Parlors, Kitchens, and in fact, for every place where a Clock is required—which will be sold at WHOLESALE OR RETAIL, at such prices as will give satisfaction to the purchaser, and enable the most humble to obtain them.

The Mantel Clock is quite as attractive, and at one half the usual price of the French Clock, which has been in so general use in the first dwellings in the city.

Since the death of the celebrated Aaron Willard, formerly the most eminent and meritorious Clock Maker in the United States, no Clocks rank superior to those of PRATT & SONS, and "PRATT'S CLOCKS" may be found in every habitable part of the world—in the dwellings of the rich, and cottages of the poor.

Having been engaged in the Manufacture of Clocks for the last twenty years, we have obtained a reputation for making Clocks of the first quality, and will assure the public that all time-keepers made by us will be WARRANTED to give satisfaction.

Also, on hand, parts of Clocks necessary to repair those of the most expensive, as well as the common kind. All Clocks cleaned and repaired by us will be done in a workmanlike manner.

Clocks put up in good order for exportation.

DANIEL PRATT & SONS.

293. Daniel Pratt & Sons, Boston, Massachusetts; the third paragraph reads: "Since the death of the celebrated Aaron Willard (1844), formerly the most eminent and meritorious Clock Maker in the United States . . ."; ca. 1850.

Clocks of New York State

There were eight distinct clock types produced in whole or in part in New York State. They are:

1. Torsion pendulum timepieces, by Aaron Crane, of New Jersey, invented and patented in 1829. These ran for a whole year on one winding and were the "forefather" of the twisting pendulums, lately one of our major imports from Germany.

Examples were made in New York City by the Year Clock Company (dates at work confused) and J. R. Mills & Company.

2. A considerable number of clocks sold in the New York market were made in Connecticut, either as a whole, or at least the movements. The entire story has been lost. "Smith's Clock Manufactory—17½ Nassau St." is one of these, in the early 1840's.

3. "Kroeber" was a fine clockmaker of New York City. He was at work from the 1880's to late 1890's. His clocks are particularly noted for the capable rugged movements of their designs.

4. In Auburn, New York. The Mungers, sometime in cooperation with Benedict, made their own forms of shelf clocks, weight driven; with "ye sore finger" seconds hands and eagle pendulum bobs. The hollow column stove pipe was another specialty.

5. The Ithaca two-dialed calendar clocks are justly famous. Produced in that city in volume from 1866 for 50 years, several of them are shown in the calendar clock section.

6. Timby Solar "Clocks" were the earlier of the two New York globe time machines. T. R. Timby (1822–1909) made them at Saratoga Springs, then at Baldwinsville; the patents are dated 1863–65.

7. Louis Paul Juvet, at Canajoharie, New York, made his patent time globe timepieces from 1867 to 1886 when his factory burned to the ground.

8. The Sidney Advertising Clock was made at Sidney for a time after 1885. They were unique, large wall clocks.

294. J. R. Mills & Company, New York City. Torsion pendulum one-month shelf clock. Basic design by New Jersey's Aaron D. Crane; ca. 1845.

JAMES W. GIBBS COLLECTION

295. Asa Munger & Company, Auburn, New York. Eight-day weight shelf clock. Flying eagle pendulum bob, wall paper case lining, and heavy weights; *ca.* 1830.

JAMES W. GIBBS COLLECTION

296. Cottage type 30-hour shelf time-piece. Unusual pendulum suspension; scape wheel on bottom right of movement. Label reads: "HENRY SPERRY, Clock Manufacturer, 18 Maiden Lane, New York City." Probably of Connecticut origin. 11¾ inches high; *ca.* 1860.

JAMES W. GIBBS COLLECTION

297. T. R. Timby, Saratoga Springs and
Baldwinsville, New York. Solar timepiece, hour and minute revolving dial
above globe, seconds dial in base.

HENRY FORD MUSEUM

298. The Juvet Time Globe, made in Canajoharie, New York. A 30-hour spring brass movement in several sizes, this one is 45 inches high to dial.

299. Shelf timepiece made by the Year Clock Company, New York City; *ca.* 1903.

JAMES W. GIBBS COLLECTION

300. Sidney Advertising Clock, made in Sidney, New York. At five-minute intervals, a bell sounds and the three lower panels turn to another set. 69 inches high; *ca.* 1888.

CHARLES O. TERWILLIGER COLLECTION

Connecticut Shelf

The variety and number of Connecticut shelf clocks has never been estimated. They began with Terry's Pillar & Scroll; then came Jerome's Looking Glass, the Transition, and then the OG. With the development of the American coiled spring, designers of clock cases were freed from having to provide space for the fall of weights. Thus all shapes and sizes were produced as production and styles of decoration changed. The American "marine" —using balance wheel control, like a watch instead of a pendulum—later turned into the Alarm of even more variety and style. Some of the more popular varieties are shown here.

301. Two rippled front shelf clocks by J. C. Brown. (L.) Standard type steeple. (R.) Twin steepled round gothic.

WALTER M. ROBERTS COLLECTION

302. Clarke, Gilbert & Company, Winchester, Connecticut. OG entablature on hollow columns which guide the weights. 30-hour brass clock movement; *ca.* early 1840's.

JAMES W. GIBBS COLLECTION

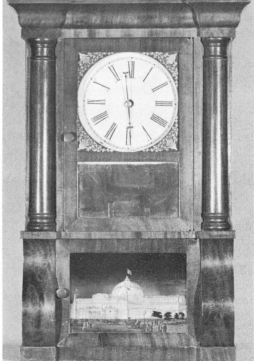

303. E. O. Goodwin (1852–55), Bristol, Connecticut. Eight-day spring brass clock movement, Empire case, Crystal Palace decal tablet.

JAMES W. GIBBS COLLECTION

304. Waterbury Clock Company. Iron front with patriotic motifs. 30-hour movement.

305. Seth Thomas iron front decorated with painting and stenciling. 30-hour movement.

306. American Clock Company. Acorn iron front eight-day spring clock. Frontal hand painted scene; case, colored mahogany. 19″x14″x3½″; *ca.* 1855.

307. Ingraham "Spectacle" tin-plate clock; *ca.* 1859.

308. The inside of the case, showing the Ives tin plate movement.

309. E. Ingraham & Company, Bristol, Connecticut. "Venetian" type round top shelf clock. 18 inches high.

1959 SWAMPSCOTT CONVENTION

310. The movement, showing the tin plates, iron gears, rolling pinions, and an unusual squirrel cage rolling escape. Patent 1859 by Joseph Ives. The name came from the tin plates of the movement.

311. Close-up of the rolling pinions.

312. E. Ingraham & Company, Bristol, Connecticut. "Doric" eight-day alarm shelf clock, two-sided top. 16½"x10½"x 4¾"

C. S. PARSONS COLLECTION

313. The Elias Ingraham "Doric." 16″x9″   314. The Elias Ingraham "Venetian."
AMERICAN MUSEUM OF TIME   AMERICAN MUSEUM OF TIME

315. E. Ingraham & Company. Small Venetian, round top one day alarm TP. 11½ inches high.

JAMES W. GIBBS COLLECTION

316. E. Ingraham & Company. Four sided top eight-day shelf clock, dial not original. 15½″x9″; 4¼ inch dial.

HENRY FORD MUSEUM

317. E. Ingraham & Company. Eight-day shelf clock; *ca.* 1874 and later.

318. Seth Thomas, Thomaston, Connecticut. Eight-day alarm clock, 15-inch cherry case, ST hands.

319. With door open.

320. D. S. Crosby, No. 1 Courtlandt St., New York City. Eight-day spring brass clock movement. 14½ inches high; *ca.* 1850.

321. Wm. L. Gilbert Company, Winsted, Connecticut. Round top alarm TP. 11"x 8¼"; four inch dial.

HENRY FORD MUSEUM

322. J. C. Brown, Forestville Manufacturing Company, Bristol, Connecticut. Miniature, 30-hour spring brass movement. Label, "Improved Brass Clocks; springs warranted not to fail . . ." 14¾ inches high.

JAMES W. GIBBS COLLECTION

323. Seth Thomas round top shelf alarm clock. 15″x10¼″; four inch dial.

HENRY FORD MUSEUM

324. Smith & Goodrich, Bristol, Connecticut (1847–52), 30-hour spring shelf clock with fusee, brass T & S movement, half-round outside door. 15½ inches high.

JAMES W. GIBBS COLLECTION

325. (L.) Forestville Hardware & Clock Company. One-day brass TP. 12½ inches high; *ca.* 1853-55.

(C.) Gilbert Manufacturing Company (1866-71). One-day alarm clock, case patent by George B. Owen, independent manufacturer, later merged with Gilbert.

(R.) No name, one-day alarm TP. Head of woman cast on pendulum bob.

JAMES W. GIBBS COLLECTION

326. The Elias Ingraham "Grecian," shelf clock; zebra case, burl base. This is an eight-day movement, with alarm.

IRVING COOPERMAN COLLECTION

327. The E. N. Welch Manufacturing Company, Forestville, Connecticut. H. J. Davies 1879 patent. Label and 30-hour round plate timepiece movement.

THE WESLEY HALLET NEWPORT, N.H. MUSEUM

328. Close-up of the movement.

329. "No. 658," made by the Wm. L. Gilbert Clock Co., Winsted, Connecticut.

AUTHOR'S COLLECTION

330. Briggs Rotary Pendulum Timepiece; patented in 1855 by John C. Briggs. Made in some volume by the E. N. Welch Manufacturing Company, Bristol, Connecticut. 7½ inches high; five inch diameter; *ca.* 1875.

C. S. PARSONS COLLECTION

331. Rear view.

332. Ansonia Clock Company, N. Y. Cabinet Antique. Solid walnut case with brass trim, corner brass finials 2½ inch and 3¾ inch center finial. Eight-day spring movement. 16″x9″x7½″; *ca.* 1880.

GLADYS LONGMIRE COLLECTION

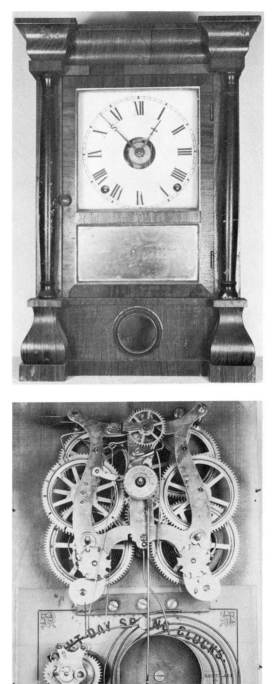

333. Seth Thomas eight-day shelf alarm clock. ST hands, mirror tablet. 16″x10″x 4″; *ca.* 1885.

C. S. PARSONS COLLECTION

334. Back board, lyre movement showing label, location of alarm, bell, and gong.

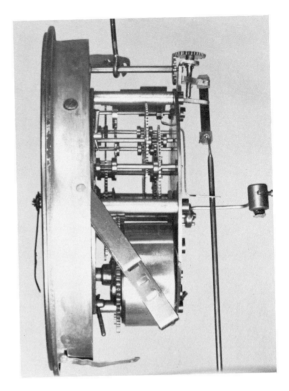

335. Seth Thomas, Thomaston, Connecticut. Small round gothic eight-day clock. Dial marked "Made in U.S.A." 11½"x 7¼"; 4¾ inch dial; *ca.* 1890.

C. S. PARSONS COLLECTION

336. The eight-day movement.

337. New Haven Clock Company. Round top eight-day table clock.

B. W. BRANDT COLLECTION

338. (L.) Yale Clock Company, New Haven, Connecticut. Early 1880's grandfather, wood case, one-day pendulum timepiece. 16 inches high.

(R.) Unmarked cast metal case 30-hour lever escape timepiece. 10½ inches high.

JAMES W. GIBBS COLLECTION

339. E. N. Welch Manufacturing Company, Forestville, Connecticut. "Lucca" eight-day shelf alarm clock. 21″x14″x5½″

C. S. PARSONS COLLECTION

340. The movement, alarm and pendulum.

341. Seth Thomas flat top with one-day weight brass movement. Probably made for Canadian trade. 25 inches high.

IRVING COOPERMAN COLLECTION

342. Seth Thomas Plymouth Hollow flat top with heavier side columns, eight-day clock spring movement. 19 inches high.

IRVING COOPERMAN COLLECTION

343. Ingraham "Oriental" eight-day shelf clock.

B. W. BRANDT COLLECTION

344. Wm. A. Bradshaw, 76 Pearl St., New York City. Flat top shelf clock with tablet in door, detached round side columns. 30-hour with flat, small light weights, brass movement. Probably made in Connecticut.

JAMES W. GIBBS COLLECTION

345. "Chauncey Jerome," New Haven, Connecticut. Flat top gold leafed side columned eight-day clock made in some quantity by Seth Thomas. Tablet shows group of unidentified buildings and a horse car in foreground. 18 inches high.

JAMES W. GIBBS COLLECTION

346. New Haven Clock Company. Empire type flat top case with side, half columns. 24″x15½″; 4½ inch dial.

C. S. PARSONS COLLECTION

347. The 30-hour spring clock movement and label showing another picture of the New Haven plant.

348. "Chauncey Jerome, New Haven, Conn., U.S." in script on dial. Flat topped case, flat side pieces. Detached fuzee movement. Label shows view of New Haven plant.

JAMES W. GIBBS COLLECTION

349. Ansonia Clock Company. Crystal Palace clock. Fourteen different models in 1880 makers catalogue. On this model, the two mirrors back of the pendulum at a 90° angle reflect the swinging motion. 17 inches high.

C. W. HALLET NEWPORT, N.H.
CLOCK MUSEUM

350. Ansonia Clock Company. "Crystal Palace Extra" with glass dome removed. Mark on dial. 17″x14″

HENRY FORD MUSEUM

351. Wm. L. Gilbert Clock Company, Winsted, Connecticut. A rare Crystal Palace type clock, eight-day spring movement. Inside, two mirrors set at 90° angle reflect the oscillation of the pendulum. "Corner A" is name on back label; *ca.* 1880.

C. W. HALLET NEWPORT, N.H.
CLOCK MUSEUM

352. Waterbury Clock Company. "Consort," small shelf clock, mirror tablet, eight-day alarm clock movement. Stamped "Pat. Aug. 30, 1870." 15½"x11¼"; 4½ inch dial; *ca.* late 1870's.

C. S. PARSONS COLLECTION

353. Waterbury Clock Company, Connecticut. China cased shelf clock of the 1890's.

AUTHOR'S COLLECTION

Mother of Pearl

These were inlay Connecticut made shelf and wall clocks, popular from the 1850's.

354. E. & A. Ingraham, Bristol, Connecticut (1852–55). Iron Front. 16¾ inches high.

355. Iron front shelf clock with inlay. Label inside reads, "American Clock Co., 3 Cortlandt St., NYC." 21½ inches high; *ca.* 1855.

HENRY FORD MUSEUM

356. Iron front eight-day shelf clock, unlabeled, hands not original. 18½ inches high.

C. S. PARSONS COLLECTION

357. The wooden box behind the iron front that contains the movement.

358. Terry & Andrews, Ansonia, Connecticut. Iron case shelf clock with gold scroll work; eight-day movement marked "Bristol, Conn." 13¾ inches high.

C. S. PARSONS COLLECTION

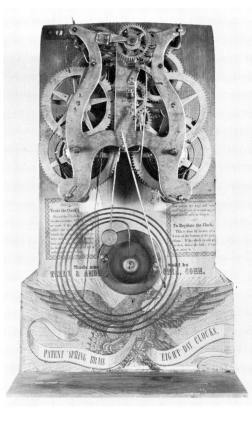

359. Backboard displaying movement and Ansonia label.

360. Forestville Manufacturing Company, Bristol, Connecticut (J. C. Brown). Pearl inlay of colored flowers and gold scroll work; case rim stamped "Pat. May 10, 1859." 15 inches high; *ca.* 1853.

C. S. PARSONS COLLECTION

361. Showing typical stamped Forestville movement.

362. C. (Chauncey) Goodrich, Forestville, Connecticut. Eight-day shelf clock
with inlay. 13¼ inches high; *ca.* after
1852.

HENRY FORD MUSEUM

363. Jerome Manufacturing Company,
New Haven, Connecticut (S. N. Botsford, of Hamden; Whitneyville). "Botsford's Improved" patent lever marine
movement, 30-hour clock. Iron case on
stand, glass globe; removed; *ca.* 1850.

JAMES W. GIBBS COLLECTION

364. From the back showing the unusual
30-hour movement with horizontal balance wheel.

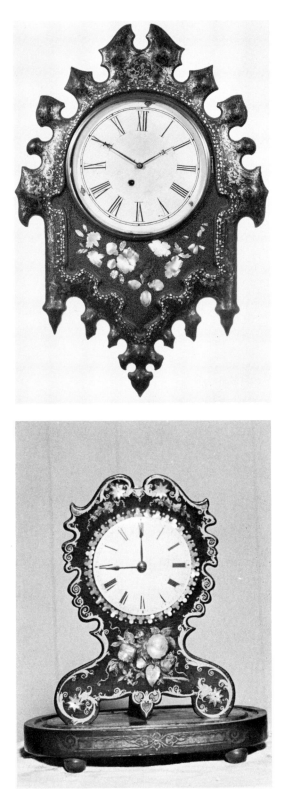

365. Iron case wall timepiece with pearl inlay. Pendulum movement, no label. 34 inches high.

HENRY FORD MUSEUM

366. Litchfield Manufacturing Company, Litchfield, Connecticut. Torsion balance shelf clock. Cache of papier-mâché with mother-of-pearl inlay.

AMERICAN MUSEUM OF TIME

Cottage

A pleasant, rather diminutive form of Connecticut shelf clocks, alarms or timepieces. Mostly 30-hour movements; wooden cases usually less than one foot in height. Now collectable, though made in some volume in the last quarter of the nineteenth century.

367. Seth Thomas, Plymouth Hollow, Connecticut. Three-sided top cottage 30-hour alarm timepiece. Off-center pendulum. 9″x5¾″

CHARLES POORE COLLECTION

368. Label.

369. Seth Thomas, Thomaston, Connecticut. Flat top cottage one-day timepiece with alarm built in to movement. 9¼"x 7¼"; 3⅝ inch dial.

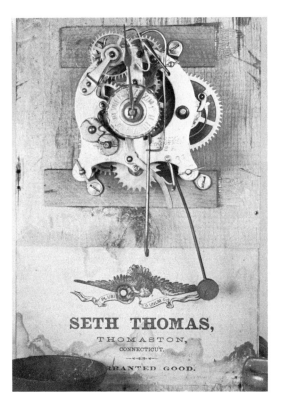

370. Back board with label, bell disconnected and removed; lyre type one-day timepiece with built in alarm, and wind stop.

371. Waterbury Clock Company. Flat top cottage 30-hour alarm timepiece; decal tablet in door, dial refinished; winds at 10:50. 11"x8"; four inch dial.

C. S. PARSONS COLLECTION

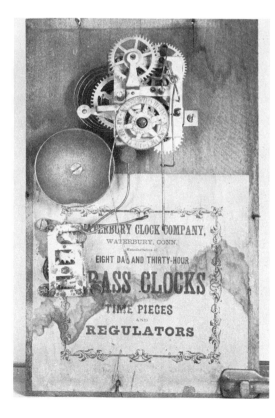

372. Back board with label, separately mounted alarm; the pendulum ball removed to show label.

373. Seth Thomas, Thomaston. Flat top rosewood case cottage eight-day clock. 12¾"x7½"x4"

IRVING COOPERMAN COLLECTION

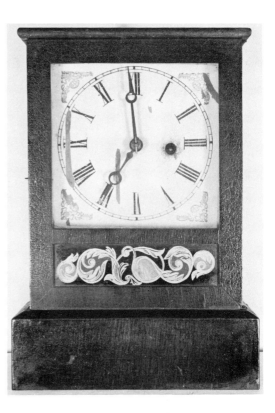

374. No maker's name. A customary flat top wood dialed cottage 30-hour timepiece with decal tablet in door. 11"x7"; four inch dial.

AUTHOR'S COLLECTION

Connecticut Wall

These were made in great volume for use in schools, offices, churches, and public buildings. Some were labeled "Regulator," whose definition in the dictionary reads "a timepiece with a superior mechanism." They represented an honest value but some were not made to give split second accuracy. Many happy examples survive.

with single door having large mirror over small tablet at bottom. Eight-day weight movement with iron plates, rolling pinions, and gears with distinctive Ives teeth. Believed to be first of a series of inventions by Joseph Ives. 40½"x16½"; *ca.* 1818–22.

JAMES W. GIBBS COLLECTION

375. Merriman, Birge, & Company, Bristol, Connecticut. Long wall mirror clock

376. With door open.

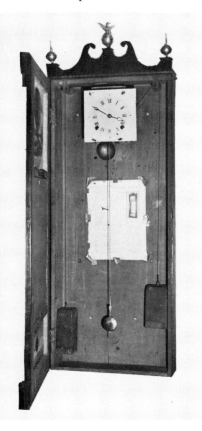

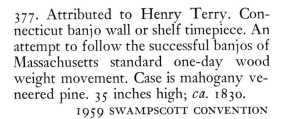

377. Attributed to Henry Terry. Connecticut banjo wall or shelf timepiece. An attempt to follow the successful banjos of Massachusetts standard one-day wood weight movement. Case is mahogany veneered pine. 35 inches high; *ca.* 1830.

378. "Conn. Banjo" with two tablets.

379. George Hills, Plainville, Connecticut. Large single mirrored door with OG type molding. 30-hour brass movement with time and strike run by single spring; *ca.* 1842.

378A. Doors open showing inside arrangement.

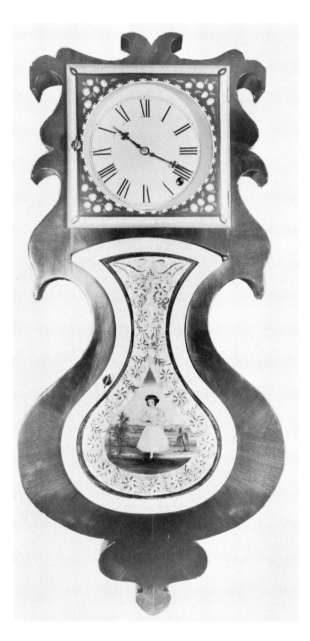

380. Connecticut wall lyre (formerly "wall acorn"). Eight-day spring timepiece of unusual design. Another J. C. Brown creation; *ca.* 1850.

JAMES W. GIBBS COLLECTION

382. With door open from the front, dial off. Has "east-west" eight-day spring timepiece movement and overhead suspended pendulum.

383. Chauncey Jerome, New Haven. Round gallery eight-day spring timepiece in heavy cherry wood case. Winds at 6.

IRVING COOPERMAN COLLECTION

384. From the back with the door open. Overhead suspended pendulum, barrel spring fuzee, heavy brass plates. Bottom case section removable for minor adjustments. Label on door.

385. Seth Thomas, Thomaston, Connecticut. Drop octagon clock, two-sided base; gold leafed border. Eight-day spring movement. May have been made for the English market.

IRVING COOPERMAN COLLECTION

386. Seth Thomas. Drop octagon time-piece. Three-sided base; oak case. Winds at 4:30.

387. Eight-day spring timepiece movement with Geneva stop; stamped "9½."

388. Waterbury Clock Company. Drop octagon. Two-sided base with 12 inch drop. Winds at 6.

389. Eight-day movement stamped "10."

390. Seth Thomas, Thomaston. Regulator type 12-sided top eight-day weight timepiece. Bottom glass door. Winds at 2:30. 41½″x19½″; six inch dial.

C. S. PARSONS COLLECTION

391. Trapazoid shaped brass plated eight-day weight timepiece movement.

392. The Elias Ingraham "Ionic" wall
clock; round head, round drop.
AMERICAN MUSEUM OF TIME

226

393. E. Ingraham & Company. "Ionic" round drop, round base eight-day time-piece. Winds at 6:30.

IRVING COOPERMAN COLLECTION

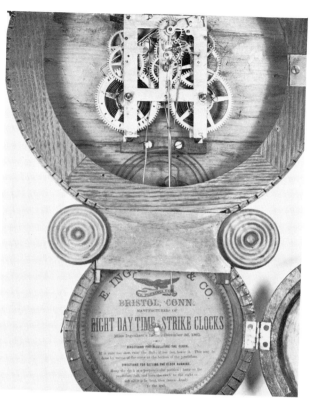

394. Door open showing eight-day full clock movement and label.

C. S. PARSONS COLLECTION

395. New Haven Clock Company. Miniature 18 inches round drop, round base eight-day spring clock.

JAMES W. GIBBS COLLECTION

396. Seth Thomas, Thomaston, Connecticut. Hooded wall clock with moon dial. 36"x17"; 6¾ inch dial.

397. Moon dial and eight-day chain weight movement.

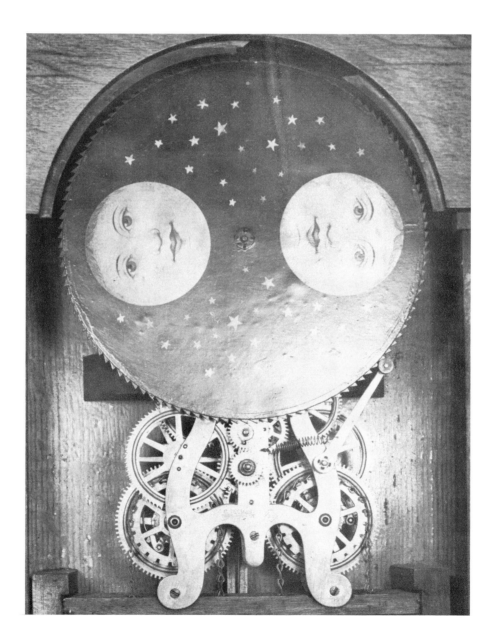

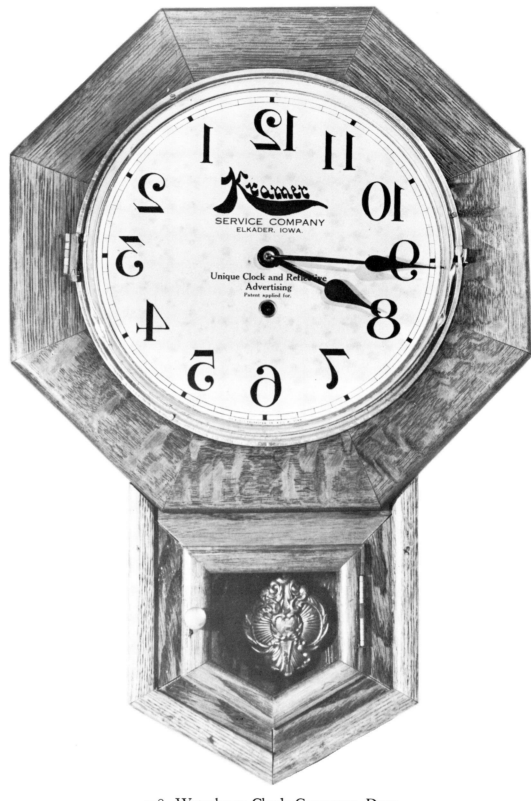

398. Waterbury Clock Company. Drop octagon advertising timepiece with reversed dial and hands moving counterclockwise. For barber shop mirrors. Winds at 6; eight-day timepiece movement.

JAMES W. GIBBS COLLECTION

Calendar

Adding some form of calendar recording as basic was not new here. Americans did invent and then make ingenious additions to a clock's time telling and striking the hours. The calendar variations, as will be here seen, are many-varied. Some add only the day of the month; others give as well the month and the day of the week. Most of the principal American calendar clocks follow.

399. Seth Thomas, Plymouth Hollow, Connecticut. Calendar clock; center tablet shows eagle in gold holding an American flag with 33 stars. Rosewood case. 30¼"x18½"x5"; *ca.* 1860–61.

IRVING COOPERMAN COLLECTION

400. Inside weight driven eight-day Seth Thomas calendar clock, showing mechanism of No. 399.

C. S. PARSONS COLLECTION

401. Direction label of Seth Thomas calendar, on back of door.

C. S. PARSONS COLLECTION

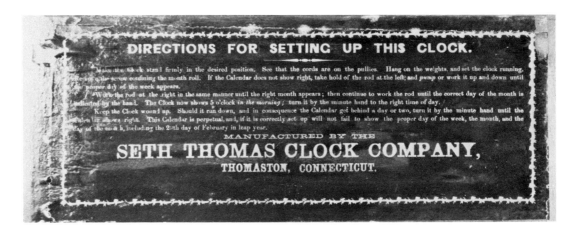

DIRECTIONS FOR SETTING UP THIS CLOCK.

Make the Clock stand firmly in the desired position. See that the cords are on the pullies. Hang on the weights, and set the clock running. Release the screw confining the month roll. If the Calendar does not show right, take hold of the rod at the left; and *pump* or work it up and down until the proper day of the week appears.

Work the rod at the right in the same manner until the right month appears; then continue to work the rod until the correct day of the month is indicated by the hand. The Clock now shows 5 o'clock *in the morning*; turn it by the minute hand to the right time of day.

Keep the Clock wound up. Should it run down, and in consequence the Calendar get behind a day or two, turn it by the minute hand until the Calendar shows right. This Calendar is perpetual, and, if it is correctly set up will not fail to show the proper day of the week, the month, and the day of the month, including the 29th day of February in leap year.

MANUFACTURED BY THE

SETH THOMAS CLOCK COMPANY,
THOMASTON, CONNECTICUT.

402. Seth Thomas, Plymouth Hollow, Connecticut. Wall eight-day "Regulator" weight calendar timepiece. Patent dates on lower dial from Sept. 14, 1854 to March 4, 1862. Head of case has nine sides. 40½"x19"x6½"

C. S. PARSONS COLLECTION

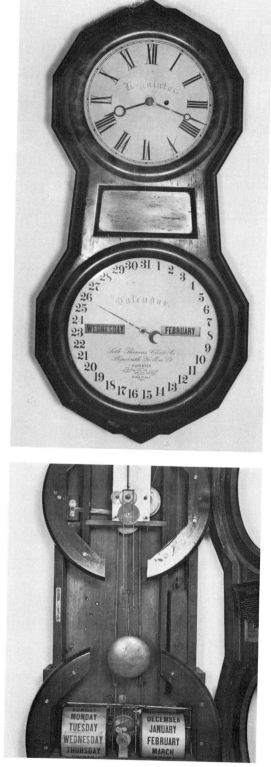

403. With door open and dials removed; showing timepiece movement, the weight on side, and ST calendar mechanism.

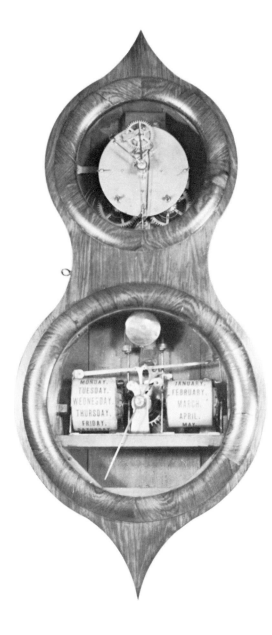

405. Ithaca eight-day shelf calendar clock with three top finials. Last patent date Aug. 28, 1866. 23″x12″x5¾″

HENRY FORD MUSEUM

404. Seth Thomas, Thomaston, Connecticut. ST wall calendar timepiece with both dials removed, showing movement and calendar mechanism. Double spring movement, eight-day. Rosewood case. 24 inches high.

IRVING COOPERMAN COLLECTION

406. Ithaca eight-day calendar shelf clock with single finial. 25 inches high.

407. Ithaca eight-day round top shelf clock with alarm. 22¾"x11½"x4"

C. S. PARSONS COLLECTION

408. With back of case removed, showing arrangement of mechanisms; the eight-day spring movement, the hour wire gong and calendar parts, and the alarm.

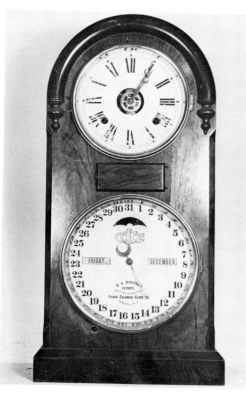

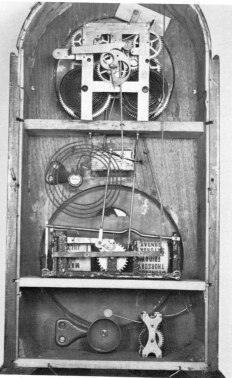

409. Ithaca Black Walnut cased Parlor calendar with black dials and clear glass pendulum bob. 19 inches high.

IRVING COOPERMAN COLLECTION

410. Ithaca eight-day calendar clock. White time dial, black calendar dial with clear glass pendulum bob. Can be either a wall clock; as shown here, or a shelf clock; the bottom bracket is removable. 22 inches high without bottom bracket.

IRVING COOPERMAN COLLECTION

411. Ithaca wall calendar eight-day clock in iron case.

JAMES W. GIBBS COLLECTION

ITHACA CALENDAR CLOCK CO.
ITHACA, N. Y.

DIRECTIONS.

The pendulum Ball and Key will be found fastened either at the bottom or top of the clock.

The time now stands at 5 minutes before 11 P. M.

If the clock is to be set IN THE MORNING, turn the minute hand forward until the right hour is reached.

If the clock is to be set IN THE AFTERNOON, turn the minute hand forward through TWELVE HOURS and then to the right hour.

The calendar changes at midnight.

Set the clock in position and attach the pendulum ball.

The clock must be perpendicular to insure a perfect beat.

NEVER MOVE THE HOUR HAND by itself, as the calendar would not change at the proper hour.

To SET THE CALENDAR—Raise the wire on the top of the clock and turn the calendar hand forward [never backward] until the right month and day of month is shown.

Still holding up the wire turn the day of the week UPWARD till right.

CAUTION—USE NO OIL ON THE CALENDAR. It is not needed, and will work only injury when used by attracting dust and clogging the machine.

To REGULATE THE TIME—Raise or lower the pendulum ball by means of the nut below it.

☞ If the clock does not strike correctly, raise the small wire at the left under the seat on which rests the time movement, and repeat until it strikes correctly. But this cannot be done within 15 minutes of the striking hour. This clock strikes the half hours.

THE BEST TIME TO CORRECT THE STRIKE IS IMMEDIATELY AFTER THE HOUR IS STRUCK.

This Clock is set for 19___

Every clock before leaving the works is tested thoroughly, both as to time and Calendar, and the Calendar being set on the right year when the clock is packed, will give the Leap year and other Februarys correctly unless interfered with, or worked ahead of time. But if this should occur, it can readily be set right as follows: Raise the wire as above, turn the pointer forward until a February is shown, and then place the pointer on the Figure 29, drop the wire and if the pointer cannot be moved you have a Leap Year February. If the pointer is not held fast on the figure 29, continue the process until it is. Calling this the Last Leap Year, work forward as before to the right year and month.

No women or children are employed in these works.

X 2944

412. Direction label for Ithaca calendar clock on the outside of the back of the clock.

C. S. PARSONS COLLECTION

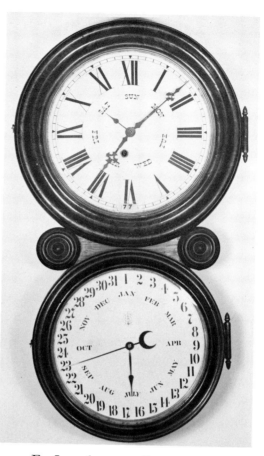

414. E. Ingraham & Company, Bristol, Connecticut. Wall calendar timepiece. Round head case with Ingraham rosettes. B. B. Lewis, calendar mechanism. 29½"x-16¼"x4½"; *ca.* 1879.

C. S. PARSONS COLLECTION

413. Ithaca four-sided top eight-day calendar shelf clock.

B. W. BRANDT COLLECTION

415. The Ingraham timepiece movement; patent dates: "Oct. 8, 1878 and Nov. 11, 1879" stamped in.

416. Part of Lewis calendar mechanism and instruction label.

417. Calendar mechanism behind Lewis calendar (lower) dial.

418. B. B. Lewis calendar. All known are eight-day spring brass movement clocks or timepieces. Day of week shown by extra hand at center of time dial, the month and day indicated by two hands on calendar (lower) dial; *ca.* from 1864.

CHARLES POORE COLLECTION

419. Welch, Spring & Company, Bristol, Connecticut. Lewis shelf calendar eight-day weight driven, with double decker case. 36½″x20¼″x7″

C. S. PARSONS COLLECTION

420. Eight-day brass weight movement.

421. E. N. Welch Manufacturing Company, Forestville, Connecticut. Daniel Jackson Gale eight-day clock model "Arditi." (Gale's calendar clocks were patented "Best Calendar Clock in Existence." They have complete calendars on lower of two round dials. Center sweep hand points to date on rim; left small hand to day of the week; right to the month.) 27″x17½″x6″; *ca.* 1870.

422. Door open and dial off showing eight-day brass spring movement and label.

423. Welch, Spring & Company, Bristol, Connecticut. Round wall calendar timepiece, Gale patent; *ca.* 1870.

424. Gale calendar label.

425. Back cover plate of a B. B. Lewis calendar mechanism.

C. S. PARSONS COLLECTION

426. Southern Calendar Clock Company, St. Louis, Missouri. Fashion calendar eight-day brass spring clock with perpetual calendar made by Seth Thomas. Upper dial carries "Patented Dec. 28, 1875" and calendar dial "March 18, 1879."

JAMES W. GIBBS COLLECTION

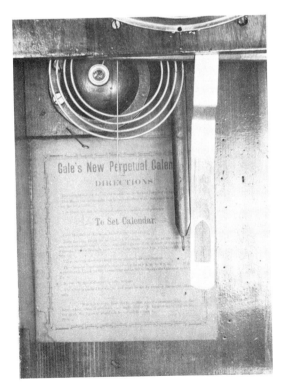

427. Wm. L. Gilbert Company, Winsted, Connecticut. Prentiss calendar shelf clock. The calendar is displayed in openings below the time dial. The glass on door is marked "The Fashion. Southern Calendar Clock Co." Prentiss Clock Company, New York City, 1887–1892 got patents on calendar April 5, 1887 and May 20, 1890.
LLOYD CARNER COLLECTION

428. Wm. L. Gilbert Clock Company, Winsted, Connecticut. Day of the month calendar shelf clock. The date runs on the perimeter of the time dial. The day of the month is indicated by a third hand. No month, or day of the week is indicated. Should the month have less than 31 days, manual adjustment is needed for accuracy. 25"x15"x4¼"
HENRY FORD MUSEUM

429. E. Ingraham Company, Bristol, Connecticut. Connecticut wall regulator, eight-day timepiece. 38"x17"x4¼"
C. S. PARSONS COLLECTION

430. Eight-day timepiece movement of Connecticut wall regulator.

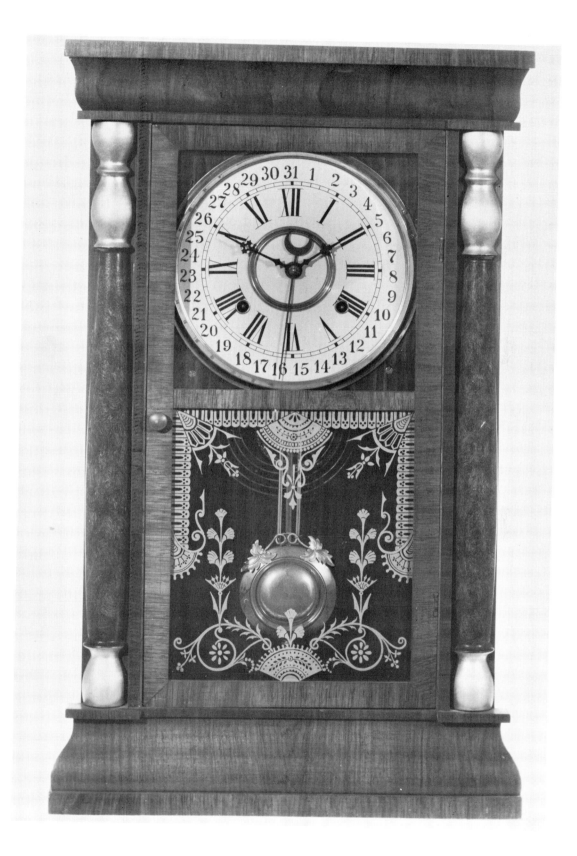

431. New Haven Clock Company. Drop octagon 12 inch wall timepiece.

432. Eight-day timepiece movement.

433. The E. Ingraham Company, Bristol, Connecticut. Round drop wall clock. Patent Oct. 8, 1872 and Nov. 4, 1873.

434. The clock movement.

Novelties

Following are examples of timepieces of the last quarter of the nineteenth century. Lacking a better term, we may call them "Novelties."

435. Burglar & Fire-Detective Alarm Clock, patent, Aug. 7, 1860. Four clock papers: back, inside door, inside base, and inside back. Back reads "Made & Sold by Seth Thomas, Plymouth Hollow. This clock answers the triple purpose of a timepiece, burglar and fire alarm, and lights a lamp at the moment the alarm strikes. Arranged on an entirely new principle, it is warranted to do more work than any other clock on the market. Simple, it is not liable to get out of order. Put up in a neat rosewood case [11¼ inches high] and warranted to keep good time. Manufactured by G. K. Proctor & Co., Beverly, Mass."

FREDERICK FRIED COLLECTION

436. "Illuminated Alarm—Patent applied for. Manufactured by H. J. Davies, 5 Cortlandt St., N.Y." Paper on back gives operational directions. Clock paper inside: "Ansonia Brass & Copper Co., Ansonia, Ct"; *ca.* 1877.

JAMES W. GIBBS COLLECTION

437. Seth Thomas round metal cased eight-day double spring drive with a lever balance wheel movement. 6¼ inch diameter.

C. S. PARSONS COLLECTION

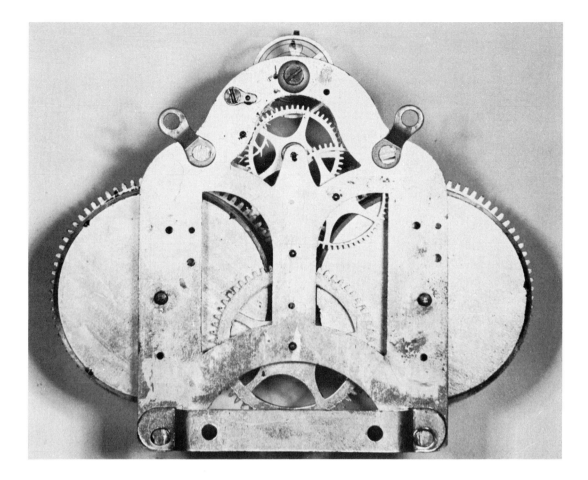

438. Eight-day double spring drive movement.

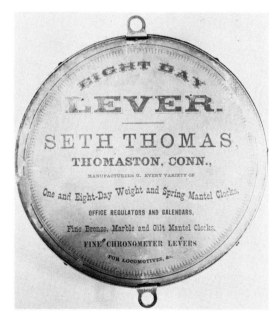

439. Label on back of case.

440. Seth Thomas 30-hour ships bell clock with metal case, bell below. Strikes ships bells, not the hour.

IRVING COOPERMAN COLLECTION

441. Group of clocks.

B. W. BRANDT COLLECTION

442. E. N. Welch Manufacturing Company, Bristol, Connecticut. Glass paperweight timepiece (also made as clock and repeater). These were mostly 30-hour timepieces, some with eight-day movements. Made in clear, amber, green, and blue glass. From the 1870's 20 different examples are in the Bernard Brandt Collection.

JAMES W. GIBBS COLLECTION

443. Seth Thomas Sons & Company, Thomaston, Connecticut, and New York. Candlestand clock. Eight-day brass spring movement; *ca.* 1875.

JAMES W. GIBBS COLLECTION

444. Bradley & Hubbard, Meriden, Connecticut. Blinking eye 30-hour timepieces. The eyes of the dog and the lion move with the beat of the pendulum. Two of many iron castings; these are rare. "Patent applied for, 1858"; *ca.* 1875.

JAMES W. GIBBS COLLECTION

445. Ansonia Bobbing Doll 30-hour timepiece; "patented Dec. 14, 1886." The up and down motion of the doll acts as the pendulum.

JAMES W. GIBBS COLLECTION

446. (L.) Ansonia Striking Doll timepiece.

(R.) Ansonia Swinging Doll timepiece; patented "April 29, 1889." The doll swings back and forward.

JAMES W. GIBBS COLLECTION

447. Violin Clock, made by Seth Thomas Clock Company; *ca.* 1892.

JAMES W. GIBBS COLLECTION

448. "Ignatz." This is one of four models pictured in the New Haven Clock Company 1884–85 catalogue, under the label of Jerome & Company. They were made only the one year. Patented by the inventor, A. C. Clausen, Oct. 9, 1883, and called "the craziest clock in the world." The small tether ball winds and unwinds on the two posts. Example of replica made in the 1960's through C. O. Terwilliger.

449. Bostwick & Burgess, Norwalk, Ohio. Columbus clock. One hand one-day weight driven wall timepiece, wood movement. Torsion bar escape does not make it very accurate. Dial is marked "Columbus" "Anno 1492." Distributed at World's Fair, Chicago, 1893. Type of timepiece and date on dial are a frequent source of confusion as to age; *ca.* 1892.

C. S. PARSONS COLLECTION

450. Movement of Columbus clock.

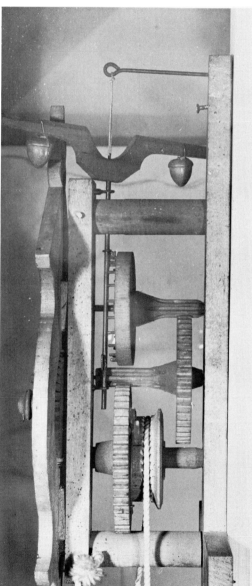

451. Chess game timer, by Yale Clock Company. Twin timepieces to check intervals between moves. Patent model at Smithsonian.

HALLET MUSEUM, NEWPORT, N.H.

452. Chelsea Clock Company, Boston, Massachusetts. Shelf clock, with fine eight-day spring driven movement with balance wheel. Has either hour–half hour or ship bell strike. Pleasant round top mahogany case made during the era of the gee gaw. 16"x7⅛"; ca. 1900.

WALTER MUTZ COLLECTION

453. Loheide Manufacturing Company,
St. Louis, Missouri. "Slot Machine" clock.
Black wood case with metal appliqué.
Coin slot is made to take $2.50 gold piece;
ca. early 1900's.

454. Jeromes & Darrow, Bristol, *ca.* 1828,
with 30-hour wood movement; Ingraham
Steeple clock; and alarms of Western
Clock Co.

455. Gas light (or table) timepiece. The back arm hooks over the gas cock; the milk glass dial is translucent, time can be read all night with only a small gas flame. By day, the arm is used to balance the timepiece on a shelf or table.

IRVING COOPERMAN COLLECTION

456. Standing as a shelf timepiece. The gas jet is seen above, not connected.

457. American Waltham Watch Company. Gas light timepiece in travel case. 4¾ inch dial.

458. The watch movement.

459. Bensel's Acme night alarm time-piece. The hand is stationary, the glass globe revolves on a platform. The right pointer is for the alarm. A kerosene lamp illuminates at night when lit. 9 inches high.

IRVING COOPERMAN COLLECTION

460. The lamp without globe.

461. (L.) Ansonia "Bee" alarm.

(C.) Briggs rotary pendulum timepiece.

(R.) Yale Clock Company's "Pendulette"; 3″x2″x1½″

IRVING COOPERMAN COLLECTION

462. Wm. L. Gilbert Clock Company. One of many types of metal cased clocks; *ca.* 1900.

HENRY FORD MUSEUM

463. Ansonia Clock Company, New York. Metal cased clock, copied from European models, with casting of human figure. 10¾″x14½″

HENRY FORD MUSEUM

464. Group of three metal cased timepieces, in style at turn of century. Center clock is stamped "The Jennings Brothers Mfg Co. Bridgeport, Ct." Left and right stamped "New Haven Clock Co." Patents date from Jan. 18, 1878 to Jan. 17, 1891.

C. S. PARSONS COLLECTION

465. Annual Wind Clock Company, Chicago, Illinois. Another of the timepieces that run a year on one winding. No exact data.

466. Ansonia Clock Company. Metal case, 30-hour clock; 14″x9¼″; 3¼ inch dial.

467. No maker's name. Jig Saw fret work
30-hour wall timepiece. A style popular
at the end of the nineteenth century. A
Mr. Pomeroy of Hartford, Connecticut,
reportedly made some from 1885 to 1900.
JAMES W. GIBBS COLLECTION

468. No maker's name. Twin glass columned 30-hour timepiece. "Made in U.S.A." Several extant, two in James W. Gibbs collection.

469. (L.) Teddy Roosevelt alarm time-piece; "Made in U.S.,"; 10½ inches high.

(R.) Ansonia Clock Company, New York. "Victory" (dog and trumpeter). No casting mark on case. 10¾ inches high.

Both are cast iron clock cases; *ca.* 1900.
FREDERICK FRIED COLLECTION

470. (L.) No maker's name. Wm. Mc-Kinley. Casting reads: "born Jan. 29, 1843–died Sept. 14, 1901. His last words were 'It is God's Way. His will be done.'" "Patent, Sept. 22, 1885"; 12½ inches high.

471. (R.) New Haven Clock Company. Copyright 1887, Muller & Sons, New York. 17 inches high.
FREDERICK FRIED COLLECTION

472. (L.) Ansonia "Bee" alarm.

(C.) Seth Thomas, Plymouth Hollow, Connecticut. Early small mantel clock. The 30-hour movement has springs made of brass.

(R.) Carriage type alarm timepiece. Often the alarm is a musical tune.
IRVING COOPERMAN COLLECTION

473. Plato, described as a Time Indicator and patented by its inventor, Eugene L. Fitch, New York, in 1902. This is one of four basic models made in 1904–06, by Ansonia Clock Company; *ca.* 1905. Production totaled 40,000 units. Time told by numbered turning leaves. Modern replicas are made in Germany for The Horolovar Company.
IRVING COOPERMAN COLLECTION

474. Wm. L. Gilbert Clock Company. Tambour mantel clock. One of many styles from the 1900's, and still being produced. 9½"x19"; five inch dial.

HENRY FORD MUSEUM

475. Ansonia Gravity 30-hour timepiece manufactured in the first quarter of this century. The back of the timepiece is lead-weighted. Lifted to the top it keeps time as it descends on the double geared legs.

VAN BELKNAP COLLECTION

476. A 24½-inch-high reproduction of Model No. 4 Mouse clock with eight-day balance wheel spring-driven movement. Produced by the Horolovar Company.

CHARLES TERWILLIGER COLLECTION

477. There were five models of the Mouse clock. Illustration shows Model No. 2, 43 inches high. Made for Dungan & Klump (Phila.) by New Haven Clock Company; *ca.* 1910.

478. New Haven Clock Company. Mission black oak case eight-day clock. 13¾"x11¾"x5½"; *ca.* early twentieth century.

C. S. PARSONS COLLECTION

479. The movement.

480. Tiffany Never-Wind Clock Corporation, Buffalo, New York. Glass domed torsion timepiece with a magnetic battery powered pendulum. "Patent March 8, 1904." 11 inches high; 6½ inch dial.

HENRY FORD MUSEUM

481. One Hand Clock Corporation, Warren, Pennsylvania. (1918–30) One hand clock. 30-hour brass spring timepiece, 9 inch dial with single hand. All records of the One Hand Clock Company were reportedly destroyed on the death of the president in 1935. Two other sizes known: 10 inch and 12 inch diameter dials.

JAMES W. GIBBS COLLECTION

482. 2¼ inch diameter brass cased Ansonia. "Pat. Apr. 28, 1878." Wound by turning back of case.

3 inch Parker & Whipple (Meriden, Connecticut) pendulum controlled desk timepiece.

3¾ inch brass case duplex escape movement (like Waterbury Series) of long wind watches by Waterbury Watch Company, Waterbury; ca. 1880.

2¼ inch diameter, Wasp bell on top alarm, Waterbury Clock Company, "Pat. June 4, 1907."

2¼ inch portable carriage type, Waterbury Clock Company. Patent dates May 6, 1890 through Apr. 27, 1897.

All 30-hour timepieces.

JAMES W. GIBBS COLLECTION

483. Lux "Pendulette," popular in the 1930's. 30-hour spring timepiece with rocking bird. 6½"x3⅞"

484. The movement.

"Walnuts"

Four forms of American timekeepers, if not necessarily beautiful, often amazing in case design, "took over the market" in the last quarter of the nineteenth century. The Industry knew one as "Walnuts," a wood out of favor from the seventeenth down to the mid-nineteenth century. "Walnuts" came into vogue in the late 1870's and lasted until 1900.

"Blacks" were in favor from 1880 to just before 1920.

"Oaks" were popular from 1890 until well into the 1900's.

"Alarms" were popular, and because of their usefulness continue to be so. Their vogue began about 1875.

Each form had its characteristics and, price of purchase considered, were good values, if the owner could look at them without shuddering.

485. New Haven Clock Company. Walnut eight-day alarm clock, pendulum ball marked for adjustment. 20"x14"; five inch dial.

486. Waterbury Clock Company. Walnut eight-day clock. 20"x13½"; 4¾ inch dial.

487. Ingraham Walnut cased eight-day alarm clock, heavy upper section. 24"x 16"; five inch dial.

488. E. N. Welch Manufacturing Company. Black walnut miniature, hands painted white for contrast; 30-hour alarm clock. 21"x13"; five inch dial.

489. Wm. L. Gilbert Clock Company, Winsted, Connecticut. Black walnut eight-day shelf clock. 19″x10½″; 4¾ inch dial.

HENRY FORD MUSEUM

490. F. Kroeber, New York City. Black walnut eight-day shelf clock with cut crystal pendulum ball. 21″x14½″; five inch dial.

HENRY FORD MUSEUM

491. Ingraham "Liberty" walnut eight-day calendar clock. 22"x14½"; five inch dial.

HENRY FORD MUSEUM

492. New Haven Clock Co. Walnut eight-day shelf clock. Pendulum ball marked to adjust changes. 20½"x13¼"; five inch dial.

HENRY FORD MUSEUM

493. "C. Jerome" (used by New Haven Clock Company). Walnut case with religious motif eight-day clock. 21"x 21"x3½"

L. W. PETERSON COLLECTION

494. E. N. Welch Mfg. Company. Walnut, Victorian motif; two knights in armor on horseback on glass door tablet. Eight-day alarm clock. 23"x14½"x5½"

L. W. PETERSON COLLECTION

495. George Owen, Winsted, Connecticut (at Gilbert). Walnut, kidney dial opening; three finial top. 23"x14"x5"; *ca.* 1880.

L. W. PETERSON COLLECTION

496. Seth Thomas, Walnut case; thermometer in center of head piece; level mounted in base. Eight-day alarm clock.

L. W. PETERSON COLLECTION

497. Wm. L. Gilbert Company. Walnut eight-day shelf clock with side down-swept finials. 24″x14½″; 5½ inch dial.

HENRY FORD MUSEUM

498. Seth Thomas, Walnut case eight-day clock. 22″x13″; 5½ inch dial.

JAMES W. GIBBS COLLECTION

499. Seth Thomas, Walnut wall eight-day clock. Some walnuts were made as wall clocks. 26¼"x14¾"; five inch dial.

HENRY FORD MUSEUM

500. Welch, Spring & Company. Platform topped walnut case, eight-day alarm clock with "compensating pendulum." 19"x12½"; 6¼ inch dial.

HENRY FORD MUSEUM

501. E. N. Welch Company. Walnut eight-day shelf clock with up-standing side columns entwined with twisted wood ribbons. Plain glass door not original. 23″x17″; five inch dial.

HENRY FORD MUSEUM

502. E. N. Welch Company. Walnut eight-day clock. 26″x15½″; five inch dial.

HENRY FORD MUSEUM

"Blacks"

These were a popular American favorite for nearly forty years after 1880. Production and sales records proved their appeal to the public. They came in a myriad of styles; the materials were of three kinds: marble, black iron, and black enameled wood.

There was no limit placed on the imaginations of the case designers. A representative selection is presented here.

The movements were soundly built, mostly eight-day, some with alarms, and with half hour and hour strike, pendulum controlled. Most manufacturers made them. They continue in use today, still keeping good time. "The Enameling process produces a surface and lustre of superior appearance and durability equal to the finest imported work" (from a sales catalogue).

Here are examples of marble, iron, and wood.

503. Ansonia marble case, flat top, no feet. Patent dates run to 1882. Escapement on face of dial.

C. S. PARSONS COLLECTION

504. Typical Ansonia movement, this with rather solid plates.

505. Ansonia iron cased "Unique" with black dial and gilt hands and chapter numbers. 10½"x9½"; five inch dial. "Patent applied for" stamped on case.

506. The movement by Ansonia.

507. F. Kroeber, New York. "Cairo" cast iron case, flat top, metal feet, porcelain dial. Escapement on dial face. 11½"x 12¾"; six inch dial; *ca.* 1875.

C. S. PARSONS COLLECTION

508. The movement by F. Kroeber.

509. Ingraham "Count" black iron case; half hour bell and hour Cathedral Gong Strike. 12¼"x10"; five inch dial.

HENRY FORD MUSEUM

510. Waterbury Clock Company. Black flat top wood case, no applied ornaments or feet, escapement on dial. 10"x11½"; 5½ inch dial; *ca.* 1881.

C. S. PARSONS COLLECTION

511. The movement, with rack and snail strike.

512. Ansonia (N.Y.) black wood flat top case and feet. 10½″x18″; 6½ inch dial.

HENRY FORD MUSEUM

513. The E. Ingraham Company. "Luzon" black wood flat top case, single marbleized column on each side, feet. 10¾″x14¾″; seven inch dial; *ca.* 1888.

C. S. PARSONS COLLECTION

514. The movement and inside back label.

515. New Haven "Monarch" black wood case with flat top, twin marbleized columns on each side. 12″x17½″; 6½ inch dial.

HENRY FORD MUSEUM

516. Ingraham "Albany" flat top black wood case with three reeded columns, capitals on each side, metal feet. 11″x17″; five inch dial. (Mint condition from Gibbs Collection, now at American Museum of Time.)

JAMES W. GIBBS COLLECTION

517. Ingraham "Gypsy" (in 1911 catalogue) flat top black wood case with three flat columns, capitals on marble insert on each side, feet and down swept side ornaments. 11″x17″; five inch dial.

HENRY FORD MUSEUM

518. Waterbury "Mosaic" black wood case with scalloped top and four reeded columns, capitals on each side, feet. Dial is arabic. 11″x17″; six inch dial.

C. S. PARSONS COLLECTION

519. The movement by Waterbury. Added time adjustment by pin through dial.

520. Sessions Clock Company. Black wood case with two side arched columns containing statues, feet, arabic dial. 12″x 16¼″; 5½ inch dial.

HENRY FORD MUSEUM

521. Ingraham "Alamo" black wood flat top case showing the movement, gong disconnected.

C. S. PARSONS COLLECTION

522. Back board of the case with back label.

"Oaks"

The "Oak" or "Kitchen" was popular for a time from the late 1890's to about 1915. There were so many different patterns for front design, no one could collect all of them. The larger clock companies made them, with perhaps Ingraham the largest producer, followed by Welch, Seth Thomas, Waterbury, Ansonia, New Haven, and Sessions.

The heights were about 23 inches; substantial eight-day long-wearing; striking movements were used.

The origin of the embossed oaks is not exactly known, possibly helped along by those who made molds and embossing dies many of which were located then around Cincinnati.

An interesting variant were those with figures or buildings on the middle top front of the clock. These were manufactured for a short time from 1899 to 1905. Ingraham had the "Army–Navy" line, six styles consisting of McKinley, Dewey, Lee, the Maine, Peace (a dove), and Emblem from 1899. This was replaced by their "National" line—six more as Mt. Vernon, Capitol Dome, Freedom (old oaken bucket), Union (doves around a bird bath), Peerless (a lion rampant), and Banner.

Welch had Sampson, Schley, Dewey, Lee, Wheeler, the Maine, and President Theodore Roosevelt.

523. Admiral Dewey, one of six of the "Army–Navy" line of the Ingraham Company. Battleship and four American flags stenciled on glass door; *ca.* 1899.

AMERICAN MUSEUM OF TIME
PHOTO BY EDWARD GOODRICH

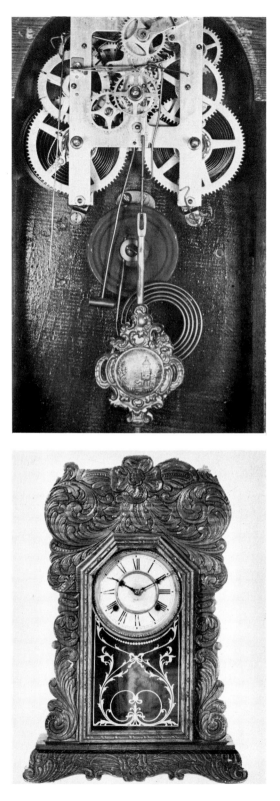

524. Inside the case view of a standard Ingraham Oak with the fine eight-day half hour strike spring movement and "cathedral gong." Domed building on pendulum ball.

C. S. PARSONS COLLECTION

525. Waterbury Clock Company. Brighton oak; *ca.* 1902.

HENRY FORD MUSEUM

526. Gila, famous Ingraham oak from their "River" line. At the left of the base a barometer; on the right, a thermometer calendar dial; *ca.* 1903.

AMERICAN MUSEUM OF TIME

527. Ingraham oak wood shelf clock with calendar. 23 inches high; *ca.* 1894.

H. BENTON GARVIN COLLECTION

528. Seth Thomas oak shelf clock. 23¼ inches high; *ca.* 1896.

SAMUEL KUTNER COLLECTION

529. Six oaks: Admiral Dewey, President McKinley, Admiral Schley—all Ingraham; middle row, Theodore Roosevelt, Admiral Sampson—by Welch; top, Capitol Dome—Ingraham.

DR. H. R. COATES COLLECTION

Alarms

The round, nickel cased, 2 front legged alarm clock, originally with its bell on top of the case, later with its bell at the back is an American symbol. These raucous but efficient and useful timepieces have been made in countless numbers by most manufacturers from about 1880. Once they retailed for as low as 39 cents. Early models are properly collectable as Americana; few of them are still in existence.

530. Seth Thomas heavy bronze cased one-day long alarm. "20 minutes on one winding, can be switched off at pleasure." 9¼ inches high; 4½ inch dial; *ca.* 1900.
AUTHOR'S COLLECTION

531. New Haven Clock Company. Sentry 15 second alarm; one-day, bronze or iron cases, in red, blue and green enamel. 10¼ inches high; 4½ inch dial; *ca.* 1900.

C. S. PARSONS COLLECTION

532. The movement.

533. Ansonia's Repeater. Typical alarm, bell on top.

C. S. PARSONS COLLECTION

534. Waterbury Clock Company. (L.) Three inches high; (R.) 5½ inches high. Patent dates stamped from Jan. 15, 1878 through Jan. 13, 1891.

C. S. PARSONS COLLECTION

535. Flyer, bell on top, top shut off alarm.
5 ¾ inches high.

536. Waterbury Clock Company. Sunbeam alarm. 6¼ inches high.

537. Alarm, bell on back, local jeweler's name on dial. (Manufacturers would do this if ordered in sufficient quantities.) 5¾ inches high.

HENRY FORD MUSEUM

538. Western Clock Company. Sleep Meter; bell on back alarm. 5½ inches high.

HENRY FORD MUSEUM

539. Sessions Clock Company. Columbia, bell on back alarm, left hand shut off with indicator. 5¼ inches high.

540. Western Clock Company. Big Ben, famous alarm type first introduced in 1910, and still being manufactured. These are two original types showing plain and radium dial.

541. Western Clock Company. Baby
Ben, smaller companion of Big Ben,
first introduced in 1915. Illustration
shows what are believed to be the
various case forms. Front row: "3A";
1927–35 / original; 1915–27 / "61 N"
1935–39 / back row: "61 Y"; 1956–64 /
"61 R"; 1939–49 / "61 V"; 1949–56 / "8-
535-32" / current, 1964 on.

AUTHOR'S COLLECTION

542. Front row, left to right:

Ansonia Clock Company. Rouser, with intermittent alarm; eight inches high.

Ansonia's Bee, several models; top winds like a carrousel; bell winds on top. Five inches high to top of ring.

Wm. L. Gilbert Clock Company. Double top-belled alarm; seven inches high; "Pat. July 7, 1885."

Ansonia. Liberty Bell type; seven inches high.

Parker Clock Company, Meriden, Connecticut. Two alarm bells under clocks; bottom wind under bell; heights 7 inches and five inches.

Top row, left to right:

Wm. L. Gilbert Clock Company, Winsted, Connecticut. Two top bell carriage type alarms.

Wm. L. Gilbert Clock Company. Single side column alarm, nine inches high; *ca.* 1897.

Wm. L. Gilbert Clock Company. Rocking back and forth bell on top alarm. Bell rocked by cords inside side hollow columns. 8½ inches high.

FREDERICK FRIED COLLECTION
PICTURES BY ERNST BEADLE

543. (L.) F. Kroeber Clock Company, New York City. Bell on top alarm time-piece with calendar; 3¾ inch dial.

(C.) Ansonia locomotive iron cased time-piece. The back turns to wind the spring.

"Pat. Apr. 23, 1878."

(R.) One-day alarm with unusual dial marked "Goldsmith Co., Phila." four-inch dial.

JAMES W. GIBBS COLLECTION

544. Electric Battery Alarms:

(L.) Darche Electric Clock Company, Chicago, Illinois. Get-Up alarm; 12 inches wide. Patent on clock, March, 1911; on casting, August 10, 1904 and March 13, 1906.

(C.) Searchlight electric alarm, patent,

Jan. 29, 1901; on battery box, July 12, 1916. 8¾ inches high.

(R.) Flashlight electric alarm. Combination timepiece and deposit box. Patent March 19, 1889 on clock; July 12, 1910 on casting. 8¼ inches high.

FREDERICK FRIED COLLECTION

545. Lux Manufacturing Company. Show Boat; the paddle wheel on steamboat revolves with balance wheel.

United Electric Company. Bartender; the arm shakes as if mixing a drink; *ca.* 1933.

Maker not known. Early Bird; the bird keeps trying to pull a worm from the ground.

FREDERICK FRIED COLLECTION

A/C's

The earlier A/C's are from 1916. Some are shown here. Many of these are found with worn motors, some repairable, some replacable. These are believed to be worth preserving.

546. Henry Warren, Ashland, Massachusetts. Battery operated timepiece. "Not too many made" (J. E. Coleman). He is credited with the successful development of time by A/C current, in widespread use today.

GENERAL ELECTRIC CO. COLLECTION
EDWIN C. PEASE

547. Warren Telechron Company, Ashland, Massachusetts. Telechron A/C wall timepiece. Model MI, motor #76659A. Patent dates from Oct. 29, 1918 to July 14, 1925; *ca.* 1927.

JAMES W. GIBBS COLLECTION

548. Hammond A/C bichronous and synchronous timepieces. These continue in operation for a while after current has been cut off; *ca.* 1931.

549. Two Telechron A/C wood cased timepieces of the late 1930's.

Museums

There has been an excellent development of horological museums in the United States. Here can be found a great assortment of the finest of clocks and watches —collections today probably beyond the abilities of an individual to acquire. Four of these museums are shown on the following pages.

550. American Museum of Time, Bristol, Connecticut. The 1801 Miles Lewis House, with the Barnes Wing on the right.

551. Inside the Barnes Wing, looking north.

552. Magill Jewelry Shop at the Henry Ford Museum, Dearborn, Michigan. Moved there from Detroit in October, 1935.

553. Inside the Magill Shop: some of the timepieces at the Henry Ford Museum.

554. The Grimm Shop at the Henry
Ford Museum. Moved there in 1940.   555. Timepieces inside the Grimm Shop.

317

556. Some of the fine clocks in the collections at Sturbridge Village, Massachusetts.

557. Hagans Clock Manor Museum, Bergen Park, Colorado. Mr. and Mrs. Orville Hagans, Directors.

558. Part of the interior of the Hagans Clock Manor Museum.

List of Makers

ABBREVIATIONS

A/C: alternating current tps. & clocks
adv.: advertised
A.J.: *Antiques Journal*
A.L.P.: Albert L. Partridge
AM.: American
ANT.: the magazine *Antiques*
apt.: apprentice
astro.: astronomical
aw.: at work
b.: born
BAC.: *Book of American Clocks*
B.C.C.: Boston Clock Club, 1934-1940
Bir.: Harry Birnbaum
Brandt: Rose and Bernie Brandt
bro.: brother
Buhler: Mrs. Yves Henry Buhler
Bul.: Bulletin of the National Association of Watch and Clock Collectors
Burt: Edwin B. Burt
bus.: business
C.: clock or clockmaker
ca.: circa (about)
cal.: calendar
Cent.: Century
Childs: Andrew L. Childs
C.S.P.: Charles S. Parsons
chron.: chronometer
Co.: company
Coleman: J. E. Coleman
Col.: Collection
Conn.: Connecticut
C.T.: Charles O. Terwilliger
Currier: Dr. Charles Currier
dau.: daughter
D.: dealer

d.: died
Dir.: directory
Dis.: dissolved
D.K.P.: Donald K. Packard
E.I.: Edward Ingraham
engr.: engraved
estab.: established
E.T.S.: Earl T. Strickler
Ex.: example
f.: failed
ff.: continuing
F.M.S.: Frederick Mudge Selchow
Ford: Henry Ford
Franks: Robert Franks
FT.: *Furniture Treasury*, by Wallace Nutting
Gibbs: (J.G.)-(J.W.G.) James W. Gibbs
G.: goldsmith
g.: gold
G.F.: grandfather clock
H.G.F.: Henry G. Fried
Hist.: town history
hr.: hour
I.C.: Irving Cooperman
ill.: illustration
Imp.: importer
insts.: instruments
J.: jeweler
j.: jewels
J.W.G.: James W. Gibbs
L.B.: Lockwood Barr
L.G.: looking-glass clock
mar.: married, marriage
mfg.: manufactured
mfr.: manufacturer

Milham: Willis I. Milham
min.: minute
M.M.A.: Metropolitan Museum of Art, New York City
movt.: movement
N.A.W.C.C.: National Association of Watch and Clock Collectors
n/d: no date
n/p: no place
Pat.: patent
Pend.: pendulum
P & S.: pillar & scroll clocks
pos.: possibly
Pres.: president
prob.: probably
pub.: published
q.: quarter
R.R.: Railroad
rpr.: repairer, repair
rcd.: received
rep.: repeating
R.H.-J.W.G.: Ralph Himmelright, J. W. Gibbs, study Pa. clockmakers
S.: silversmith
sd.: signed
sig.: signature
Smiths. Inst.: Smithsonian Institution
spg.: spring
str.: striking
Twp.: township
tp.: timepiece (a clock that does not strike)
(tx.): tax records
W.: watch or watchmaker
wgt.: weight
W.R.M.: Willis R. Michael

LIST OF MAKERS

The list of makers in The Book of American Clocks *contains more than 6,000 entries. The list below is an extension and, to some degree, correction of the original list. It is doubtful that any list can ever be complete. History tends to become cloudy through the years. But, thanks to the many who have helped, information continues to be absorbed and classified.*

"Makers" is defined fully on page 14 of The Book of American Clocks. *Again, there is no intent that those listed actually made some form of timekeeper. The added data are to try to help in the identification and dating of American timepieces.*

An asterisk (*) before an entry means that the listing originally appeared in The Book of American Clocks.

*Abbott, Henry: (1850–1943). b. Danbury and educated there. To Newark, N. J., apt. to Gabriel Spense for W. Estab. own business in downtown N.Y.C., 1871. Inventive, rcd. more than 40 patents, 3 on "stem-winding devises," and on enameling W. dials, typewriters, eyeglasses, telephone meters, calculagraph, etc. 19 yrs. Treas., W. A. Mfrs.; Pres. Calculagraph Co. till d. at age 93 in 1943. (*Mrs. J. L. Dill; Jeffrey Granger*)

Abbott, John: Portsmouth, N. H., adv. 1843 as W. and J. "Wooden clocks some as low as $3, warranteed to keep time."

*Abbott, Samuel: Boston, *ca.* 1810–33, and also at Dover, N.H. Adv. 1814; Concord, N.H., and Montpelier, Vt. From 1827–33, Boston addresses as 11 Pitt St., 64 Hanover St., and 33 Merimack St. Prolific maker of good clocks as G.F. (few), banjo, shelf and N. H. Mirror.

"Accutron": Name used by Bulova Watch Co., N.Y.C., 1960 and later, for electronic battery-powered tp. (*H. Titchell*)

Adam, William Wallace: (1817–77). Alexandria, Va. Son of John Adam (1780–), S., J., and W. and accried on his business after his death. Adv. 1846 "W. by trade. Good assortment of W., g., and s. will be sold low. Music boxes rpr." Two sons, Robert L. and Charles, continued the business. (*Cutten*)

Adams, A. S.: Boston at 8 Winter St., 1850 and later. W. and j rpr.

*Adams, Charles F.: Erie, Pa., "about 1870." Marketed Calendar C. with Statue of Liberty on tablet. Type of cal. not described.

Adams, H. E. & Son: Burlington, Vt., 107 Church St., n/d. Bus. card said W., D., J. and rpr. (*H. Birnbaum Col.*)

Adams, H.: Litchfield, Conn., 1830s. Printer of labels for Northrop & Smith of Goshen. Not C.

Adams, John: Cincinnati, Ohio. Adv. 1808, "W. & Rpr.—continues to clean etc. at his shop on 3rd St." (*Gibbs*)

*Adams, Nathan: (1755–?). Danvers, Mass. Prob. apt. at Newbury Port. In Revolutionary War from Andover, then Newbury. (*Charles Currier*)

Adams, Smith: (1828–after 1895). Apt. to Charles Morse and J. Davis. Estab. Bangor, Me., at 4½ Exchange, 1851, began recording all his C. rpr. 1864 to St. John, N. B., to operate C. dept. of Fairbanks & Co. 1866 to Milltown, Me., where he pub. book on *Practical Horology.* 1866 built 24-hr. dial C. with unusual strike. (*Charles Currier*)

Adams, W. P., Springfield, Mass., n/d. name on dial of "American Lever" key wind W. #22. (*J. E. Quayle, Jr.*)

"Addison": Name used by New England Watch Co. having duplex escapements. *Ca.* 1898. One in author's Col. (*H. B. Fried*)

Aiken, David S.: Yarmouth, Mass., n/d. G. F.'s with rocking ship dials reported.

*Aird, David: Portsmouth, N.H., 1780s. "From

Edinburgh—worked for William Parker of Portsmouth, a S. (*C. S. Parsons*)

ALABAMA CALENDAR CO., Tuskegee, Ala. Etched in glass tablet on door of walnut "kitchen type" cal. shelf C. *ca.* 1890. (*T. J. Groiffen*)

ALBRIGHT, THOMAS F.: Phila., High St. Dir. 1843–47. (*J.W.G.*)

ALCOTT (ALCOX), OBED: Plymouth, Conn., *ca.* 1811. Made wood clock pinions and cord for Thomas & Hoadley.

ALDEN, WILLIAM: Fitchburg, Mass., 1885. W. paper extant with "Look Well to Your Time" and date Mar. 15, 1885. (*Joseph Sternfeld*)

ALLEN, S. D.: Westfield, Mass., *ca.* 1835. Shelf clock with label reading "Made for——by D. D. & R. Day." Prob. sales only.

ALLEN, WILLIAM FREDERICK: (1846–1915). Promoted the Time Zone System in 1883. Sec. and Treas. Gen. & So. Time Conventions. Devised system of dividing 5 zones of 15° latitude with all time within the zone the same. Formerly local sun or mean solar time was used. Adopted and accepted Nov. 18, 1883. On Mar. 19, 1918, Congress enacted the first "Standard Time" Act. Bronze tablet on Union Station, Wash., D.C., honors him and the American Railway Managers for their 1883 contribution to standardizing time in the U.S. Now extended throughout the civilized world. (*Association of American Railroads*)

ALMY, H. R.: N.Y.C., 1878–82. Supplied iron-casted clock cases to Mfgs.

ALMY, JOHN C.: Exeter, N.H., 1824. Adv. for an apt. to Derry, N.H., 1830. (*C. S. Parsons*)

"AMERICA" on dial of thick inexpensive American-type back-wind pocket watch with "M. C. & K." (*Hagans Clock Manor Museum*)

AMERICAN BANK PROTECTIVE CO.: Minneapolis, Minn., 20th Cent. A 6-ft.-high tp. with 2 At. movts. operates on batteries. At *Hagans Clock Manor Museum.*

AMERICAN CHIME CLOCK CO.: Nicetown, Pa., 1916–22. Sold clock cases for G.F. and banjo in knock-down packages. Put together and movts. supplied by purchasers. Louis Breitinger of Germantown, Pa., was pres. Blueprint sets in E. F. Tukey Col.

AMERICAN CLOCK CO.: Bristol, Conn., and N.Y.C., 1849–79. Distributor for all Conn. mfrs. "Sold all forms of C—from iron case, cottage, blinking eye, etc."

AMERICAN CLOCK & BRASS CO.: N.Y.C., 6 Warren St., 1879 and later. Had branches in Japan and China. Files now at American Clock & Watch Museum. (*Edward Ingraham*)

AMERICAN CLOCK CO.: Chicago, n/d. Made battery tps. Two in Terwilliger Col., one 13″ high, other 10″.

AMERICAN ELECTRICAL NOVELTY & MFG. CO.: N.Y.C., 304 Hudson St. Adv. 1905 "Improved 'Ever Ready' PLATO Clock—no hands, no dial—wound and set like any clock [tp]. Watch the time fly." Four styles ill. (*J. E. Coleman*)

AMERICAN EVERREADY CO.: N.Y.C., 1904–06. May have financed production of *ca.* 40 thousand PLATO tps. Conrad Hubert, pres. This Co. mfg. Ever Ready batteries. Was sold to National Carbon Co., 1914. (*J. E. Coleman*)

AMES, EZRA: (1736–1836). Aw. 1790 and later. Not C. Did ornamental work for Benjamin Willard— "5 days @ 5/" 1791–92, also the Nathan Hale, Rindge, N. H., and Stephen Sibley of Great Barrington, Mass. He recorded "1797—lettering C faces at 2/ and painting clock face @ 16/." "1800 guilding hands on a church clock." Later at Worcester, then Albany, where he became a distinguished painter of portraits.

ANDERSON, HENRY C.: Charleston, Va. Adv. 1828 as C., W., and S. Mar. 10-2-1830, Philena V. Whittaker. 1831–35 as Anderson Whittaker as dry goods, hardware, groceries, watches, J. and S. (*Cutten*)

ANDERSON (HENRY C.) & WHITTAKER (WM. F.): Charleston, Va., 1831–35. Conducted a varied line business. (*Donald Anderson*)

ANDRE, JOHN A.: (?–1880). Pottstown, Pa., 1862–74. C. and W., active in politics. Bought David Leigh's business. (*R. Hammond*)

ANDREAS, ABRAHAM: (1725–1801). Bethlehem, Pa. To Bethlehem, 1736; mar. the dau. A. Boenfer; succeeded him in 1793. Henry was son; a W.

ANDREAS, HENRY: (1762–1802). Bethlehem, Pa. Apt. in Phila., to Bethlehem 1800. (*Gibbs*)

*ANDREWS, FRANLIN C.: Bristol, *ca.* 1848. His label reprinted by Liveseys Yankee Presses,

74 Fulton St., N.Y.C.–"Improved/Clocks–" Was later as Terry & Andrews. (*E. F. Tukey*)

*ANDREWS, L. (LUCIUS) AND F. (FRANKLIN): 1835–43 on label in Barney Col. with standard 30-hr. wood movt. in flat OG case.

ANDREWS, WILLIAM N.: Cheshire, Conn., *ca.* 1852. With R. T. Andrews of Plymouth, Conn., patent #9267, 1852, for "alarm for lighting lamps." (*A. L. Partridge*)

ANGELL, J. A.: Providence, R. I., 1034 High St., n/d. W. Decorated business card in Birnbaum Col.

ANGSTADT, ADAM: Richmond Typ., Berks Co., Pa. *ca.* 1790. Made clocks. (*J.W.G.*)

ANNUAL WIND CLOCK Co.: Middletown, Conn. Inc. 1901. Adv. 1904 8 styles shelf clocks, one wall. 2 movts. ill.; 1 pendulum, 1 marine. Extensive factory pictured "Clocks & clock movts that run one year on one winding; no electricity; each guaranteed to keep accurate time." A N.Y. agent mentioned. (*J. E. Coleman*)

ANSONIA CLOCK Co.: Ansonia, Conn., 1851–78; then Brooklyn, 1879–*ca.* 1930. Prolific producer of many good American C.'s, tps and W.'s, some very unique. Names used were:

ANSONIA CLOCK Co.– the principal company name.

ANSONIA BRASS Co. in Conn., n/d, pos. 1851–*ca.* 1878.

ANSONIA BRASS & COPPER Co. [in Conn. Mfrs. of the H. J. Davis lamplighter alarm]

ANSONIA BRASS & BATTERY Co. in Conn. n/d. The "Battery" referred to the process of making brass, not to an electrical storage unit.

Co. inc. May 7, 1850, capital $100,000. Estab. at Derby, Conn. and named for Pres. Anson G. Phelps, Theo. Terry, and Franklin C. Andrews (each 1334 ss –" to make various kinds of C., tps, C. cases, and C. movts. H. F. Terry was Co. Sec. Mfg. soon started. Then (Hist.) "1854, the Co., but recently located was burned out with a loss of $20,000. Factory stood on Main St. 'Twas a heavy blow to the prosperity of the Village as young as Ansonia was. Subsequently, the business was continued there till 1878, when it was removed to the Co.'s factory in Brooklyn, N. Y." Lewis I. Coojin said "help make dies and jigs for their 1st alarm tp. and went

along to work in the new Brooklyn plant." Made Plato tps. 1904–06. Symbol on dials and movts. is a Capital "A" inside a diamond, inside a circle.

ANSONIA, CONN.: Among those making clocks there were: Ansonia Clock Co. (and associated Co.'s): 1851–78. Ingraham, E. and A.: *ca.* 1855–56. Gardner, John B.: 1857–80. Gardner & Son: 1880——. Phelps & Bartholomew: 1881– (inc. 1886). Terry, Theodore: "from 1850 to *ca.* 1852." The plant did burn. Then merged with P. T. Barnum. Terry, William A.: "Sold mfg. rights to his cal. C. (Pat. 1–25–1870) to Ansonia Clock Co.

ARIS, SAMUEL: Portsmouth, N.H., Pitt St. Before 1783. W. (*C. S. Parsons*)

ATKINS, M. (MERRITT) W.: Bristol. 30-hr. brass spg. shelf steeple with label without "& Co." (*Amos Avery*)

ARZENS, LAWRENCE: Youngstown, Ohio, 1867. W. from Italy. (*J.W.G.*)

ASHBY, L.: Cincinnati, Ohio, 1888. Rcd. patent on "stem wind & set W." (*J.W.G.*)

ATKINSON, NATHANIEL P.: 1753 at Newbury, Mass. Adv. 1807 from Boscawen, N.H. G.F. clocks–examples extant. (*Parsons*)

ATTLEBORO CLOCK Co.: Attleboro, Mass., n/d. No data available, though 2 shelf clocks known so marked. (*G. E. Clifton*)

*ATWOOD (STEPHEN) AND BRACKETT: Littleton, N.H., 1850–70. "Dealt in many articles." (*Hist.*)

*ATWOOD & BRACKETT: Littleton, N.H., 1850–70. Stephen W. Atwood was J., later merchant, including sale of C. and W. (*Hist.*)

*AVERY, JOHN: Boston, *ca.* 1726. G.F. 8-day brass 2 wgt. silvered dial with moon and engr. "Plainfield" in L. Sack Col.

BABCOCK, JAMES F.: New Haven, *ca.* 1834. Printer, not C. incl. labels for Mark Leavenworth. (*J. E. Coleman*)

*BACON, CHARLES E.: (1832–98). Dover, N.H. Central St., *ca.* 1867. With bro. Horace– orange or yellow W. paper. (*Am. W. Papers*)

*BADGER, FRANKLIN: (?–1935). Concord, N.H. *ca.* 1890. Two 8-day brass G.F.'s and 3 banjos known. Founder, E. Concord. (*F. M. Selchow*)

*BAGNALL, BENJAMIN, JR.: Boston. First mar. 1737 to Anne Hawden (FT), second mar. Ann Peaslee, Haverhill, Mass., 1742. 1752–

entry Suffolk County Records Real Estate Sarah Dennis "for cleaning a Clock—6 lbs." (*Mrs. Yves Buhler*)

*BALDWIN, JEDIDIAH: "Bro. Jabez, apt. T. Harland," to Northampton 1791; then Hanover, N.H., where he adv. Dresden, Vt., *Journal & Eagle* "aw Hanover. March 15, 1806." Later Postmaster at Hanover, where records Dartmouth College record his death, but to Morrisville, N.Y., 1818–20; Fairfield, N.Y., and Rochester, N.Y., where Dir. 1834–44.

*BALDWIN, MATTHIAS: (1795–1866). Phila. Apt. at 16 to Woolworth Bros. J., Phila., 1817 to Charles Fletcher, J.; 1819 for self as C. and J. College Ave., Phila., to 1823. 1825 made machinery for bookbinding. By 1828 needed a steam engine for power, which he then made. 1831 made model steam engine for R.R. which ran on a track at Peale's Museum, Phila. 1832 rcd. order for a locomotive from Phila. and Germantown R.R. Then made steam locomotives till his death, and good ones.

BALL, H.: (1818–1902). Nashua, N.H. A clock-maker, violin maker, and J. Also at Alstead, Walpole, and Westmoreland, N.H. Extant W. Roberts Col. 49″ banjo tp. with case of Howard style, but wood movt. 8 day and dial "Made by Westmoreland." (*Walter Roberts*)

BALLARD, BARTHOLOMEW: (?–1830). Antrim, N.H. From Asby, Mass., 1795. G.F. wood movts.; 1806 to Columbus, Ohio. (*Hist.*)

*BAILEY, BANKS, & BIDDLE Co.: Phila. 1894ff.: Bailey & Kitchen at 136 Chestnut St., estab. 1832–46; Bailey & Co. 1846–78; Bailey, Banks, & Biddle, 1878–94. All records destroyed by fire, 1893, then present name.

BAIRD, R. A. and ALVA F.: Ravena, Ohio, 1851–71. W. (*Gibbs*)

BAKER, THOMAS: (?–1820). Concord, N.H. Took over shop of Abel Hutchins, Jan. 1, 1819. (*C.S.P.*)

BAKEWELL, JOHN P.: Pittsburgh, Pa. Son of Benjamin, an early glass mfr. Patent Oct. 1, 1830, for "Glass wheels for C."

BALDWIN, EZRA: Winsted (Winchester), Conn., 1841–49. "A Clockmaker." Partner with Wm. L. Gilbert & Lucius Clarke ("Clarke was a merchant") as "Clarke, Gilbert & Co."

BALLARD, S.: Antrim, N.H., n/d. "Made G.F.'s with enormous gears of wood," one owned by Dr. S. D. Hart.

BANTA, W. C.: Springfield, Ohio. There estab. as C. 1867. For his shop, built a C. embedded in cement to minimize vibrational interference. (*J.W.G.*)

BARBER, C. W.: Middlebury, Ohio, *ca.* 1840. OG with 30 hr. wgt. movt. extant.

BARCHETTE, CHARLES M.: Clarksburg, Va. Adv. (Oct. 24) 1824 as C., W., S., and J. "in a shop lately occupied by His bro. [in-law?] Albert Montanden at Mack's Hotel." Only data. (*Cutten*)

BARBER, GEORGE: Unionville, Conn., 1830s. "Shelf clock with 30 hr. wood movt.; case with curly maple pilasters and fret work on headpiece and label reading 'Patent Clocks with Brass Bushings etc.'" was from the press of Hulburt & Williams, Hartford. (*The Amos Averys*)

BARKUS, SIMON: (?–1805). Burlington Bay, Vt. Adv 1793 "made Clocks." (*Joseph Sternfeld*)

BARNES & BAILEY: Berlin, Conn., "1831." Only mention is in *F*.

BARNES, BARTHOLOMEW & Co.: Bristol, Conn., 1833–36 (tx.). Made clocks with wood wgt. movts. Plant was in Edgewood section. Took over from E & G Bartholomew (Eli, Geo. W.) (1828–32), who also made "Hollow Cols." Then became Upson, Merriman & Co., 1836–38, which continued to make mirror wood movt. shelf C. Eli Bartholomew sold his interest in 1836 and joined to become Philip Barnes & Co., 1836–38. These men were the 1833–36 Co.: Eli Bartholomew, Rensselaer Upson, Henry Geo. Merriman, and Philip Barnes (of Great Barrington). They bought a factory near North Main and North sts. and mfg. C. 8-day brass wgt. C. known.

BARNES, HENDRICK & HUBBELL: (W. B., E. M., LaPorte): Bristol (tx.), 1849–53. Same as Hendrick, Barnes & Co., & Hendrick, Hubbell & Co. Hist.: "At the old original Manross shop, later the property of LaPorte Hubbell, made the first marine clock (sic) invented by Bainbridge Barnes." This is the forerunner of the American wind-up alarm tp.

BARNES, L. M. & Co.: North Adams, Mass., *ca.* 1850.

BARNES & WELCH: Bristol. No data—not on tax lists. (*L.B.*)

BARNES, ASHEL M. SR.: Chimney Pt., Vt. and Addison, N.Y., *ca.* 1830. Shelf clocks extant so labeled, which printed by *Vergennes Aurora*, newspaper dating 1825–31. (*C. E. Hall; D. Cooley*)

BARNES, B. D.: Oswego, N.Y., 1850s. C. and rpr.

BARNES, EDWARD M.: (?–1871). Bristol, 1834–46. Was partner in Barnes & Bacon; also made clocks with own name. *OG* mirror shelf C. wood movt. in Olin Nye Col. with label reading: "Improved Clocks/Mfr. & Sold by/—" Joseph Hurlburt, Hartford, printer.

BARNES, HARRY: (1855–). Bristol, Conn. Bro. of Carlyle F., son of Wallace. In The Barnes Brothers Clock Co. 1880–84. (*E.I.*)

BARNES, HORACE: Boston. Dir., 1854, "of Terry & Barnes-boards at Lynn."

BARNES, MATTHEW: Richmond, Va., *ca.* 1820 W. (*Massey*)

BARNES, PHILIP: Bristol, Conn., 1833–37. "Of Great Barrington, Mass."

BARNES, PHILIP & Co.: Bristol, Conn. (tx.) 1836–37. Successor to Barnes, Bartholomew & Co. Transition shelf C. carved side cols. and splat, claw feet 31½ x 18½ in American Museum of Time. Henry E., George Merriman, and Rensselaer Upson in Co.

BARNES, THOMAS: Litchfield, Conn., 1760–90. Only American "Barnes" listed in Baillie—pos. meant for Timothy.

BARNES, TIMOTHY: (1749–1825). Litchfield, Conn., 1780–1825. Maker of clocks with both brass and wood movts. and S. B. Branford, son of Timothy and Phebe Barnes. Parents moved to Litchfield soon after his birth. Spent rest of his life there. In Revolutionary War, mar. Eunice Munson of Wallingford. His sister, Lois, mar. Lemuel Harrison; became mother of James Wooster Harrison, who was prob. his apt. One by this same name a C. at Clinton, N.Y., 1825 and later. (*Hoopes*)

BARNES, W. B.: Bristol, Conn., *ca.* 1840 and later. Credited with successful "marine" movt. as early as 1842—at the plant of Stever & Bryant, Whigville, Conn. Made improvements in a shop in Plainville southeast of old grist mill opposite side of bridge (shop later *ca.* 1850s destroyed by fire). Later, at Wolcott, Conn., Barnes made a further developed model tp. in Plainville. According to his son William A. it became part of the assets of Hendrick, Barnes & Co. in 1848. This Co. made only movts., prob. marines in the old Manross Shop. Were very successful. Some sold to C. Jerome at New Haven, stamped with Jerome's name, since he refused to allow the others' to be used. Before this, one of the Terrys patented a coiled brass spring of "peculiar composition, which was rolled very hard, as it was necessary that it be rolled continuously in one direction, as otherwise it would be granulated and break." (From a 1911 letter by Wm. A. Barnes of Bridgeport, son of W. B., and pub. in *Keystone Magazine*). (*J. E. Coleman*)

BARNSTEIN, JOHN: Phila. Dir., 1791. "C." (*J.W.G.*)

BARBECK, C. G.: Phila. Dir., 1835–36. (*G.K.E.*)

BARBER, JAMES: Phila. Dir., 1841–50. "C. Maker and Dealer."

BARRETT, MOSES: Amherst, N.S., n/d. Name on label of *OG* of Conn. mfr. with 2 repairmen —Mass. and Me.—overpasted. (*C.O.T.*—Amos Avery)

BARRINGTON, J. DUMFRIES: Va. Adv. 1792. "C and W. long experience in both theory and practice—C. in particular are made to wind themselves keeping regular motion during the performance, and regulate themselves according to the inclemency of the weather to so great an exactness that there is scarce a perceptible variation—also musical and astro. C." Same adv. from Salisbury, N.C., 1792.

*BARTON, BENJAMIN: (?–1816). Alexandria, Va. Arranged a C. mechanism to operate the shutters on his shop window, raising them at 8 A.M. and lowering at 6 P.M. "Many years kept the town clock." Retired, succeeded by son, Thomas (?–1821). (*Cutten*)

BARTON, BENJAMIN, II: Alexandria, Va. Son of Thomas who d. 1821. Took over father's business as W. and S. 1823—adv. left old stand and removed to shop of John Adam. Also C. and all kinds of work in his line. Adv. 1836 "Fresh Supply of g. & S. Watches have been rcd." (*Cutten*)

BARTON, T. H.: (n/p, n/d). "The American Watch" engr. on movt. "like very early Waltham but top plate 3/64″ larger diameter —wheels hand made." (*E. A. Battison*)

BASSETT & GIBBS: Litchfield, Conn., 1830s. 30 hr. stenciled split ½ Col. and splat shelf clock with mirror tablet, wood movt. Label says:— "Mfg. by and printed by H. Adams, Litchfield." In Col.'s of both C. Wesley Hallet and J.W.G.

BATCHELDER, K. L.: Concord, N.H. G.F. with wood movt., n/d. (*C.S.P.*)

*BAUGH, VALENTINE: 1820–30. "Rumour only." (*Cutten*)

BAUMANS, G.: Columbus, Ohio. Dir., 1845. C. and W. rpr. (*J.W.G.*)

BAY STATE WATCH Co.: Boston, n/d. "Sold Howard movt. W.'s—" #56,993 in Henry Fried Col.

*BEACH & BYINGTON: Bristol. 1840s. Over-pasted label in fuzee alarm steeple shelf C. with etched glass tablet "Brewster & Ingrahams" in script printing on dial and "Terryville" on label. (*In Ray Walker Col.*)

*BEALS: Boston. For a protracted period of time in the C. business in Boston at varying addressses with varying firm and individual names from 1838 to 1874 and later. Two principals were J. J. and William Beals. Label in Howard banjo reads: "J. J. Beals/ Clock Mfr./Wholesale & Retail Dealer in American C. and C. Materials/Particular attention paid to C. spring/16 Hanover St. Boston." (*Charles Terwilliger Col.*)

BEAR, J.: Lexington, Va., *ca.* 1800. G.F. 8 day clocks known. (*H. P. Davis*)

BEARMAN, E. H.: Honolulu, n/d. W. paper in Hamilton Pease Col.

*BEATTY, GEORGE: Harrisburg, Pa., "1808–50." Made G.F. clocks. b. Ireland; apt. to bro.-in-law. (Samuel Hill & Estab.) 1808 (*R.H.*)

BECKTEL, CHARLES F.: (1801–80). Bethlehem, Pa. 1826–30 apt. of John S. Kramer and J. Weiss. His apt. was Henry Bishop who took over his C. & W. when he built a foundry.

BENEDICT, PHILIP: (1771–1862). Lancaster, Pa. Made at least 1 C. Worker in metals, making stoves, etc. (*J.W.G.*)

BECKWITH, JABEZ: Newport, N. H., 1878. "Made 1st 8 day clocks in town, and came from Lempster, N. H." (*Ed Burt & Wes Hallett*)

*BEITEL, JOSIAH O.: (1811–98). Nazareth, Pa., *ca.* 1835. 30 hr. brass wgt. G.F. clock known. (*R.H.*)

BEHRENS, S.: Baltimore, Corner Front and Gay Sts., n/d. C. & W. (*H. B. Fried*)

BEIDERMAN, JOHN: Hamburg, Pa., *ca.* 1820. (*Hist.*)

BEITH & ELLERY: Boston, *ca.* 1800. G.F. in D. K. Packard Col.

*BELKNAP, EBENEZER: Boston. Dir., [1809]–30.

Fine maker of Mass. shelf C. (*Van F. Belknap*)

*BELKNAP, WILLIAM A.: (1798–1841). Boston. Dir. 1818–32, then Exeter, N. H. "W. and J." white and pink W. papers. (*Am. Watch Papers*)

*BELL, WILLIAM: Gettysburg, Pa., before 1805. Then to Phila. Dir., 1805 at 11 South Front St. "C. and W." Made G.F.'s with sweep second. "Wm. W. and William, Phila.," prob. the same.

BEMIS, SAMUEL, KEENE: N. H. Adv. 1803, "Returned and will revise and correct watches." (*C.S.P.*)

BENNETT, W. O.: Phila., n/d. His W. paper reads "Clock and Watch Maker/504 Race St./abt. 5th/W. and tp./carefully rprd." In same W.-W. paper Ziba Ferris "Sept. 23, 1840" in E. F. Tukey Col.

BERNHARD, LOUIS: (1839–1927). Bloomsburg, Pa. b. Germany and to U.S.A. 1840 with parents to Wilkes-Barre where he apt. John J. Jordan. Estab. own business as C. W. and J. in Bloomsburg. "A master craftsman, had 11 apts.; also architect." (*C.O.T.*)

BERRGANT, PETER: Phila. Dir., 1825–33.

BEST, DANIEL: Cincinnati, Ohio. 1804 ff. "Mar. Dec. 13, 1804–is W. and S. of this town." (*J.W.G.*)

BEST, SAMUEL: Cincinnati, Ohio. Adv. 1802, "1st C. here—not many clocks here now—cabin corner Front and Walnut Sts." Adv. 1806, "Wanted, immediately, a smart, active lad about 12 or 14 as apt. to the C. and W.-making and S. Business. One from the Country, and well recommended would be appreciated." (*J.W.G.*)

BEST, ROBERT & SAMUEL: Cincinnati, Ohio. Adv. 1811 and 1812. G.F. known—white dial with round, laughing moon—on map of world Asia and India were *"Tartory"* and for Australia–"New Holland." 7-ft.-high wood case with inlay, name on dial. (*J.W.G.*)

BEVINS (BEVANS) WILLIAM: (1755–1819). Phila. Dir., 1810–16, Norristown, Pa., 1816–19. Adv. 1818, "C. and W. Maker—will barter 1 or 2 Eight-Day Clocks for Hickory Wood." (*J.W.G.*)

BILLS, E. (ELIJAH) & E. A.: Colebrook River, Conn. *OG* 30 hr. brass wgt. movt. wood dial. In Amos Avery Col. Seemingly, many clocks made in this area, part of which now (1966) under water. (*Thomas Blake*)

BIND, WILLIAM: Phila. Dir., 1829–33 did make clock dials. (*J.W.G.*)

*BINGHAM, B. D.: Nashua, N. H. Dir., 1849 at 54 Pearl St. After C. for L. W. Noyes—master W. and model maker, Nashua Watch Co., 1859–62. Invented dust ring for W. and horse nail machine. (*F.M.S.*)

BINGHAM, P. L.: Nashua, N. H., n/d. Banjo extant "Almost identical with Howard with seconds Pend., but wind post 'twixt '6' & center arbor." (*Ray L. Walker*)

*BIRGE, MALLORY & Co.: Dayton, Ohio. Overpasted label in a shelf clock. (*Sam W. Jennings*)

BISHOP, HENRY: Bethlehem, Pa. 1830 ff. Was apt. and successor to C. F. Bickel and his C. and W. business.

*BISHOP, JACOB: Allentown, Pa., *ca.* 1810. His dau. Margaret mar. Jacob Mohr, cabinet-maker. (*Louis Mohr*)

*BISHOP, MORITZ: Easton, Pa., 1780. Tax list as C. and W. "And for long time thereafter."

BIXLER, ARTHUR B.: (1882–1945). Easton, Pa. May be the last of 6 generations of this family in C., W. and J. (*J.W.G.*)

BIXLER, C. WILLIS: Easton, Pa., n/d. Son of Daniel who continued the Bixler Business. Succeeded by Arthur Bixler.

*BIXLER, DANIEL: Reading, Pa., 1810–25ff. Son of Christian III. Entered father's business 1810 and took it over in 1825.

BLACK, JOHN: N.Y.C. at 75 Fulton St. Printer —not C.—of clock labels for, among others: Henry Smith, Plymouth, Conn.; Joseph Smith N.Y.C., and Hotchkiss & Fields, Burlington, Conn. (*E. F. Tukey*)

BLACKMAN, JOHN STARR: (1751–1851). Danbury, Conn. C. and S.; shop south of Court House. Sons, John Clark B. (1800–72) and Frederick Starr B. (1811–98) were apts. F.S.B. succeeded his father, J.C.B. to Bridgeport, Conn., where he estab. his own business. Levi Clark (b. 1801) later estab. at Norwalk, also apt. (*Lockwood Barr*)

BLACKMAN, J. N.: New Milford, Conn. 1880's. Adv. card in Harry Birnbaum Col.

BLAISDELL (BLAISDEL): fine family of C.

*BLAISDELL, JONATHAN E.: Kingston, N. H. G.F. in F. M. Selchow Col. in flat-top pine case 30 hr. brass movt. and dial marked "MCDDLXVIII."

BLAISDELL, ISAAC: Mar. 27, 1738, Amesbury. d. Chester, N. H. (Oct. 9, 1791). "A clockmaker, settled in Chester, 1762." (*Hist.*) Marker, N. H. historical markers–, "located on E. side of Rte 121 in Chester just north of the junc. Rts. 121 and 102 near the Congregational Church–" "Chester–(14)–Early American Clocks"–"Isaac Blaisdell–1738–91 — son and father of clockmakers settled in Chester in 1762 and commenced mfg. one day striking, wall and tall case clocks with one wgt. and metal works. He was an Association Test signer, Revolutionary War Soldier, Selectman, and Member of the Committee of Safety."

BLACKESLEE (BLACKESLY), GILBERT H.: Bristol, Conn., Jan. 18, 1878. Patent 205, 037 used by F. Kroeber, N.Y.C. (*J. E. Coleman*)

*BLAKESLEE, M. (MILO) & Co.: Terrysville, Conn., *ca.* 1840. "At the Old Stand of Eli Terry, Jr. Movt. made by H. Welton—Finished & sold by—."

*BLAKESLEE, R. & Co. JR.: 54 John St., N.Y.C. OG marked, "With Davies Patent Lever, 1846. Mfg. in Plymouth, Conn. by Morse (Myles) & Blakeslee, (R. Jr.)." 1 day brass wgt. movt. (*J.W.G.*)

BLANCHARD, JOSHUA: Cincinnati, Ohio, *ca.* 1835. (*J.W.G.*)

BLODGET CLOCK Co.: Boston. "1898–Patent." Master Electric Battery wall tp. which can drive slaves, with seconds pendulum, 6' high case. (*Roy McKinney Col.*)

BLOOMER, WILLIAM: Mt. Victory, Ohio, *ca.* 1860. (*J.W.G.*)

*BLUMER, JACOB: (1774–1830). Allentown, Pa., aw. *ca.* 1798–1820. b. Whitehall Twp., Pa., a son of Rev. Abraham Blumer. Lt. in War of 1812. Joseph Graff a partner for a time; a Blumer & Graff G. F. dated "1799" extant.

*BOARDMAN (CHAUNCEY) & WELLS (COL. JOS. A.): Bristol, Conn., (tx.) 1832–43. Prolific, good C. of Bristol.

BOARMAN & WELLS: Warren, Ohio, *ca.* 1840. Shelf clock labeled: "Extra Clocks, with brass bushings, Made & Sold by —," an unexplained oddity; cf. Boardman & Wells.

*BOARDMAN, CHAUNCEY: (1789–1857). Bristol. Adv.: standard steeple shelf clock with 8 day brass movt. ½ hr strike, label reads: "PATENT/Equalizing and Power Maintaining Springs/Brass Clocks/Warranteed—etc. by—/Bristol, Conn. U.S.A./The superiority of said Clocks, consists in the EQUALIZING and MAINTAINING power of the springs/which are so constructed as to give the same weight or pressure upon the moving parts at all times, from the time the Clock is wound up/until it is run down, rendering it capable of being regulated so as to keep perfect Time./ Said springs being made of superior quality of Steel/and mfr. by the most celebrated Spring Maker in the/City of New York./ They can be warranted not to break, or to lose their power./"—Printed by Elihu Geer, 1 State St., corner of Main, Hartford (1847–50). This clock one of the final period of C. by one of the most prominent men of Bristol. This followed the 1844 dissolution of the Boardman & Wells Partnership, each continuing in his own name to make C. The "U.S.A." on label denotes invasion of the markets of the world for American Clocks then; many were sent all over the globe. Note the secured springs in N.Y.C.—good ones were then being made in Bristol.

BOARDMAN, JOHN: (1826–73). Newburyport, Mass., where he was b. and d. Son of Richard. W. and C. (*Charles Currier*)

BOEHNER, JOHN: Georgia, 1736. To Bethlehem, Pa., 1748 ff. C. from Gruenberg, Bohemia, where trained. (*R.H., J.W.G.*)

BOEMPER, ABRAHAM: (1705–93). Bethlehem, Pa., 1748–93. Apt. in Germany and Holland. To South America, then to N.Y.C. There after first wife d., to Bethlehem in 1748 and mar. widow of Isaac Ysselsteyn. There estab. own C. and W. Business. Succeeded by son-in-law Abraham Andreas. (*J.W.G.*)

BOND, WM. & SON: Boston. Dir., 1813; Dir., 1842 and later. In Dir. 1869 at 17 Congress St.

BONNET, JACOB: Zanesville, Ohio, 1835–90. C. and W., apt. in Germany.

BONNET, JOHN M.: Zanesville, Ohio, *ca.* 1855. (*J.W.G.*)

BOOTH, H. B.: Rochester, N.Y., n/d. W. paper in Birnbaum Col.

BORNEMAN, HENRY H.: Boyertown, Pa., 1840–89. C. and rpr.

BORNEMAN, JOSEPH H.: Boyertown, Pa., after 1850. Apt. of Henry H. Borneman.

BOSS, JAMES: Phila., 1859. "Had factory at Chestnut & 5th Sts. One W. case marked 'Inv. & Pat.'" (*R.H., J.W.G.*)

BOWEN'S PRINT, H.: Boston, 19 Pearl St. 1840s

label on *LG* 30-hr. wood clock reads this way. (*H. B. Fried*)

*BOWER (other spellings), HENRY O.: (1807–67). Phila., *ca.* 1830–45. b. Douglas Twp., Pa. "Made *ca.* 130 clocks, last in 1845." (*R.H., J.W.G.*)

*BOYD, THOMAS: Phila. Dir. 1807–09 at 41 Cannonhill St., then 315 North Front St. (*R.H., J.W.G.*)

BRACE & FRENCH: Granville, Ohio, 1828. Knowles Linnell's clock factory moved from St. Albans, Ohio, to Granville and Linnell left Co. These two were bros.-in-law. C. extant.

BRADFORD & CONANT: Auburn, Me., after 1865. Succeeded Bradford & Pinkham. *OG* with 30-hr. brass movt. in American Museum of Time. Pos. only case makers. (*E. E. Runnells*)

BRADFORD & PINKHAM: Auburn, Me., *ca.* 1845. Two OG's known—1 with wood movt., one brass. Pos. dealer or sales only. (*E. E. Runnells.*)

*BOSTON CLOCK CO.: Boston (Chelsea), 1888–97. Was Eastman Clock Co. 1886–88. Became Chelsea Clock Co. 1897. Continuing today, making fine clocks. Patent rcd. Dec. 28, 1880, covered: "Compensated balance wheel movt., one wind post for both time and strike (L and R wind)." Some in marble cases of French style, one in author's Col. (*Walter Mutz*)

"BOSTON—No. 6" name of oak kitchen clock made by Ingraham as one of their "City Line," which included "N.Y.C., Chicago, St. Louis, Washington, and Atlanta." Listed at $4.75; made 1897–1900. (*E.I.*)

BOWEN, J. B. (R.): Waltham, Mass., n/d. Banjos with bezels of wood, painted iron dials, roman chapters, spear-type hands. Waist of case with beveled-type borders; throat box tablets using "Constitution and Gurriere." Conventional movt. 8 day wgt. tp., single bridge. In Burt, Wollman, and Charles Currier Cols.

BOWEN, NATHAN: Marblehead, Mass., 18th Cent. "Responsible for looking after the town clock including its rpr. at the New Meeting House." (*H. M. Failes, Essex Ins.*)

*BRADLEY & HUBBARD: Meriden, Conn., *ca.* 1854–*ca.* 1915. Many unusual clocks made—source of most "Blinking Eye" which was patented 1856. Also, small "box clocks *ca.* 7 x 9¼." Also used "West Meriden" address. (*Charles Parker*)

BRADLEY MFG. CO.: Southington, Conn. Shelf clock with slight step–back, 15″ high 9¼″ at base 8-day brass spg. movt. strikes hours, count wheel control. Door has decal spandrels at corners of glass, making round opening for painted white-zinc dial. Below on door is panel, 2¼″, decal of early scene of White House. Label reads: "Plain, Ornamental, Inlaid Pearl & Fancy. Eight and One Day Brass Clocks and Marine Time Pieces, mfg. & Sold by—" Label printer, Elihu Geer, 10 State St., Hartford (1850–56.)

BRADSHAW, WM. A.: N.Y.C. at 76 Pearl St., n/d, "near Coentes Slip, up-stairs." Pos. D. only, buying Conn.-made clocks and labeling. "Mfr. and Dealer in Brass and Wood Clocks." Also used a Courtlandt St. address.

BRAISCH & LARSON: Telluride, Col., n/d, name on watch dial. (*Orville Hagans*)

*BRANDT, ADAM: New Hanover, Pa., *ca.* 1780ff. "Made many G.F.'s." Most extant have white iron dials, though 1 engr. brass dial known. (*R.H., J.W.G.*)

BRANDT, CHARLES & Co.: Phila., Dir.,· 1816–17. (*G.K.E.*)

BRANNAN, G., 3RD.: Columbus, Ohio. Dir., 1853. "Mfr. of C." (*J.W.G.*)

BRASSINGTON, JOHN: Alexandria, Va., Fairfax St. 1820 Adv. (*Cutten*)

BRECHT, ELIAS, BURKS CO.: Pa. *ca.* 1820. Grandson was Joseph T. Bright, a C. rpr. at Springtown, Pa., *ca.* 1907. (*R.H., J.W.G.*)

BRENEISER, (N.) GEORGE: Adamstown, Pa., *ca.* 1800–20. Bro. of Samuel. (*G.F.C.*)

BRENEISER, (N.) GEORGE: Wormelsdorf, Pa., *ca.* 1820. Bro. of Samuel. (*G.K.E.*)

BREWER, C.: Middleton, Conn., *ca.* 1800. W. paper. (*M.M.A.*)

*BREWER, WM.: Phila. Adv. 1774; Dir., 1825. Also on Chestnut, Front, and Walnut Sts. (*G.K.E., R.H., J.W.G.*)

*BREWSTER, E. (ELISHA) C. & Co.: Bristol, Conn., 1840–43 (tx.). "One of first coil spring users." Label read: "Patent Springs/ Brass Clocks/made and sold by—" Geer labels, no date. (*E.I.*)

*BREWSTER & INGRAHAMS, (ELISHA, ELIAS, AND ANDREW): Bristol, Conn., 1844–52 (tx.). Followed E. C. Brewster & Co. Many fine extant Conn. shelf clocks after designs of Elias Ingraham, including the twin-steepled gothics. Did use brass-coiled springs.

*BREWSTER, GEORGE G.: Portsmouth, N. H., *ca.* 1826–34. Extant are 3 banjos "similar to the Willards," dated 1826, 27, and 33 and one 1834 in "primitive case."

BREWSTER, WALTER: Canterbury, Conn., n/d. Did make some clocks with metal plates and gears, and wood winding drums, slightly tapered. Could have been before 1800, but no data.

BRICE, JAMES: Cincinnati, Ohio, n/d. "Shelf clock extant." (*J.W.G.*)

BRIDGEPORT BRASS CO.: Bridgeport, Conn. Stamped on front plate of 8-day spring brass alarm clock movt. in small wood case and "Pat. Aug. 6, 1876." Purchased "new in 1878." (*Maurice Walter Col.*)

BRIERLY, JAMES E.: Birmingham, Conn., 111 Main St., 1885. Adv., "sole agent for Columbus Watches."

BRIGDEN, C. H.: Canton Junction, Mass., 1890. Did make a 1-wheel gearless tp. operated by steel balls through tubes running 72 hrs. on a winding. Was shown at Paris Exposition 1900 and won gold medal. Example at Hagans Clock Manor Museum Col.

BRINSMAID, ABRAM: Burlington, Vt., 1809. Adv. (*Dustin Cooley*)

BRISTOL WATCH CO.: No data. A key wind and set W. #982-406 in H. B. Fried Col.

BROOKLYN WATCH CO.: Brooklyn, N. Y., n/d. Key wind and set W. #5896 in gold filled case in H. B. Fried Col.

BROWN & BEECH: Columbus, Ohio, 1850. Adv. "Prob. D." (*J.W.G.*)

BROWN BROS.: Minneapolis, Minn., *ca.* 1879. In the 1940's, reportedly made *ca.* 100 side walk post C. Later, O. B. McClintock. (*J. E. Coleman*)

BROWN, GEORGE: New Haven, Conn., at 120 Chapel St. Dir; 1859–68.

*BROWN, J. C.: Bristol, Conn. Quote from *The Boston Cultivator*, Jan. 29, 1853—"A few nights since, the clock factory of J. C. Brown, at Bristol, Conn. was destroyed by fire with all it's machinery, stock, and a number of finished clocks. Loss estimated at $35,000, with $30,000 Insurance." (*C. W. Burnham*)

*BROWN, JOHN JAMES: Andover, Mass., "before 1839." C., mar. Emily Fisk Willard. W. and G. to *ca.* 1850ff. (*Charles Currier*)

BROWN, JOHN ROGERS: New England, *ca.* 1850. Made tower C. Invented first automatic machine for graduating rules. 1852, Inv. vernier caliper to 1/1000 of an inch. Later, built first universal grinding machine. (*Charles Currier*)

BROWN, JOHN W.: Newbury Port, Mass., *ca.* 1830. W. paper in Whitford Col. (*H. B. Fried*)

BROWN, NELSON H.: Boston, at 90 Franklin St., *ca.* 1900. Did issue 3 catalogues on G.F.'s and "Mantels" clocks "fitted with the Elite movts., with maintaining power and rust proofed by a secret process." (*E. I.*)

BROWN, PHILIP: Hopkinton, N.H. before 1820. Also made inlaid mahogany clock cases for G.F.'s. Won $25,000 lottery, and then built mills and in R E Business. (*C.S.P.*)

BROWN STREET CLOCK CO., THE: Monessen, Pa., aw. 1913. (*M. Massey*)

BROWN, SETH E.: (?–1850). Concord, N.H. Succeeded by Moses M. Chick. (*C.S.P.*)

BRUCKMAN, V. C.: Atlantic City, N.J. Between Atlantic and Pacific Aves. Last q. 19th Cent. W.–adv. card in Birnbaum Col.

BRYANT, JEREMY: Andover, N.H., (1800–60) "A dyer and finisher–not C." Hist. (*C. S. P.*) at East Andover *ca.* 1830. "C. & W." (*E. B. Burt*)

*BRYANT THOMAS: Rochester, N.H. (not N.Y.) First q. 19th Cent. Was associated with E. G. Moulton.

BULKLEY, DAVID: Litchfield, Conn. Adv. 1839. Made some clock cases. A Cabinet maker, not C. "2 doors W. of Court House." (*Floyd Thoms*)

*BUDD, JOSEPH: Pemberton, N.J., *ca.* 1808–32. Then to Hamilton, Ohio, G.F.'s extant. (*J.W.G.*)

*BULOVA WATCH CO.: N.Y.C., 1875–continuing. Extensive tp. mfr. and other products. American made W. 1946ff. Trade mark names used include "Bulova," "Caravelle," and "Accutron"–a tuning fork controlled electronic tp. (*Haskell Titchell*)

BUNDY MFR. CO., THE: Binghampton, N.Y., 1889. See I.B.M. Inc. as first Time and Recording Co.; mfr. their clocks using Seth Thomas movts. To Endicott, N.Y., 1907.

BUNDY, WILLIAM L.: Auburn, N.Y. A jeweler, devised a key time recorder. See I.B.M.

*BUNNELL, EDWIN: Bristol, Conn., *ca.* 1850. In Whigville Section built a shop later called "The Mills Turning Shop," used for a clock factory. Later, built a second shop "further N. on the corner." (*Hist.*)

BURGE, J.: Circleville, Ohio. 1872. Rcd. patent for time lock. Later assigned to Yale Lock Mfr. Co. (*J.W.G.*)

BURLINGTON WATCH CO.: Chicago, "20th Cent." 21 j. double roller W. in E. F. Tukey Col.

BURT, E.: Cleveland, Ohio, 1864. Then rcd. a W. patent. (*J.W.G.*)

BUTLER, NATHANIEL: (1760–1829), Utica, N.Y., *ca.* 1795–1815. From Conn. W., J., and rpr. W. paper *Am. Ant.* Society Col. (*Miss Dorothy Spear*)

*BURWELL, ELIAS.: Bristol. (tx.) 1851–67 "Lewis' Perpetual *cal.* C. mfr. by–" (*C. J. O'Neil Col.*)

*BYINGTON LORIN (Lawler-Lawyer): Newark (Valley) N.Y. 1830's LG, Conn. origin 30 hr. wood movt., bell mounted on top of case behind splat; label, printed by 'Leonard, Owego, N.Y.' "Improved/Clocks/made & sold by/–" (*Herbert Rand*)

*CABLE, S. (STEPHEN): 25 Albany St., N.Y.C., *ca.* 1848. Beehive, 30-hr. lyre spg. movt. labeled: "Made and Sold by Terry & Andrews, Bristol," and overpasted label: "S. Cable's Old Established Clock & Looking Glass Store; 384 Grand St. N.Y."

*CAIRNS, JOHN: Providence, R.I., 1784. "Mostly aw. though brass movt. G. F. and shelf C. extant with his name, with fine toothed gears. May have used a watch gear cutter for making his C. wheels." (*Hamilton Pease*)

*CALAME, OLIVER: Charlestown, Va., 1819. Adv. in Fredericktown, Md., then to Harpers Ferry as C. & W. (*Cutten*)

CALDWELL, EDW. F. & CO. INC.: N.Y.C. D. and Importer name on dial of small marble shelf C. (*Mrs. Samuel Haft Col.*)

*CALDWELL, J. E. & CO.: Phila., 1836 ff. At Chestnut and Juniper Sts. since 1916. James E. Caldwell to Phila, 1836 as C. & W. Became, 1839, Bennett & Caldwell; 1848, James E. Caldwell & Co., at several Phila. locations.

CAMPBELL, JAMES: Steubenville, Ohio, 1808. Adv. as C., W., S., J., and Engr. near Red Lion Tavern. "Has just rcd. elegant assortment of j.; also complete materials for C. and W. clocks made and rpr." (*J.W.G.*)

*CAMP, HIRAMS (1811–93), New Haven,

Conn. Adv. Original MSS of his "Sketch of the Clock Making Business" now in the Howard Sloane Col.

CANADA CLOCK CO.: n/p, n/d. *OG* with 30-hr. brass movt. so stamped on front plate, also on printed label. (*John Sinclair*)

CANFIELD: Conn. Prolific label printed for C.'s.

*CANNON, WILLIAM: (–1753) Phila., 1720's. Later to Burlington, N.J. where he d. Joseph Hollingshead *Adm* of his Estate. (*J.W.G.*)

"CARAVELLE": name used by Bulova Watch Co., N.Y.C., 1960ff. (*Haskell Titchell*)

CARMINE, H.: Coatesville, Pa., 1884. Name on W. dial of W. #7276 made by Fredonia Watch Co. In H. B. Fried Col.

CARNEY (KEARNEY), HUGH: Wolcottville, Conn. not "Ind."-(BAC-165) P & S and other shelf C. known.

CARPENTER, SAMUEL: Flushing, N.Y., 1858. Patent 20252 on "Improved chron. escape for ws. and tps." Also Patent in England. Example at Newport N.H. Clock Museum. (*Wesley Hallett*)

CARTER, L. F. & W.: Bristol, 1860's Cal. C. label reads: "E. Pluribus Unum—(under an eagle)—B. B. Lewis Pat. *cal.* C; 8, and 30 day Office and Mantle C.—Made expressly for ——" (See E. Burwell) (*E.I.*)

CARVER, JACOB: Phila. Dir., 1785–1833 at several addresses as C. and W. (*J.W.G.*)

CASE, TIFFANY & Co.: Hartford, Conn. on Pearl St. Printers of labels for C. as Elisha Hotchkiss and others. (*Victoria Warren*)

*CATE, COL. SIMEON: (1790–1845), Sanbornton, N.H., *ca.* 1820ff G.F.s, wood movts; also made chairs and cotton hats. (*Andrew L. Childs*)

"CAVOUR": name used on duplex escape size Ow's by New England Watch Co. Example author's Col.

"CENTENNIAL-PHILADELPHIA": 1876 name stamped on w.-full plate 18s, 7 j. with solid balance and "Centennial" on dial. (*E. A. Battison*)

CHAMBERLAIN, JOHN DRESSER: (1779–1870), Cincinnati, Ohio, 1811ff. "Walked there from Goshen, Mass." Joined in forming Read & Watson; also known as Read, Watson, & Chamberlain. Engaged in the mfr. and sale of C. (*J.W.G.*)

CHANDLER, TIMOTHY & Co.: Concord, N.H. 1824–29; then A. Chandler & Co. till Dec. 4, 1830. (*C.S.P.*)

CHANDLER & WARD (AUSTIN M. ?): Concord, N.H., *ca.* 1840. 2 large inlay cased 8-day C. with moon dials marked "Made & Sold by Moses Hazan." (*F.M.S.*)

CHAPMAN, HENRY: Otis, Mass., n/d. Label in *OG* 30 hr wgt. C. reads: "Cased and Sold By——/E. J. Bull's Print Shop, Lee, Mass." (*Ray Durham Col.*)

CHARTERS, GEORGE: (1835–1910), Xenia, Ohio, 1875. Adv. Son of John—"a skilled & practical W." (*J.W.G.*)

CHASE, JOHN W.: Hopkinton, N.H., 1810. C. (*C.S.P.*)

CHENEY, ASHEL: 1808. Adv. Royalton, Vt., then 1816 Rochester, Vt. Made G.F.s

CHENEY, MARTIN: Windsor, Vt., 1801. Adv. (not "1790"). (*D. Cooley*)

CHENEY, RUSSELL: Woodstock, Vt., 1806. Adv. "from E. Hartford, Conn." (*D. Cooley*)

CHENEY, SILAS: (?–1820). East Hartford, Conn., 1748. G.F. with 30-hr. 2-train wood movt. hr. strike with white metal dial with cast spandrels and silvered chapter ring. Also at Litchfield, Conn. Bought Cheney Homestead 1788 "only one in County for Many Years." May have made some clock cases. (*Sherman Haight*)

*CHESHIRE CLOCK Co: Cheshire, Conn., 1884. Inc. with A. E. Hotchkiss, Pres.; C. B. Ferrell, Sec. Stock certificates ill. marine C. with "A.E.H.-Patent" on dial.

*CHESHIRE WATCH Co: Cheshire, Conn., 1883–*ca.* 1893. "Some W.'s made." (*Albert Partridge-Edward Ingraham*)

"CHINNOCKS": n/p, n/d. Cast on back of church-style iron front with mother-of-pearl inlay, the clock made by Terhune & Botsford, N.Y.C. (according to the label). (*Nelson Booth Col.*)

CHRONOMETER STAMP Co.: N.Y.C. at 34 Park Place, 1880. Ill. catalogue at American Museum of Time, Bristol, showing forms of time stamps. (*E. I.*)

*CHURCH, JOSEPH & Co.: Hartford, Conn., *ca.* 1830. ("1825–38" B.A.C.) W. paper M.M.A.

CHURCHILL, JOEL H.: Bristol, 1830's (no tx). 2-decker 8-day brass wgt. movt. shelf C. extant. (*Camille Condon*)

C. L. & J. B.: Newburyport, Mass., "1841" dated W. paper in Am. *Ant.* Soc. Col. (*Miss Dorothy Spear*)

CLARK, HORATIO: Vermont, 1795–1803. As

partnership with Jonathan Hunt as C. W., and S. Then alone. (*John E. Moore*)

CLARK, (THOS. W.) & HARTLEY: Phila. Dir., 1839–41.

CLARK, JESSE: Phila. Dir. 1809–14. C. & W.

CLARKE & BROWN: Manchester, N.H. at 877 Elm St. Last q. 19th Cent. Adv. card as W. In Bir. Col. (*No Parsons*)

CLARKE & DIXON: Manchester, N.H. at 977 Elm St., 1880's. Adv. card in Bir. Col. (*No Parsons*)

CLARKE & PLUMB (OLIVER–EBEN, JR.): Litchfield, Conn., 1797. Adv. cabinet makers who took over shop later occupied by Mr. O. Lewis. Pos. some C. cases. (*Sherman Haight*)

CLARKE, GEORGE H: N.Y.C., n/d. Label: "Made and Sold at 46 Courtlandt St." (*Henry Kuels*)

CLAUSEN, ADLER CHRISTIAN: Minneapolis, Minn., 1883. Patent #286,521, Oct 9, 1883—the "Flying Pendulum Clock." Made and ill. one yr. only in 1884–85, New Haven Clock Co. Catalogue with "Jerome & Co" label. Four models ill. (*C. O. Terwilliger*)

CLAYTON, ELIAS, B.: Phila. Dir., 1848–50 "W." (*G.K.E.*)

CLOISTER MFR. CO.: Buffalo, N.Y., early 20th Cent. Made battery tps. for Tiffany Never Wind. (*C. O. Terwilliger*)

COBB, J. L.: Winchester, Conn., n/d. OG, brass 30-hr. wgt. movt., wood dial, extant so labeled. (*H. E. Shaw Col.*)

COBURN & CLARKE: Bristol. Printers of labels for C. as Atkins Clock Co. (*Haskell Titchell*)

COE, RUSSELL: N.Y.C., 87 Pearl St., n/d. 'flat' OG wood movt. case with tablet in C. O'Neil Col.

COFFIN, HENRY T.: Nobleboro, Me., *ca.* 1850. OG 1-day standard brass wgt. movt. so labeled. (*E. E. Runnells*)

*COLE, JAMES C.: (1724–1815). Apt. of Edw. Moulton G.F.'s (*Burt*)

COLES, JOHN: Boston at 62 Back St., 1800's. Heraldic painter and did dials for S. Willard Banjos. (*Conlon; B.C.C.*)

COLLINS, G. E. & CO.: N.Y.C. at 335 Broadway, 1870. Adv. Godey's Lady's Book, Jan. 1870: "Celebrated Imitation Gold Hunting Case Ws–Collins Metal (Improved Oriode) at $10–15–20. We have just commenced making a very fine AMERICAN WATCH, full j., patent lever, chron. *bal. adj.* to heat, cold and position. Equal in appearance and time

to a gold W. costing $250.–for $25–thoroughly tested last 4 yrs/To Clubs—where 6 W.'s are ordered at one time, we send a 7th W. free——" etc. (*Albert L. Partridge*)

COLLINS, OZRO: Prospect, Conn., *ca.* 1830. Shelf C. 8-day brass wgt. movt. rack and snail strike. (*Bryson Bugbee Col.*)

COLLINS, PELEG: Cincinnati, Ohio, 1825. Dir. as "W." (*J.W.G.*)

COLONIAL CLOCK WORKS: pos. Mich., 20th Cent. may have been used by Colonial mfr. Co., on G. F. (*E. E. Runnells*)

*COLONIAL MFR. CO., THE: Zeeland, Mich., 1914. Adv–still extant.

COLT, JOHN: Patterson, N.J., 1825–33. Dir. (*E. E. Raym*)

*COLUMBUS (COLUMBIA) WATCH CO.: Columbus, Ohio. Succeeded Gruen & Savage who originated 1876. By 1882 imported W. movts. Sold to South Bend Watch Co., 1902.

COMSTOCK & MINOR: Plymouth, Conn., 1830's. OG 27" high wood movt. with label printed by Case, Tiffany & Co. reading–"Extra Clocks——" (*Nelson Booth Col.*)

COMSTOCK, L. F.: Plymouth, Conn., n/d. 8-day brass movt. G. F. extant. (*John A. Sinclair*)

*CONANT & SPERRY: N.Y.C., at 112 Fulton St. *ca.* 1840. "C. & Looking Glass mfrs." Flat OG, wood movt., in C. O'Neil Col.

*CONANT, W. S.: N.Y.C., at 177 Pearl St., *ca.* 1810. Address formerly given as "177 Pine St" which at that time would reportedly have been under water in East River; 8-day brass lyre-shaped movt. OG cased bears label at 177 Pearl St. Nearer date 1840s. (*Walter C. Robinson Col.*)

CONCORD, MASS.: C. Excellent American Cs. were made in this historic place. Data about the famous makers was difficult to obtain, now clarified and available. Fine display at Concord Historical Society, Spring, 1966 with assistance from various members N.A.W.C.C. Many hitherto unseen clocks were on view. (Catalogues of the exhibit available) The following were Concord Makers: and from *ca.* 1791 and for about 35 years. The types: G.F., banjo, girandole, lyre, N.H. Mirror.

CURTIS, LEMUEL: (1790–1852); 1811–21.

CURTIS & DUNNING: 1813–21.

DUNNING, JAMES NYE: 1813–21.

DYER, (DYAR) JOSEPH: (1795–1850); 1818–25.

MULLIKEN, JOSEPH: (1765–1802); 1791–1802 d.

MUNROE, DANIEL, JR.: (1775–1859); 1796–1808.

MUNROE, NATHANIEL: (1777–1866); 1798–1817.

MUNROE, WILLIAM: (1779–1861); 1800–19.

WHITING, SAMUEL: 1808, ca. 1820.

CONGER, JOHN: Bristol, Conn., ca. 1830 (no tx.). 30-hr. wood movt. shelf C. has label reading: "Made by Samuel Terry; for——" (*Mary P. Williams*)

CONNECTICUT CLOCK CO.: N.Y.C., 1872. Dir. Label on 9" round marine tp. reading: "mfrs. and D. in C. and C. trimmings of every Description at 28 and 30 John and 69 Nassau Sts., corner John and Nassau, N.Y." as printed Russell's American Printing House 30 Centre St., N.Y.C." in C. O'Neil Col.

"CONQUERER": name on W., resembling early Illinois-Spflg's "Hoyt" marked "Iowa Watch Co." (*H. B. Fried Col.*)

COOK & JAQUES: Trenton, N.J., 1880's. "Horologists—The Standard R. R. Clock" is on label of brass movt. *spr.* pendulum movt. in walnut cased wall tp. (*Stewart Dow*)

COOKE, SAMUEL: Waterbury, Conn., ca. 1830. Minature *P & S* wood movt. reads: "Improved Clocks—Mark Leavenworth/Invented & Made by——" (*R. Crichton*)

COOPER, DANIEL M.: Rochester, N.Y., 1894. He patented first card Time Recorder. Previously had invented laundry machinery. See I.B.M. (*Arthur Willex*)

*CORNELL, WALTER: Newport, R.I. G.F. at Ford Museum. (*Wm. Distin*) Banjo with dead beat escape known. (*Theodore Waterbury*)

CORYTON & LYNN (JOSIAH; ADAM): Alexandria, Va., 1795–96. Shop opened on Fairfax St. and "intended to carry on C–W–G–S." Each on own 1797. (*Cutten*)

CORYTON, JOSIAH: (–1810) Alexandria, Va., Royal St., 1766. Did C. & W. gilding, silvering, & kept for sale W. chains, keys and necklaces. 1797 Adv. "furnished self with articles necessary to mfr. C. offering to make all kinds of C. 1798, adv. employed W. rpr. Mar. Catherine Lynn before 1795. Brass movt. 8-day bracket C. 17x7 was ill. Ant. Jan. '52. (*Cutten*)

"COSMOS": name used by Rockford Watch Co. #580-018 is *18s* and 17j. (*H. B. Fried Col.*)

COUCH, STOW & CO.: Rock Springs, Tenn. LG with wood movt., with label with identical printing to Reeves & Co., Youngtown, Tenn. "D.—sold Patent C." (*J. E. Coleman*)

COWLES, DEEMING, & CAMP: Farmington, Conn., n/d. Shelf C. so labeled. (*Richard Bernheim*)

COWDERY, SHEREBIAH: Westmoreland, N.H., 1815. Adv. "Mfg. & Sold wood movt. C". (*C.S.P.*)

CRAWLEY JOHN: Phila. Dir., 1803–26 at South Front St. and other addresses. (*James Merrill*)

CRISSY, W.: Poughkeepsie, N. Y., at 209 Main St., 1858. "W.–J.–S.–rpr." One of 3 listed there on 1858 map. Dutchess County. (*Arthur Stout*)

*CRITCHETT, JAMES (1761–1849). Candia, N.H., n/d. Wood movt. C's. and N.H. Mirror C.'s known.

CRANDELL, J. R.: Salem, Mass. at 7 North St., 1870s. "W.–J.–D." Old bus. card in Birnbaum Col.

CROKER, WILLIAM S.: Harpers Ferry, W. Va., 1839. Adv. that he did rpr. C. & W.—had long experience meriting patronage. (*Cutten*)

CROOKS & PHELPS: Northampton, Mass., n/d. W. paper M. M. A. as "W.–J."

CROSBY, MORSE & FOSS: Boston, n/d. Name on black marble shelf C.—pos. French movt. (*Joseph L. Taubman*)

CROSBY & VOSBURG: N.Y.C. ca. 1860 (not Wasburg).

CROSBY, D. S.: N.Y.C. at 1 Courtlandt St., ca. 1850. Pos. of Crosby & Vosburg. OG standard metal movt. wgt. powered, with label printed by "Liveseys Print," 74 Fulton St., N.Y.C. (*R.H., J.W.G.*)

CROWLEY & FARR: Phila. Dir. 1823–25 as "C. & W." (*G.K.E.*)

CROWLEY, E.: Phila. Dir., 1833. "W." (*G.K.E.*)

*CURRIER, EDMUND: (1793–1853). Hopkinton, N.H., 1815–25. His *a/c* book for that period as C. extant. To Salem, Mass. Dir. 1837–53. Alone there, and with Foster from 1831–40; then alone. (*Charles Currier*)

CURRIER, T. D.: Waldoborough, Me., ca. 1820 as "C." (*L. S. Sheffield*)

*CURTIS & DUNNING (Lemuel, J. N.): Concord, Mass. ca. 1814–21, then Burlington, Vt., 1821 ff. and there, 1822 adv. "shop also near Branch Brook Bridge, Montpelier, Vt." Adv. 1827. Continuing mfd. 8-day tps. with mahogany or gilt cases; $25–35 each and warranted to keep time. After Dunning's death "Curtis continued alone."

CURTIS, CANDY (prob. Candace) & Co.: Bristol, Conn., n/d. (No "Candy" listed at Bristol.) *OG* "Jerome type" brass movt. so labeled; and at American Museum of Time, gift of Nelson Booth.

CUSHING, GEO. D.: Braintree, Mass., n/d. G. Mother C.—hood slides off—extant, at Sturbridge Village. (*E. C. Dunfee*)

CUSHMAN MFR. Co., H. T.: New Haven, Conn., *ca.* 1910. Mission-type slated black wood floor tp. with New Haven movts., one owned by Charles Rampe. (*E.I.*)

DAGGETT, GILBERT: Providence, R.I., *ca* 1860. Son of Thomas. Continued his business 7 rpr. after death of father "for some yrs." (*Theodore Waterbury*)

DAGGETT, THOMAS: Providence, R.I., at 70 Point St., *ca.* 1835. Father of Gilbert. Manifold rpr. tps. near Providence, leaving his name thereon in ink or chalk.

DANNER, JACOB: Lancaster, Pa., *ca.* 1820. An 8-day G.F.—white dial with moon extant. (*R.H., J.W.G.*)

DARCHE ELECTRIC CLOCK Co.: Chicago, at 830 S. Halstead St. and 306 Central Ave., Jersey City, N.J., 1886–1916. Pat. March 19, 1889. Made electric battery alarm tps. (*Fred Fried*)

*DARLINGTON, BENEDICT: (1786–1864). West Town Twp., Pa., *ca.* 1810. Pos. C.—also case maker, mechanically inclined, seeming mfr. G.F. wood wgt. movts. like those of Conn. Some extant.

DAVIES, H. J.: N.Y.C. (not Davis) 5 Courtlandt St., *ca.* 1858–86. Ill. alarm and several patents. Example of ill. Alarm in I.B.M. Col. has label on back of back board—"Ansonia Brass & Copper Co. Ansonia, Conn." (*Thomas Jones*)

DAVIES, THOMAS: Plymouth, Conn., and N.Y.C., 1846 ff. With Myles Morse at Plymouth. Patent on "Lever Clock." Extant examples: "Made by R. Blakeslee, Jr./C. & H. S. Sawyer—Colebrook River, Conn./Naraganset Clock Co., N.Y.C." His count wheels have horizontal pins, not vertical; no "lever" evidence. One *OG* extant labeled "Ansonia Brass & Clock Co., N.Y.C." and, stamped on front plate of movt. "J. J. Davies"; and also—same *OG* a back label reading "Successor to

Geo. A. Jones & Co., 5 Courtlandt St., N.Y.C." Estab. 1858. Albert L. Partridge has stated: "No patents recorded to one Thomas Davies."

DAVIS, PETER: Jaffrey, N.H., 1786. "From Rindge, N.H., a C." (*C.S.P.*)

DAVIS, ROBERT: Concord, N.H., 1812–15. W., C., and J. "One month in 1814 in Abel Hutchins shop."

DAVIS, ROBERT, JR.: Concord, N.H., 1824–26. as C. and W.; then a "conexion with Seth Eastman." (*C.S.P.*)

DAWE & MCIVER (PHILIP; COLIN): Alexandria, Va., *ca.* 1785. W. and S. "for a short time." (*Cutten*)

"DAX": name used by Westclox [1935] and later. mostly for non-j. "American Vertical Lever" pocket watches. (*Author's Col.*)

DAY, D. D. & R.: Westfield, Mass. *LG* shelf c. so labeled. Some with Masonic dials (*F.M.S.*)

DAY, BENJAMIN: Euclid, Ohio, n/d. "Clock case maker—examples extant." (*J.W.G.*)

DELONG ESCAPEMENT CO., INC.: N.Y.C., 1915. Inc. 1934 (Dis.) by C. W. Geiling; J. J. Thompson; and E. A. Hamilton. "See Chamberlain." (*J. E. Coleman*)

DEEMAN MFR. Co.: Chicago(?), 1890–1900. Name cast in case—outer—of early Westclox alarm tp. May have mfr. black iron stoves. Both these tps. in quantity; cased them in 2 piece cases in iron to match the stoves. Dials marked "A. L. Swift, Chicago." (*C. E. Durfee*)

DEMING, PHINEAS: Vienna, Ohio, *ca.* 1830. P. and S. so labeled, ill. ANT. March, 1965. Also extant a wood movt. 1-day G.F. marked "P. Deeming." (*The Amos Averys*)

*DENNETT, CHARLES: (1788–1867). Rochester, N.H., *ca.* 1825. His inlaid G.F. C. cases extant. (*Hist.*)

DEUBLE, G. M.: Phila., 1825 ff. Apt. at Baden, Germany. To Phila., 1825; then to Manahoy City, Pa. "where he made C." 1831 to Canton, Ohio, as C., W., and rpr. 4-dialed tower C. known; 1854 rcd. patent on "Striking Part for Tower C." (*J.W.G.*)

DEY TIME REGISTER CO., THE: Syracuse, N.Y., 1893. Inc. and made dial type time recorders. See I.B.M. Col. (*Arthur Willex*)

DEY, DR. ALEXANDER: Syracuse, N.Y., 1888. "Scottish Physician distinguished mathematician." Patented a time recorder "radically different from Bundy's dial type." See I.B.M. Col.

DICKEY, THOMAS: Harrisburg, Pa., 1793. Adv. 1814. Adv.—"begs leave to inform the Publick that he has commenced the business of a C. and W. maker, next door above the Tavern." (*R.H., J.W.G.*)

DIFFERENTIAL CLOCK Co.: Grand Rapids, Mich., *ca.* 1910. Name on dial "One Year Differential Clock; Pat. 1910." (*E. B. Burt*)

DOANE, JOHN: Situate, Mass., "before 1800." One G.F., brass movt. extant. (*C. H. Jones*)

DODGE, GARFIELD & Co.: Chilicothe, Ohio, 1840s. Conn. mfg. shelf Creads "Birge, Mallory & Co." (aw. 1838–43—BAC) Prob. D. (*E.I.*)

DOLE, DANIEL NOYES: (1775–1841). Hallowell, Me. "Maker of G.F.'s." (*L. R. Sheffield*)

DORESEY & OWENS (D. & M.; GEORGE): Mt. Vernon, Ohio, n/d. of the No-Key Clock Co., of which little is known. (*J.W.G.*)

*DOW, DAVID: Pittsfield, N.H., 1800s. "C. with Jacob B. Jones. Did experiment with movts. of wood, but best known for metal ones." (*Hist.*)

*DOWNES, EPHRAIM: (1787–1860). Bristol. Aw-1810–42. Some labels spelled "Downs." "Important C." "Did not fail in 1837 Depression." (*Lockwood Barr*)

DOWS & FULLER: N.Y.C. at 153 Pearl St., "cor. of Wall." Prob. D.—label in standard *OG* in Col. Thomas F. Burke.

*DOULL, JAMES: Charlestown, Mass. G.F., white dial with moon, mahogany case in William Osgood Blaney Col.

*DRAWBAUGH, DANIEL: (1847–1911). Eberly's Mills, Pa.—"7 miles from Harrisburg." Inventor and C. Made electric magnetic battery powered impulse tp. 7' high. His telephone instruments, transmitting speech, exhibited in his shop, 1869. The tp. exhibited at Phila. Centennial, 1876; patented, 1889; 125 patents granted him before his death at age 84. (*J.W.G.*)

DRAYER, WILLIAM E.: Hamilton, Ohio. 1834–53. "C. & W. at the signe of the Big Watch." (*J.W.G.*)

DROWN & BARNABY: Dover, N.H., 1850 ff. W. and J. (*C.S.P.*)

DUBLE, CHARLES: Zanesville, Ohio, 1815. Adv. "Commenced the C. and W. business on Main St." (*Hist.*) (*J.W.G.*)

DUCHENE, ANDREW: Portsmouth, N.H., 1798.

Adv. "W.—from Geneva, in Switzerland, will tarry in Towne a few days—has for sale a large assortment of French and Eng. silver W.'s at very low prices." (*C.S.P.*)

*DUEBER HAMPDEN WATCH Co.: Canton, Ohio, 1888–1925. A combining of the Dueber Watch Case Co. and Hampden Watch Co., of Springfield, Mass., *ca.* 1886. Operations at Canton from *ca.* 1888. Prior history: 1864—Mozart Watch Co.: Providence, R.I. 1867—New York Watch Co.: Springfield Mass. *ca.* 1877—Hampden Watch Co.: Springfield Mass. 1888—Dueber Hampden Watch Co.: Canton. *ca.* 1927—W. mfr. suspended. *ca.* 1930—Machinery sold to Russian interests. Numbering of W.—James W. Gibbs, formerly of Canton, a specialist in the Co. history, said: "Many employees I interviewed years ago and none knew the system of watch numbering. Relying on my research and a letter from F. Earl Kackett of Vancouver, Wash., Sept. 30, 1859—quote:—'Consecutive numbers used from the start of N.Y. Watch Co. in 1867; thru Hampden at Canton (1877)." About 10,000 by 1870. Full plate model introduced 1871 numbers about 10,000 to 100,000 (1877); some numbers below 100,000 have dials marked "Hampden Watch Co."—but not the movt. plate. Springfield numbers to about 500,000 *ca.* 1886. First Canton *W's* number about 600,000 by 1888. Webb C. Ball used numbers in the 800,000 series in 1892. Data from catalogues indicate movts. made *ca.* 1900 from 1,300,000. Early 1902 model size 6 about 1,500,000. 3,000,000 made by about 1920. Last numbers were about 4,000,000. Trade Names used as compiled by J.W.G. were:

At Springfield

John L. King	H. G. Norton
Homer Foot	J. L. King
Albert Clark	Charles Haywood
Theo E. Studley	John Hancock
Fred K. Billings	Geo. Sam Rice
Chester Woolworth	J. C. Perry
State Street	Lafayette

At Canton

Railway	Josephine
Molly Stark	Man O'Fashion
Gen'l Stark	Gladiator
John Hancock	Dueber Grand
Diadem	Special Railway
Wm. McKinley	Champion

Paul Revere
No. 302
Upper Ten
The Minute Man
The Dueber Watch
   Co.
The Hampden Watch
   Co.
No. 300
No. 304
No. 308
No. 314
New Railway
No. 105
Nathan Hale
Beacon

The Four Hundred
Hampden 300
No. 307
Ohioan
8-0
John C. Dueber
No. 306
No. 310
No. 312
3-0
No. 109
No. 104
Aviator
5-0
Mary Jane
Playboy

DUFFEY, GEORGE: (1820–96), Alexandria, Va., *ca.* 1850. Adv. as W. Did keep town records intact during Civil War. (*Cutten*)

*DUNGAN & KLUMP (ELMER E.; CHARLES M.): Phila. at 1208 Chestnut St., 1909–12, when Klump d. "Mouse Clock" 3 models made by New Haven Clock Co., the fourth by Sessions under 1910 Patent. There were also a fifth model and minatures. "Dickory, Dickory Dock;—The Mouse Ran Up the Clock ——" (*C. O. Terwilliger*)

DUNGAN, ELMER ELLSWORTH: (1862–1930), Phila. and Flowertown, Pa. "self-taught—self-made Inventor." Mar. Margaret E. Murray 1893. See Dungan & Klumpf, "The Mouse Clock." Fort Washington, Pa., 1909. Rcd. patent #912-833 (Feb. 1909) which covered the "MOUSE" Clock (tp). (*Bary—C. O. Terwilliger*)

DUNLAP. MAJ. JOHN: (1746–92) Bedford, N.H. Oldest of family of cabinet makers. Example at Amherst College, some with brass dial Mulliken movts. (*C.S.P.*)

*DUNNING, JOSEPH NYE (J.N.): (1793–1841) Concord, Mass. *ca.* 1814–21. To Burlington, Vt. with Lemuel Curtis 1821 as Curtis & Dunning. Adv. 1827 "Continuing mfg. 8-day tps, etc. Mar. 1st—Charity Conant, 1827. She d. 1829. Second mar. 1837: Frances Hulbert. Adv. 1840. (*Mrs. Dustin Cooley*)

DUNYON, AUGUSTINE: Portsmouth, N.H., 1843. Adv. as C. and W. (*C.S.P.*)

DURFEE, WALTER H.: (1857–1939) Providence, R.I. Aw. 1878–1939 d. Started at C. business at 295 High (now Westminster) St. with Dexter C. Cheever. *Ca.* 1885 to 151 Pond St.; 1920 on at 270 Washington St. Nephew,

Elisha continued after 1939 to retirement in 1962. (Street addresses to try to help date C.) (*J. E. Coleman*)

*DURGIN, CLARK: (1814–93) Andover, N.H. 1842ff. "long a C." b. Plymouth, N.H.; to Andover, 1815 where he d. Mar. Drusilla Bryant in 1842, dau. of C.—Jeremy Bryant. Labels extant in N.H. Mirrors, some with 1 wheel striking brass movts. with large, 3½″ fan in front of face plate "in odd shaped case." (*E. B. Burt*)

DURGIN, GERSHAM: (1750–1827) Andover, N.H. *ca.* 1790 ff. "A noted C., first in town." (*Hist.*) Grandfather of Clark Durgin to whom he apt.

DURKIN, JOHN FRANCES: (1859–?) Akron, Ohio, n/d. b. Ireland; "became chief of Police in 1900." One large G.F. extant with his name on dial. (*F. O'Neal*)

*DUTTON, DAVID: (1792–1862) Mount Vernon, N.H., 1830's and later. Wood movt. L.G's in numbers extant with some of his labels dated.

DUTTON, HILDRETH: (1787–?) Lyndeborough, N.H.; then to Greenfield, N.H., in 1812. Bro. of Reed Dutton. (*C.S.P.*)

DYAR, HARRISON GRAY: (1805–?) Concord, Mass., 1820ff. Bro. of Joseph to whom apt. Was b. Harvard, Mass. Reportedly sent electric impulses over a wire, pos. before S. B. Morse. Devised a converted 8-day C. using a rotary lever that cut down on the number of wheels from a half dozen to two.

DYAR, JOSEPH: (1795–1850) Concord, Mass., before 1816. There continued the Curtis & Dunning business after their move to Vt. To Middlebury, Vt. where he adv. 1822 and adv. 1824. "Respected citizen. Killed by a runaway horse & team, startled by a whistle of the R.R. locomotive." Bro. who was his Apt. was H. G. Dyar.

DYER, W. & V: Savannah, Ga., *ca.* 1835ff. Triple Decker shelf C. labeled "Patent Clocks/Invented by Eli Terry/made by——" Pos. outgrowth of the then local taxing situation in certain areas of products not generally made in the South. (*Ray Walker*)

EASTMAN, CYRUS: (1787–1862) Amherst, N.H., *ca.* 1814. To Amherst after 7 yrs. apt. to T. Chandler at Concord, N.H. Also patent rcd. on "making lead pipe." (*Hist.*)

EASTMAN, EDWARD: Sanbornton, N.H., *ca.* 1804. C. then to Cato Four Corners, N.Y. d. prior to 1855. (*Hist.*)

EASTMAN, JOSEPH: Boston and Chelsea, Mass. Trained as C. by the Willards, providing link from them to modern-day C.-making. Did devise a "watch-type" escapement" for ship and house clocks, differing from the "marine" type escape used in Conn. Organized 1886 Eastman Clock Co., building first factory in Chelsea, to make C. with his patented improvement. 1888 became Boston Clock Co. In 1897–Chelsea Clock Co. This business continues today, making fine C. and tps. (*Walter Mutz*)

EASTMAN, SETH: Concord, N.H. Dir., 1830–34 as W. and J. W. paper extant.

EATON, ISAIAH C.: Walpole, N.H., 1793–Adv. for apt. C. Some of his spoons, and a clock ill. (*Hist.*)

ECO MAGNETO CLOCK CO.: Boston. First q. 20th Cent. Made Eco Portable Watchman's tps. with aluminum cases, dial glass covered; 10 station punches within tp. Differs from Kimhauser. Movt. marked "Germany, 11 j.–Pat. June 25, 1907." (*Example Ray Walker Col.*)

ECONOMY FARM RECORD CO., THE: Newton, Iowa, 1907. Did mfr. giant window C.–"this movt. is made especially for us by one of the largest C. mfrs. in U.S.A." Now at Newport, N.H. C. Museum. (*Wesley Hallet*)

EGE, JAMES: Fredericksburg, Va., 1832. Adv. (only 1) as "C. & W." (*Cutten*)

ELECTRO CLOCK CO.: Baltimore, Md., n/d. Wall battery tp. 37″ high in C. Terwilliger Col.

ELGIN NATIONAL WATCH CO.: "gave up mfr. men's j. watches at Elgin 1964." (*Business Week–6-5-65*)

ELLIOT, J. R.: Minneapolis, Minn. Last q. 19th Cent. Adv. card in Birnbaum Col. as "D. J. W. etc"

ELLIOT, LUTHER: (1794–1876), Amherst, N.H. Employed by Thomas Woolsen, Jr. to build town C. (*Hist.*)

ELLIS, ARNOLD: Londonderry, N.H. (?), n/d. G.F. with brass movt. having unusually large and heavy skeleton plates. (*D. K. Packard*)

ELSWORTH, DAVID: Windsor, Conn. Name on dial of G.F. Ill. [ANT.] Apr. '56 with "case made by Chapman or Parsons" only one extant. (*Charlotte Hamilton*)

"EMPIRE SPECIAL": N.Y.C. "Name used on some 18s watches Swiss made." (*H. B. Fried*)

EMPIRE CALENDAR CLOCK CO.: Genoa, N.Y., n/d. Mfg. various styles of Pat. cal. C. of

J. E. Youngs. 8-day movts. by Wm. L. Gilbert Clock Co. "Cal. of G.F. type plus month and day of week indicator, in dial slots; 1-31 on perimeter outside time circle. Adjusts for Leap Year." (*W. E. Woernley*)

ENGLE, JACOB: (1845–) New Bedford, Ohio. 1881ff. b. Germany. To Millersburg, Ohio, 1881, where "made & rpr. C. & W., some C. with name on dial" Was time inspector of railroads. (*J.W.G.*)

ENGLE, STEPHEN D.: Hazleton, Pa., *ca.* 1878. W. Made the "Engle C." copies of 4 page booklet (5¢) showing photos of the clock, Engle and Capt. J. Reid in Col. Elisha Durfee at Columbia (Pa.) Museum of Antiquities. (*Earl Strickler*)

ENGLEHART, C. W. & SON: Phila. at North 2nd St. Last q. 19th Cent. Adv card "W.–J." (*Bir. Col.*)

EQUITY WATCH CO.: Boston. 20th Cent. "a less expensive W. 3/0–12 @ 16 sizes of Waltham type." (*H. B. Fried.*)

ERICKSON, LAURENCE: Evanston, Ill. 1899 "Rcd. Patent #602.635 on 'Specially Designed Clocks' later produced in some volume." (*J. E. Coleman*)

ERWIN, EDWARD F.: Bethlehem, Pa., 1882–90's "Took over bus. of John M. Miksch" (*R.H. –J.W.G.*)

"EUREKA": name used by E. N. Welch Co. on 8-day alarm C. 16″ x 8″ all-glass front. One in H. B. Fried Col.

EVANS, ELIJAH: Fredericktown, Md., n/d. Brass-dialed 2 wgt. 8-day brass movt. G.F. so marked. (*John Myers Col.*)

EVANS, SEPTIMUS: Doylestown, Pa., 1807ff. There built a dwelling which later became the Green Tree Inn. Mar. Catherine Haupt of Durham, 1811. To Jenkintown, 1821; later to Delaware.

FABER, GEORGE: (1778–?) Sumneytown, Pa., *ca.* 1791ff. Son of Rev. John Theobold Faber. Uncle and godfather was C. Daniel Rose of Reading, Pa. who taught him C. His dates aw. have some confusion. (*Lucille Lehman*)

FAIRBANKS & CO.: New Brunswick, N.J., *ca.* 1830. LG so marked. (*E. E. Runnells*)

FAIRCHILD, G. W.: Bridgeport, Conn. at 2 Citizen's Bldg., Main St. Dir. 1868 C. and W. (*Leopold Gregoire*)

FAIRHAVEN CLOCK CO.: Fairhaven, Vt., 1897–1910. Made glass-sided cased shelf C. with marine movts. among other C.'s. "At peak production, employed several (not "400") workmen. (*E. B. Burt*)

FARMER'S EXCHANGE MFG. CO.: n/p, *ca.* 1890. "Kitchen type shelf C. (oak) 27 x 16½ x 4″ with typical 8 day spg. ½ hr. strike movt. (*Herbert A. McIngvale*)

FARMINGTON: Plainville, Conn. Adjoining towns. Some confusion on Conn. C. labels. One Ives C. in Edward Ingraham Col. has *both* town names on same label.

"FASHION": Name used by Southern Calendar Clock Co., St. Louis, 1875–89 and revived briefly early 1890's.

FEARIS, I.: Pittsburgh, Pa., early 1800's. G.F.s case maker. (*Don Shaffer*)

FENN, GIBE: (1808–93) Brimfield, Ohio. *ca.* 1850 "maker of C. cases". (*J.W.G.*)

FENTON, GAMALIEL: Walpole, N.H., 1798. Adv. Town C. and bell foundry. (*C.S.P.*)

*"FILBER, JOHN": Error and remove from list. Was mistake for John Fisher (Fischer): York, Pa. aw. *ca.* 1759–1808, from misreading the script German "S." *ANT* Dec. 1865.

"FINNEMORE": Birmingham, Eng., *ca.* 1800. Made dials for and were imp. to U.S.A. for G.F.'s. Name found on back or on false plate when used.

FISHER, THOMAS: York, Pa., 1779–83. "Pos. a C. —no exact data." (*R.H.–J.W.G.*)

FISHER, WILLIAM: Charleston, Va. at Main St., 1841ff. Adv. 1845 "added C. rpr." (*Cutten*)

*FITCH, EUGENE L.: (1846–?) N.Y.C. To Iowa 1881; back to N.Y.C., 1901. Patents on "Thread Case" Type Writing Machine" and 4 on "PLATO" tps. as:– 733,180 7/7.1903 :: 715,776;-Dec. 16, 1902 :: 724,466; Apr. 7, 1903 :: and 726,276; Apr. 26, 1903. (*C. O. Terwilliger*)

*FITCH, JONAS: (1741–1808) Pepperell, Mass., C. n/d. Reportedly made G.F.'s with wood movts. of which several extant in Fitchburg. (*E. B. Burt*)

FLAGG, SETH: Springfield, Mass. *ca.* 1840 W. paper, Fried Col.

*FLEICHTINGER, CHAS. W.: Sinking Spring, Pa., *ca.* 1900. "Inventor & Mfr." name on C. in Russell Fegley Col. (*Robert Franks*)

FLOWER CITY WATCH CO.: Rochester, N.Y., late 1890's. Gold-filled hunting case W. #1099911, stem wind and set marked with "Chalmers Patent" on dial and movt. in Henry Sayward Col.

"FLYER": name used on modern alarm tps. by New Haven Clock Co.

FORBES & TUCKER (WELLS – –): Concord, N.H., 1841–42. Partnership ended. Forbes to Bristol, N.H., alone 1842ff.

*FORBES, WELLS: Concord, N.H., 1841 then Bristol, N.H., 1842ff. 20″ high wood flat top case after style David Dutton, but smaller in Ray McKinney Col. Prob. casemaker or D. Has dated "1842" label with quaint language. Has unusual 8-day brass movt. with solid gear wheels (not cut out) complete spg. covers, and mounted on back board by well fitting iron casting.

FORD, HENRY: (July 30, 1863–Apr. 7, 1947) Detroit, Mich. C. and W. fascinated him from early in his life. This lead to his establishing a collection of over 3,500 C. and W. now displayed at the Henry Ford Museum, Dearborn, Mich.

About 1880, he planned to mfg. a pocket watch he hoped could be sold for about 30 to 50 cents each. With this, he went as far as to obtain a partner. Dies were actually cut for making watch gears. Finally decided to turn his energies to other enterprises despite the increasing interest at the time in standard time for the railroads, though watch mfr. was, with a few exceptions, not too profitable. He was quoted: "Often I took a broken W. and tried to put it together to run again, tho I had but the simplest tools. There is much to be learned by tinkering with things. I did want to make something in quantities." In 1885, he made a W. with 4 hands to show standard and sun times on the same dial. On Apr. 11, 1888 mar. Clara Bryant, who spurred him on to the heights of great success.

FOLSOM & HULBEET: Hartford, Conn., n/d. Printers of some Eli Terry Jr. labels for his C. (*J. E. Coleman*)

*FORESTVILLE MFR. CO.: Bristol, 1835 ff. An 8-day brass wgt. *OG* has these three names on label–"J. C. Brown; C. Goodrich; and S. B. Smith." (*O'Neil Col.*) Oddity in Avery Col. is a 1 day wgt. wood movt. *OG* with label "Improved Brass Bushed Clocks, Mfg. & Sold by Forestville Mfg. Co."–etc. (*P. Canfield, Hartford, Printer*)

FORRER, CHRISTIAN: (1737–83) Lampeter and Newbury, Pa. 1754–83. Swiss, came to America, 1754; in Lampeter, 1774.

*FOSTER, SAMUEL: Amherst, N.H., *ca.* 1800 "G.F. with brass wheels, wooden arbours and plates so marked." (*A. L. Partridge*) Adv. at Concord, N.H., 1810.

"FOUNTAIN SQUARE": "name used on some Swiss-made W. like 1860s American W. Co." (*H. B. Fried*)

FRANKLIN, DR. BENJAMIN: (1706-90), Phila. Great American statesman—invented a tp. with but 3 wheels and 2 pinions.

FREDONIA WATCH CO.: Fredonia, N.Y., 1884-5. "H. Carmine" name on dial of W. #7276. (*B. Robert Rand*)

FREEPORT W. CO.: Freeport, Ill., 1874–75. Purchased Rock Island W. Co.'s equipment. Plant burned to ground in 1875 (Oct. 11); 3 Patents to "E. Chapin." (*R. S. Tschudy*)

FRENCH, BRACE, & GOLDBURG: Granville, Ohio, 1828. "When Linnell factory moved, Co. became then so known." (*J.W.G.*)

FRENCH, DAVID: New Ipswich, N.H., n/d. N. H. Mirror C. with second hand, cal. day of week and week, and day of mo. 7-day wgt. brass striking movt. with alarm—3 wgts. in D. K. Packard Col.

FRICK, F. A.: Rochester, N.Y., 1894. A mortician, with J. C. Willard formed Willard & Frick Mfr. Co. See I.B.M.

FROMM, SEBASTIAN: Hamilton, Ohio, 1827. Adv. 1859, "C. & cabinet maker." (*J.W.G.*)

FROST, JESSE: Lynn, Mass., *ca.* 1835. 30-hr. wood "groaner" shelf C. extant. (*Stanley Church*)

FULLER & KROEBER: N.Y.C. at 25 John St., *ca.* 1865. 30 hr. brass spg. movt. in walnut case with oval top shelf C. 11″x 8″ labeled on back of backboard "———, Mfr. of American Clocks Oddity on front of plynth is stamped into the wood—" Pat. May 17, 1863. Above the trunk is a false drawer (see Kroeber). (*Victor Stengel Col.*)

FULLER, RUFUS: (1782–1849), Francestown, N.H. "C.—a man of good mechanical ability." (*Hist.*)

GAENSLE (GENSLE), JACOB: (1721-68). Phila., 1741-65. C. b. Germany, son of John, and there apt. To Phila., 1741. (*R.H.–J.W.G.*)

*GALES, JOHN: (1775–1853) Portsmouth, N.H., early 10th Cent. C. Grandson of cabinet-maker John Gates.

GALT, JAMES: Alexandria and Williamsburg, Va., 1801. adv. to *ca.* 1825. (*Cutten*)

GARDNER, JOHN B. & SON: Ansonia, Conn.,

1857ff. Mfg. C. dials and C. parts.—"sucessful"—"sunken dial" type. Original factory on Main St., enlarged from time to time and *ca.* 1870 "became one of the principal plants of the Borough"—"Employed up to 100 men." (*Hist.*)

*GATES, ZACHEUS: (1779–?) Harvard and Charlestown, Mass. first *q.* 19th Cent. C.— G.F.'s with rocking ship and banjos. (*E. B. Burt*)

GAWNE, W. A.: Oxford, Ohio, *ca.* 1850. Shelf C. extant so labeled, and "Printed by R. S. Ritchie." (*J.W.G.*)

GAY, LEVI B.: Nashua, N.H. "Opposite City Hall on Main St." Dir., 1864. W. (*F.M.S.*)

*GEER, ELIHU: Label printer of Hartford. "Puffin' Betsy"—engr. of fanciful old time R.R. steam locomotive—is, among many others, on a Chauncey Boardman shelf C. On this one the engr. is inscribed "Hartwell —Entered acc. to Act of Congress, etc. in the year, 1845." (*E. F. Tukey*)

GEIGER, JOSEPH: Whitehall, Pa., *ca.* 1750. Inscribed on brass dial of a G.F. (*R.H.– J.W.G.*)

GELSTON & TREADWELL: N.Y.C., n/d. Name on dial of W. of foreign origin. (*Efroim Greenberg*)

GENERAL ELECTRIC CO.: Bridgeport, Conn., and Ashland, Mass., from 1930 ff. Makers of a./c's and other electric C. and tps., radio timers, and synchronous motors: The Warren Telechron unit at Ashland merged 1951; then known as Telechron Dept. This was the Co. founded by Henry Warren who has been considered responsible for the better control of a./c. cycles, making time telling from the electric lines possible. (*Edwin C. Pease*)

"GENERAL STARK": Name used on W. by Dueber-Hampden Co. #1516725 in Henry B. Fried Col.

GENSEL, JOHN: Phila., n/d. May be son of John or Jacob G. 30 hr. wgt. movt. rope drive G.F. with one-hand extant. (*R.H.–J.W.G.*)

GEORGE, WILLIAM L.: Coal Creek, Tenn., second q. 19th Cent. W., C., and J., (1794–1887).

*GEROULD, S. A.: Keene, N.H., W. and J.— later—"S. A. & J. M. Gerould," then son joined in 1841 to become "S. A. Gerould & Son." (*Hist.*)

GERRISH & PEARSON: Portland, Me., at 74 Exchange St., 1859. W., C. and W. materials. (*Ernest Cramer*)

GERRISH, WILLIAM: DOVER, N.H., 1830s. W. (*C.S.P.*)

GERRY, JAMES H.: Newark, N.J., 1880. Patent #236–017—both time and strike wound on single arbor—left, and then right. Examples made by Boston Clock Co. *ca.* 1885 (*Author's Col.*)

GIBRALTER MFR. Co.: Jersey City, N.J., *ca.* 1940. "Oxford—Self-Starting" on dial of shelf a./c. tp. model 124D. (*Janos Weinberger Col.*)

GIFFORD, ELLIS: Fall River, Mass., n/d. Name on pocket W. with fuzee size 16, 14 j. (*H. B. F. Col.*)

GILBERT, HUBBARD, & Co.: Bristol, 1855–57. Pos. firm name then in use for Hubbard, Gilbert & Co. Records in American Museum of Time.

*GILBERT, WILLIAM LEWIS: (1806–90), all in Conn.: Farmington, Bristol, Winchester (Winsted). Important and successful clock Mfr. from 1825. Made a fortune in the business. Was: 1828–30 Marsh & Gilbert; (Geo., Wm. L.) at Bristol. 1830–35 Marsh & Gilbert at Farmington, then back to Bristol. 1835–37 Birge, Gilbert & Co. Bristol 1839–40 Jeromes, Gilbert, Grant & Co. First 1-day brass wgt. OGs made by this firm. 1841 Gilbert to Winchester at the place where Riley Whiting made C.'s. 1841–*ca.* 1851 Clarke (Lucius) Gilbert & Co. 1851–66 William L. Gilbert Co. 1866–71 Gilbert Mfr. Co. After a bad fire reorganized as:—1871–1934 William L. Gilbert Clock Co. 1934–57 William L. Gilbert Clock Corp. (Bad damage in '55 flood.) Then became General Gilbert Co. to *ca.* 1964 when clock business was sold to Spartus Co., of Chicago: Since 1806 for first time, no C.'s made at this place.

GILES, JOSEPH: Concord, N.H., 1798. Adv. "lately from Phila.; taken a part of Messrs Levi & Abel Hutchins shop" Adv., 1812 "has returned from the southward and has taken old stand of Mr. Foster." (*C.S.P.*)

GILL, ED.: Phila. *ca.* 1800. Caster of bells for G.F.s.

GILLESPIE, WILLIAM: New London, Pa., n/d. Brass-dialed G.F. at Chester Co. Hist. Soc. Museum. (*Dr. Robert Ravel*)

GILMAN, BENJAMIN, C.: (1763–1835), Exeter,

N.H. n/d. C. S. inst. maker; hydraulic eng.; etc. (*ANT–9–'43*)

GILMAN & INGALLS: Dexter, Me., at 3 Mercantile, n/d. W. paper in Hamilton Pease Col.

GIRD, WILLIAM F.: Alexandria, Va., 1799. Adv., 1805; last adv. C. (*Cutten*)

GLASS, THOMAS: Hanover, Va., 1771. Adv.— C. J. Rpr. Mar. 1773, Martha East. In 1777 paid for rifles and moulds. 1801 as W., Norfolk, Va. Dir. at 21 Market Sq.; also later, 1801, adv. as W. at Raleigh, N.C. (*Cutten*)

GODDARD, BENJAMIN: Worcester, Mass., at 174 Main St. Dir., 1849 as Mfr. J. & D. Dir., 1860.

GODDARD, D. & Co.: Worcester, Mass., at Main St. Dir., 1849. (*E. A. Battison*)

GODDARD, DANIEL: (1787–?) Shrewsbury, Mass. Son of Luther; bro. of Parley; nephew of Nichols. Apt. in father's W. shop at Shrewsbury and went to Worcester with him in 1817, staying there in business with him. (*Dr. P. L. Small*)

GODDARD, P. & D.: Worcester, Mass., n/d. Watch #8784 in coin silver case #232 with chain fuzee in Ernest Cramer Col.

GODDARD, NATHANIEL W.: Nashua, N.H., at 89 Main St. Dir., 1857 W. & J. Also: N. W. Goddard & Son same add. Dir., 1866 W.'s, mostly Swiss. One in F. M. Selchow Col.

GODDARD, NICHOLS (Not Nicholas): (1773–?), b. Shrewsbury, Mass. Apt. of his cousin, Luther Goddard. 1794 to Northampton, Mass. There mar. Charity, dau. Job White. 1779–to Rutland, Vt. There also partner of Capt. Lord as Lord & Goddard.

GODDARD, PARLEY:—b. Shrewsbury, son of Luther & Elisabeth Goddard. Apt. to Father and became partner of his in W. factory, 1809. In 1817, when father and bro. Daniel went to Worcester, stayed on at factory and made *ca.* 30 more W.'s. Finally gave up since foreign competition too severe, and became a farmer. By 1825 went to Worcester to join father and bro. in C., W., rpr. There made "a few more W.'s."

GOELET, PETER: N.Y.C. "Early adv."—"at Golden Key, 48 Hanover Sq. has imported from London a very large and general assortment of iron mongery, cutlery, hardware, all kinds of tools and materials for C. and W. makers. Also great variety of pewter spoons, coat, vest, and sleeve buttons, leather and hair trunks, bootlegs and vamps, leather soles and a consignment of playing cards." (*Renee Amy*)

GOODING, JAMES: Waltham, Mass., n/d. Son of John who trained him. Also as W.

GOODING, JOHN: (1780–1870), Plymouth, Mass., *ca.* 1802–70. Son of Joseph and his apt.

GOODING, JOSIAH: Bristol, R.I., and Taunton, Mass., *ca.* 1780. G.F.'s reportedly had his own secret touch mark on his dials—"one lone fly." Often reportedly used dials from England as "Wilson." (*Benjamin Finch*)

GOODNOW, SILAS B.: (1814–58), Fitchburg, Mass. Dir. 1838–49. (*Roy McKinney*)

*GOODWIN, WALLACE: North Attleboro, Mass., 2nd q. 19th Cent. banjo with brass bezel fine gilded eglomise work, square box brass side arms in James W. Kenna Col.

GORDON, GEORGE: Newburgh, N.Y., n/d. "C. & W.-maker." (*Catharine Tobin*)

*GORDON, THOMAS: N.Y.C., n/d. G.F. with brass dial with moon and "New York" engr. on dial. (*Sak Col.*)

GORE, JOHN: Boston, 1752. "For guilding a C." —4 pounds." (*Mrs. Yves Buhler*)

GOULD, ABIJAH JR.: (1777–1818), Hollis and Nashua, N.H., *ca.* 1810. Wood movt. G.F.'s extant. (*Robert Dickey*)

*GOVE, RICHARD: (1776–1836). Sanbornton, N.H., as C., W., and J. Sons entered business. To Dover, N.H., then Peru, N.Y. (*A. L. Childs*)

GOVE, RICHARD: (1815–*ca.* 1875). Sanbornton, N.H. Apt. in Boston. C., W., and J. (*A. L. Childs*)

GRANT & LORING: Boston, n/d. Name on dial of extant banjo. (*E. B. Burt*)

GRANT, GEORGE W.: Phila., at 3814 Lancaster Ave. last q. 19th Cent. Adv. card Bir. Col.— "W.-maker & J."

GRANT, ZELOTES: Bristol, Conn., (tx.) 1839–40. Partner in first 1-day brass wgt. OG production with the Jeromes and Gilbert as Jeromes, Gilbert & Grant. Then Jeromes & Grant, 1841–43; then each alone.

*GREANLEAF & OAKES (DAVID, JR.; FREDERIC): Hartford, Conn., at Main St., *ca.* 1804. W. paper M.M.A.

GREGG & POMEROY, (JOSEPH; HAMILTON, O.): 1828. Formerly together at Rossville, across the Miami River, then a separate town, now part of Hamilton, Ohio. C. (*J.W.G.*)

*GREGG, JOSEPH: (1766–1832). Alexandria, Va., early 19th Cent. Adv. 1803 as "Returned to City"—did W. and C. work. Sold out in 1809 to Griffith & Gaither. To Georgia, estab. first cotton factory in South. (*Cutten*)

GRIFFITH & GAITHER (GREENBERRY; JOHN): Alexandria, Va., 1809. Gaither alone by 1811 while Griffith also adv. (*Cutten*)

GRIFFITH, GREENBURY: (1787–1848). Alexandria, Va., 1809 ff. (*Cutten*)

GRIFFITH, HUMPHREY: (1791–1870). Indianapolis, Ind., 1825–34. G.F.'s, one at D.A.R. Hall, Wash., D.C. (*Mrs. L. O. Kupillas*) Earlier at Huntington, Pa., to 1818, then Lebanon, Ohio, 1819–23, then Indianapolis and Centerville, Ind. b. Wales and apt. and made C.s in London. "Good quality G.F.s extant." (*J.W.G.*)

GRIFFITH, NATHANIEL S.: Portsmouth, N.H. 1769 adv.—"make & rpr. all kinds of C.s also mend W.s"

GRISWOLD, H.: Leominster, Mass., 1788–1812. C., W., and rpr. (*H.B.F.*)

GRISWOLD, J. & W. W.: Fitchburg, Mass., *ca.* 1833. W. papers extant as "C. and W."

*GROPENGIESSER, JOHN: Phila. C. and W. and chro. Dir. 69 South Front St., 1841–42/South 3rd St., 1843–50/814 Walnut St., 1871. (*R. H.–J.W.G.*)

GROPENGIESSER, LOUIS C.: Phila. Dir. 1871 at 814 Walnut St. with bro. John. (*R.H.– J.W.G.*)

GRUBER, GEORGE: Berryville, Va., 1840. Adv. C. and W. (*Cutten*)

GUILD, BENJAMIN:—N.J., n/d. Name on dial of G.F. owned by A. C. Pierson, Bird-in-Hand, Pa.

GUILD, ISAAC: Francestown, N.H., adv. 1824, C. and W. (*C.S.P.*)

GUTH, JOHN: Whitepaint Twp., Pa., 1803–06. C. (*R.H.–J.W.G.*)

HADDON PRODUCTS, INC.: Chicago, 1960s. Making a/c's. (*R. F. Tschudy*)

HAHN IMPROVED PORTABLE WATCHMAN'S TIME DETECTOR: Phila., 1890's–1900's. "Awarded 1st prize Chicago World's Fair, 1893–" Was sold by Riggs of Phila., *ca.* 1902. (*J.W.G.*)

HAIGHT, NELSON: Newburgh, N.Y., n/d. "At the old Stand of N. B. Meyer C. and W. Maker." (*Maurice Van Buren*)

HALL & STILLMAN: Flemington, N.J., *ca.* 1770. W. paper extant. (*William S. Dilts*)

HALL, CHARLES: Lancaster, Pa., *ca.* 1770. W.

and S. Mar. Maria S. Leroy, dau. of Abraham Leroy, C., 1767. (*R.H.—J.W.G.*)

*HALL, DANIEL G.: Grey, Me., 1846, C. and W. On W. paper in A. L. Partridge Col. Also at Lewiston, Me.

HALL, IVORY: Concord, N.H., 1819. Adv. 1853, 8-day brass movt. G.F. with his name on dial, extant; also a W. paper. Had Jewelry Store on Main St. (*John Sinclair—C.S.P.*)

*HALE, NATHAN: Ringe, N.H., later Vt. C. 1800s. Also G. Ezra Ames, "ornamental painter," did work for him in 1791 Mass. shelf C. at Ford Museum. (*D. K. Packard*)

HALL (HILL) SAMUEL: Harrisburg, Pa., n/d. Am. G.F. with white dial in Reading Room, Newport, R.I. (*T. E. Waterbury*)

HALL, WILLIAM HENRY: (1809–68), Lititz, Pa. Son of Christian; continued his C. and W. business. (*R.H.—J.W.G.*)

HALLER, JACOB: Cannonsburg, Pa., *ca.* 1810, C. (*R.H.—J.W.G.*)

HALLOWELL, ROBERT: (1817–?). Baltimore Md., *ca.* 1835. "Of Quaker lineage." Son of Charles T., *ca.* 1845, made C. for Independent Engine Co. of Baltimore.

HAM, DANIEL: Portsmouth, N.H., 1804–37. W. paper in American W. Paper Col.

HAM, FRANCIS: (1828–1905), Portsmouth, N.H., aw. 1841–61. C., W., and J. (*C.S.P.*)

HAM, LEE S.: Bushnell, Ill., *ca.* 1950 ff. Made at least 3 complete C. 1 with wood movt. Also rpr. including Tower C.'s.

HAMMOND INSTRUMENT Co.: Chicago, 1960s. Making a/c's. (*R. F. Tschudy*)

HAND MADE CLOCK Co.: Piqua, Ohio, *ca.* 1930. Joseph A. Thomas designed and made about 50 novelty C. so marked and sold to a brewing Co. (*J.W.G.*)

HANKS, BENJAMIN: (1755–1824), Litchfield, Conn. "Dr. Ezra Styles, 1778, President of Yale on May 24, 1784 while viewing lands he owned at Litchfield examined Benjamin Hank's air clock. It will go 8 days without winding up. A ventilator moves with every breeze—those of two ordinary hours will wind up the whole 8 days." (*C. O. Terwilliger*)

HANSON CLOCK MFG. Co.: Rockford, Ill., 1960s. Making a/c's. (*R. F. Tschudy*)

*HARLAND, THOMAS: (1735–1807), Norwich, Conn. First to produce watches in some volume in U.S.A. His fine G.F.s highly prized. Trained many fine apts. A most important American citizen.

*HARMSON, HENRY: (?–1837). Marblehead, Mass., *ca.* 1720. b. Germany. To America; also at Newport, R.I. "after 1723" and Newburyport, Mass. G.F. at Essex Institute. (*T. S. Waterbury*)

*HARPUR (HARPER), WILLIAM E.: Alexandria, Va., 1836. Adv.; later Phila. where Dir. 1839 ff. (*Cutten*)

HARRIS & WILCOX: Troy, N.Y., at 206 River St., *ca.* 1840. Prob. D., though shelf C. labeled as "Mfr." (*Oscar Hockenson*)

HART & WAY: Brookfield, Conn., 1800s. G.F. with 30-hr. wood pull up movt. at Hagans Clock Manor Museum. (*Jo Hagans*)

HART, HENRY: Goshen, Conn., *ca.* 1830. L.G. wood movt. carved cols. "Improved C.—mfr. by T. M. Roberts, Bristol, for——" P. Canfield printed label. In Edward Ingraham Col. Now at American Museum of Time.

*HART, ORRIN: Bristol, at Peaceable St. Aw. 1824–33. Purchased the Charles G. Ives clock business and brick house of Edward Barnes. Sold both to John Bacon in 1833 and to Waterloo, N.Y., there sold C. One label, printed by P. Canfield, reads: "Improved C. Mfg. & sold by——for William Hill. Bristol, Conn."

HARTFORD WATCH Co.: Hartford, Conn., *ca.* 1895. Key wind j. W. #49,735 seen by Amos Avery. No further data.

HASEY, S.: Renselersville, N.Y., *ca.* 1855. W. paper in Fred Fried Col.

HASKELL, MOODY: Burlington, Vt., *ca.* 1820. Name on dial of C. at University of Vt. Note inside case describes him as "Maker & Donor." (*L. W. Burkhardt*)

*HASSAM, STEPHEN: (1764–1861). Charlestown, N.H., after 1790. b. Boston; d. Charlestown. "Learned C. from Daniel Burnap." (*E. B. Burt*)

HASSEM (HASLAM) JOHN: Charlestown, N.H., n/d. Son of Stephen. Tower C. in Haverhill, N.H. church has his maker's plate "1843." Movt. has pin escape one beat every 3 secs. (*Ray Walker*)

"HAVLIN ELECTRIC": on dial of brown-colored metal case non-self start a/c tp. This the only visible marking and on dial with "Made in U.S.A." *ca.* 1930. (*Charles Currier Col.*)

HAYES, ALEX W. & Co.: N.Y.C., n/d. Name

on dial of French type imported C. (*George Coggill*)

HAYES, PETER B.: (1788–1842), n/p, 1826–42. American C. extant with his name. (*Carl Dauterman*)

*HEISLEY, FREDERICK: (1759–1843). Frederick, Md., 1783–93. In Revolutionary War. Mar. Catherine Hoff. Made math instruments and C. Tower C. of his operating at Smith's Inst. 1793, to Lancaster, Pa., partner of George Hoff. 1801, to Harrisburg, Pa., then 1820s to Pittsburgh where Dir. 1837 at St. Clair St. d. Harrisburg. Two sons, George Jacob and Frederick Augustus. (*Charles E. Smart*)

HEISLEY, FREDERICK AUGUSTUS: (1792–1885). b. Frederick, Md., son of Frederick, bro. of George J. Made C., W. D. and math insts. d. Pittsburgh. (*C. E. Smart*)

HEISLEY, GEORGE JACOB: (1789–1880). Frederick, Md., then Harrisburg, Pa. Son of Frederick. Also made C., W., and math insts. (*C. E. Smart*)

HENDERSON, L. R.: Concord, N.H., 1841. Adv., 1861, W. and S. (*C.S.P.*)

HENDRICK, BARNES & CO. (E. M.; M. B.): Bristol, 1848–55. Seems also as Hendrick, Hubbell & Co. From 1848 made mostly movts. of the Bainbridge Barnes steel spring driven marines. "Jerome was principal customer and he insisted such movts. as they made for him be stamped 'Jerome'—Successful till the Jerome failure." (*W. A. Barnes— J. E. Coleman*)

HENSE, GOTTESLEBEN, & JONES: N.Y.C., at Courtlandt St., 1868. 12' high G.F. in Teller House, Central City, Col., so dated. Regular type dial, huge gridiron pendulum with mercury; and with flanking American flags engr.; plus an American Eagle and Shield. (*Jo Hagans*)

HENSE, J. E.: Central City, Col., ca. 1870. Then, C., W., and J. for this gold mining town. His name inscribed on dial of Ithaca Wall cal. C. also in Teller House there. (*Orville Hagans*)

HEPFLUFS & HARROLD: Birmingham, Eng., ca. 1800. This name cast into middle plate of 30-hr. brass movt. G.F. (*Alan Cartoun*)

HERMAN, GEORGE: Newport, R.I. "Swing C.— Pat. 1872" in Albert L. Partridge Col.

*HERON, ISAAC: N.Y.C., ca. 1771. Adv. N.Y. Gazette and Weekly Advertiser, Apr. 15, 1771, "At the Signe of the Arch'd Dial by

the upper end of the Coffee House Bridge— W.-maker;—has an assortment of Ws. and the best, second best, third, fourth, bad, and worse sorts; some very neat, some very ugly, and others, so-so. Most of them plain and a few in Engr. gold, silver gilt, and warrants for a long time, some for a Shorter Time, and others for No Time at all." (*Lockwood Barr*)

*HEYDORN, CHRISTIAN: (1786–?). Hartford, Conn., 1808–11. From Germany to Phila., 1807, there maybe a yr., then to Hartford. Also as Heydorn & Imlay. (*Nelson Booth*)

HILE, T. W.: n/d, Kansas. Designed and made the "Century Clock" for Phila. Cent. Exhibition of 1876. Heavy wgt. dropped 76″ at rate of ¾ inch per yr.

HILL, A.: Steubenville, Ohio, n/d. G.F., Hepplewhite-style case with moon dial so signed. (*J.W.G.*)

*HILL & ROSS (CHARLES; A. C.): Zanesville, Ohio, at Main St., 1833 ff. Announced Dec. 7, partnership with his former teacher as C. and W. (*J.W.G.*)

HILL, NOBLE SPENCER A.: Bennington, Vt., 1795. Adv. "C. from London." (*Robert Dickey*)

HILL, SAMUEL: (1765–1809). Harrisburg, Pa., 1785–94. B. Eng. and apt. in London. To Pa. in Dauphin Co. 1785. Mar. 1790 Nancy Beatty. Her bro. George an apt. Taxed as C. 1786 "first there." Began in shop south side 2nd St. later at shop near Bromberg's Tavern where he aw. till d. "Ingenious & Skillful; All his C. not alike." One with recoil escape just in front of back plate. On some of his G.F.s used "Osborne" dials.

HILL, W. & CO.: Chicago, at 111 Madison St., 1880's–90's. Adv. "Our Pride" stem wind and set W. in gold-plated silver cases for sale by mail for $6; 3 for $12. "Hill—he pays the express." Also at 207 State St. in 1894 adv. (*Rudolf Orthwine*)

HILL, WM. J.: Bristol, ca. 1850. L.G. so labeled "like Orrin Hart." P. Canfield printed label.

HILTON MFG. CO.: Chicago, 1960s, making a/c's. (*R. F. Tschudy*)

*HIMELY (HIMELEY, HIMLI) JOHN JAMES: Phila. before 1786, then Charleston, S.C. 1786–1810 as: adv. 1786–1789 imported W. and j. from London (at 18 Broad St.); adv. 1796 moved from 43 Broad to 117 Tradd St.; 1801–06 119 then 135 Broad St.; 1807 Dir. at

76 Church St.; 1809 at 20 Broad St. (*H. J. Barbour*)

HINTON, GEORGE: Paterson, N.J. Dir., 1825–32. C. and W. with Wm. Thompson.

*HOADLEY, SILAS: (1786–1870), Hoadleyville, Conn. Famous for his own designed wood movts. One, the "Franklin" shelf C. with upside down movt., reads "Time is Money—Franklin Clocks—with the Improvement of Bushing—the pivots with Ivory—Arranged and mfr. by——" Some such labels have 2 engrs.—Franklin, wearing eye glasses; and eagle with "E Pluribus Unum." Also 8-day G.F. wood movts., etc. (*George Ford*)

HOFFMAN, P.: Wappinger's Falls, N.Y. On 1858 map of Dutchess Co. as W., J., rpr. (*Arthur Stout*)

*HOLDEN, ELI: Phila. Dir., 1843 ff., banjos by Howard & Davis and also Riggs. (*Robert Franks*)

HOLLER (HALLER) WATCH CO.: Brooklyn, N.Y., n/d. His #80 in Whitford Col. as "Haller's Watch Co."—in keystone yellow hunting case and #239916.

HOLMES, A. B. & J. S., JR.: Newark, N.J., at 627 Broadway, *ca.* 1885. Adv. card Bir. Col.

HOLT, DAVID, JR.: Harper's Ferry, Va., 1832. Adv. as C. and W. (*Cutten*)

*HOLTON, H. A.: Wells River, Vt., *ca.* 1895. Hamilton Pease has W. in his Col. so signed. Is key wind.

*HOPKINS & ALFRED (EDW.; AUGUSTUS): Fluteville, Conn., 1816–24. In 1960, site of factory now underwater in back up from new dam. It had been previously dismantled, parts now at Smiths. Inst. (*J. L. Reeves*)

*HOPKINS, ASA: (1799–1838). Northfield and Harwinton (Fluteville), Conn., 1813 ff. Son of Harris, inventor and C. Full story of his life at Yale Library by Phillip T. Young (Watertown, Conn., 1962).

*HOPKINS, ORANGE: (1791–?), Fluteville (Harwinton), Conn., nephew of Asa. Partnership, 1816–27 ff. "He later moved to upstate N.Y." (*P. T. Young*)

HORNE, JAMES A.: Dover, N.H., 1850s. Adv. as W., J. (*Herbert Horne*)

HOROLOVAR CO., THE: Bronxville, N.Y. Third q. 20th Cent. Producer of recreated Ignatz, Plato & Mouse tps. etc. under direction of Charles O. Terwilliger.

HOSMER, ——: Hartford, Conn., 18th Cent. G.F. with maple case; dial has spandrels and

moon, 76″ high. Ill. Lockwood. (*R. Franks*)

HOSMER, JONA: Nashua, N.H. 1864 Dir., W. (*F.M.S.*)

HOSTETTER, JOHN, SR.: Hanover, Pa., 1788–1824, the to New Lisbon, Ohio, till 1831. Son was his apt. (*J.W.G.*)

HOTCHKISS, A. E.: Cheshire, Conn., 1884. Inc. The Cheshire Clock Co., President-Secretary was C. B. Farrell. A marine tp. is ill. on stock certificates with "A.E.H.—Patent" on these pictured dials. Rcd. at least 8 U.S. patents 1881 ff. for clock movts., pinion for C.-striking mechanism for C.—rep. C. etc. (*A. L. Partridge*)

HOUGH, JOSEPH G.: Hamilton & Lebanon, Ohio, 1806–11. One G.F. extant. (*J.W.G.*)

*HOVEY, S., & CO.: Manchester, N.H. Dir., 1854–58, W., J., and C. 1846–50 Dir. was "Stanford Hovey."

HOWARD & CO.: Waltham, Mass. Folding case balance wheel 8-day tp. Patent—double spg. (main) and jeweled escapement—"Mar. 19, 1912." (*Fraser Georgie*)

HOWARD, THOMAS: Phila., at 26 South 2nd St., 1775. Dir., 1791. (*J.W.G.*)

HOWE, JUBAL: (1783–?) b. Shrewsbury, Mass. Apt. to Luther Goddard at age 16 to learn C.-making. Later employed in Goddard's W. factory. Became distinguished master W. 1830 to Jones, Low & Ball at 123 Washington St., Boston, as foreman. With firm many yrs. He employed Aaron L. Dennison, "a young C. from Brunswick, Me. who wanted to learn about W.s." (Not Tubal Hone as in Moore's "Timing a Century.")

HOYT,——: Phila. Danbury, Conn., *ca.* 1830. 30-hr. wood movt. shelf C. with carved col. case extant, so labeled. (*John D. Booth*)

HUDSON & SKINNER: Hartford, Conn., *ca.* 1820. Printers of Seth Thomas labels on shelf mirror C. with wood movt. crediting Terry as "Patentee."

HUG MFG. CO.: Springfield, Ill., 1930–60s. Took over Imperial Clock Co. Made electric tps. (*R. F. Tschudy*)

HUGGINS BROTHERS: West Grandy, Conn., *ca.* 1900. "Mfg. by" on card inside door in back of oblong-cased C. where door lifts up on hinges. Brass movt. has no name or number.

HUGHES, EDMUND: Middletown, Conn., n/d. W. paper. (*Mortimer Cassilith*)

HULBURT, JOSEPH: Hartford, Conn., *ca.* 1825. Printer of labels for Henry Terry and others.

HUMPARY, WILLIAM & D. S.: Parma, Ohio, *ca.* 1830. Wood movt., 30-hr. shelf C. labeled "Approved Alarm C.—Mfg. & Sold by——at Wholesale & Retail." (*J.W.G.*)

HUNT & CLARK (JONATHAN; HORATIO): Vt., 1794–1803. A partnership till dissolved, then each alone.

HUNT & COLGROVE: Farmington, Conn. OG 30-hr. wood movt., mirrored door. Written on card found inside "Cleaned by K. Wirner Jan. 16, 1867—Geo. Mitchell—50 cts." (*Harold Smith Col.*)

HUNT, JOHN: Keene, N.H., 1825. Adv. as W. and J. (*C.S.P.*)

HUNTINGTON & CHURCH: Springfield, Mass., n/d. W. paper in M.M.A.

HUNTRESS, L.: Lowell, Mass., *ca.* 1840. Was printer of C. labels for David Dutton of Mt. Vernon, N.H. (*Chesley Bixby*)

*HUSTON, JAMES: Trenton, N.J., 1761–70. Then Phila. 1774 and later. C. Tobasco has Trenton shop where Huston made Trenton's first town C. in steeple of First Presbyterian Church. (*C. E. Smart*)

*ILLINOIS SPRINGFIELD WATCH CO.: Springfield, Ill., 1869–85. Became Illinois Watch Co. till 1927, then sold to Hamilton Watch Co. Among names used on W. was "A. Lincoln."

IMBERG, A.: Cleveland, Ohio, *ca.* 1840. Shelf C. labeled "Made & Sold by——" (*J.W.G.*)

IMPERIAL ELECTRIC CLOCK CO., THE: Granite, Ill., 1909. Started by Frank, Joseph and August Ferand. To St. Louis, 1911; to Collinsville, Ill., 1923. 1 Patent 1909 to F. Ferand. (*R. S. Tschudy—J.W.G.*)

IMPERIAL PORTABLE WATCHMAN'S TIME PROTECTOR: Phila., *ca.* 1900. Were sold by Riggs. & Bro. 1 Patent, Nov. 5, 1900. (*J.W.G.*)

*INGERSOL WATCH CO.: Adv. "A long time sales mgr. said that 1892 production was 40,000; in 1893, 100,000, and at one time up to 16,000 a day. During W.W. I, did produce about 3,000 j. watches a day in addition to the non-j.'s." (*E.I.*)

*INGRAHAM: Bristol, Conn. Elias Ingraham (1805–85) founded a C. business which continues successfully today. For identification, there are these Co. names and dates: 1831–32, Ingraham & Bartholomew. 1832–33, Ingraham & Goodrich. 1835–40, in business for self. 1841–44, Ray & Ingraham (pos.). First Ingraham C. with labels identifying. 1844–52, Brewster & Ingrahams. 1852–55, E. & A.

Ingraham (plant burned, Dec. 1855.) 1856, in Ansonia, as E. & A. Ingraham. 1857–60, Elias Ingraham & Co., in Bristol. 1861–80, E. Ingraham & Co. 1880–84, The E. Ingraham & Co. 1884–1958, The E. Ingraham Co. 1958 ff., The Ingraham Co.

In 1924, a "lot" of sharp gothic 4-column steeple shelf C.s were made under the direction of Dudley S. Ingraham and have "Elias Ingraham" name on dial and "now much sought after." (*E.I.*). In 1959, discontinued mfr. of American Lever (pin) Wrist W. (*Business Week Mag., 6-5-65*). The various Companies have made "over 76 million W., and a quarter billion tps. (1964)." (*E.I.*)

INGRAM, ALEX: Greenwich, N.Y., *ca.* 1870. Small back label on Waterbury Bee Hive C. in Gladys Longmire Col.

INTERNATIONAL BUSINESS MACHINES CORP.: Endicott, N.Y., 1924 ff. Formed by absorbing Computing & Tabulating Recording Co. This included Computing Scale Co. of America; International Time Recording Co.; The Tabulating Machine Co.; and Bundy. Time recording clocks were important in the beginnings of the Corp. Thomas J. Watson Sr. joined *CBT* in 1914.

INTERNATIONAL TIME RECORDING CO. OF N.J.: 1900. Absorbed properties of Bundy plus Standard and Willard and Frick. See *I.B.M.*

INTERNATIONAL TIME RECORDING CO. OF N.Y.: 1901. Acquired the Chicago Time Register Co., which mfg. "Merrett Autograph Time Recorder"; in 1907, Day Time Register Co., and, 1908, The Syracuse Time Recording Co.; and by 1911, Bundy, Willard and Frick, and Standard—becoming Computing & Tabulating Recording Co., Inc. Further additions were The Computing Scale Co. of America; the Tabulating Machine Co. I.B.M. was inc. on Feb. 24, 1924. (See *I.B.M.*)

IOWA WATCH CO.: Des Moines, Iowa, *ca.* 1880. W. "like 'Hoyt' of Ill. Spg. W. Co. known, one trade named 'Conquerer.'" (*H.B.F.*)

ITHACA CALENDAR CLOCK CO.: Ithaca, N.Y., 1865 to *ca.* 1914 or 1919. Two-dialed Calendar. C.

*IVES, C. & L. C. (CHAUNCEY; LAWSON): Bristol, (tx.) 1830–38. 1831 Dir. listing—"Mfr. of 8-day Patent Brass and 30-hr. wood C.s" (*Lockwood Barr*)

JACCARD, E.: St. Louis, Mo., at 517 Oliver St.

"Founded," 1829. Adv. card: C., W., J., S., and Engr.

*JACKSON, THOMAS, JR.: Norwich, Conn., 1775 ff. C. "Not much data found here." Norwich '66 Catalogue. (*Samuel Thorne*)

JACOBS, J. M., & Co.: Brooklyn, N.Y., at 136 Fulton St., n/d. Very small rectangular shelf C.—9″ high with 30-hr. brass movt. with upside down escape and pendulum attached to top of case so labeled.

JAEKEL, F. A.: Cincinnati, 1881. Patent on C. for magic lantern. "Interesting, even ingenious, but largely useless device." (*J.W.G.*)

JAMES CLOCK MFG. Co.: Oakland, Cal., at 5307 E. 14 St., 1940s. A/c timer for intervals switch alarm tp. at Ford Museum with dial so marked. (*Julie Belknap*)

JEFFERSON ELECTRIC Co.: Bellwood, Ill., *ca.* 1950 ff. Maker of a/c's including "The Golden Hour Mystery tp."

JENGENS, R.: Sag Harbor, N.Y. Name on a G.F. and also a skeleton tp. hair spg. escape, under glass dome. (*Louis Peterson*)

JENNINGS BROTHERS MFG. Co.: Bridgeport, Conn., *ca.* 1890. Pewter-type white metal-cased small desk tp. 30-hr. movt. and stamped on front plate "Waterbury Clock Co., USA," and on back plate "Patent May 4, 1890; Dec. 23, 1890; Jan. 13, 1891; May 29, 1894." Standard shelf steeple in Mrs. Maurice Walter Col.

JENSEN CLOCK Co., F. W.: Chicago. 20th Century made "Nite-Lite" a battery-powered alarm tp. (*Fred Fried*)

*JEROME, CHAUNCEY: (June 10, 1793–Apr. 20, 1868). In Conn.: Plymouth, 1816–22; Bristol, 1822–44; New Haven, 1845–55, f. Later, Austin, Ill. George Mitchell induced him to come to Bristol to continue to make C.s. 1824–33 as Jeromes & Darrow (C. and N.; Elijah), made the first L.G.s; 1834–39, C. and N. Jerome; 1839–40, Jeromes, Gilbert, Grant, & Co. (Chauncey and Noble; William L.; Zelotes). This firm was first producer of his 1-day brass wgt. movt. OG. Hiram Camp was Supt. Ended the wood movt. era. 1841–44 in Bristol as "Chauncey Jerome" and "Jeromes & Co." Two factories completely destroyed by fire. These labels often printed by E. Geer at 26½ State St. 1845 operations started in New Haven as Jerome Mfg. Co. organized with Hiram Camp as Jt. Stock Co. Then Camp organized The New Haven Clock Co., *ca.* 1853 ff. This Co. also used the

trade name "Jerome & Co." in last half 19th Cent. One label of New Haven has "Chauncey Jerome, Clockmaker" over main entrance door in an engr. of factory. This label printed by "Benham, 65 Orange St., New Haven." 1855 came the merger involving P. T. Barnum and failure. Later wrote his autobiography. Still later, pos. in the 1860's, was at Austin, Ill., where C.s are so labeled with his name, and "Warranted a good Timekeeper." (*Ex. in Fred Fried Col.*)

*JEROME, S. B.: n/p, Conn., *ca.* 1865. Small shelf tp. with marine movt. "made by La-Porte Hubbell labeled 'Patented June 16, 1863.'" (*C. J. O'Neil Col.*)

*JEROME, CHAUNCEY, INC.: N.Y.C. at 500 5th Ave., 1931. A/c tambour tp. with label on door so marked and "Factory, New Haven, Conn." Same name on dial. (*Efroim Greenberg Col.*)

*JEROME & GRANT, (NOBLE; ZELOTES): Bristol, 1842–43, (tx.). 30″ high OG with standard 30-hr. brass movt. (*D. Longmire Col.*)

*JOHNSON, ADDISON: Wolcottville, Conn. *ca.* 1825. "Old cap shop built on bank of Naugatuck River, 1831 was first used by Luther Bissel for mfg. casks and tables. Then Addison Johnson made cases for mantel C. for a short time. These were the pillar style and stood 2½' high. It was thought to be a big improvement at the time." (*J. H. Thompson*)

JOHNSON, DAVID: Limerick Twp., Pa., 1850. Census—"age 35, *W. R.E.* worth $1450." (*J.W.G.*)

JOHNSON, W. N. & Co.: N.Y.C. at 35 John St., n/d. Label in smaller (20″) wgt. 1-day OGs reads:—"Clocks & Looking Glass of all kinds made and sold by—."

JOHNS, DANIEL: Charlestown, Ohio. Adv., 1838 as C. & W. (*J.W.G.*)

JOHNSTON, JOHN: Boston, Court St. After 1800—A portrait painter who did dials and glasses for the Willards. (*A.L.P.*)

*JONES, EZEKIEL: Boston, 1790. Dir. 1813; Dir., 1825. His W. paper in James Arthur Col. reads "—Watch & Clock Maker, 10 Ann St., Boston." (*The Curator*)

*JONES, E. K. (EDW.): Bristol. On 1837 map—"Followed his bro., Lowrey, making C. in Whigville at what became known as The Jones Shop." (*Hist.*)

JONES, GEORGE AMASA: (1800-77). Zanesville,

Ohio. 1830–77. Adv. 1830, C. and W. Rcd. another addition of C., W., and J. for sale at low cost. Adv. 1836. His dau. mar. R. D. Mershon, C., W., and J. (*J.W.G.*)

JONES, GEORGE A.: Bristol, 1875ff. Bristol Press 1879 (8-28) "—in engaged on an order for 5,000 'Little Dot' Clocks prob. the smallest pend. C. mfg." (*Charles Parker*)

*JONES, JACOB B.: (1749–1835). Pittsfield, N.H. b. Amesbury, Mass. Made G.F.s *ca.* 1800. d. Pittsfield. (*A. L. Childs*)

JONES PRINGLE, & Co.: Bristol, before 1838, no tx. list. Standard 1-day metal movt. OG with eglomise tablet depicting the Capitol at Washington; label reads: "Improved C.—2." (*Col. Mrs. George Watts.*)

JOSLIN MFG. Co.: A. D. Manistee, Mich. "currently making the ECLIPSE Time Stamp tp." (*Lockwood Barr*)

JUST, WM. F.: New Britain, Conn., 185 Main St., 1890's W., J., and D., Rpr. on adv. card. (*Bir. Col.*)

KALISH, B. S.: Bangor, Me., *ca.* 1870. Bus. card in Bir. Col. as C. and W.

KAYTON, B.: Fredericksburg, Va., 1847. Adv. as C. & W. (*Cutten*)

KEELER, JOSEPH: (1786–1824). Norwalk, Conn. C. His Estate inventory showed "pivot lathe; fuzee cutting tool; files, W. case stakes and S. tools." meaning that perhaps he also might have made W. Spoons bearing his touchmark extant in Conn. (*Lockwood Barr*)

KEENE, J. B.: Ansonia, Conn., at 76 Main St. Dir., 1885 as W., J., Engr. and "rps complicated C. and W."

KEITH, WILLIAM H.: Shrewsbury, Mass., *ca.* 1810. Worked at Luther Goddard's W. factory—"Competent W.-maker and executive." Later, clerk of Waltham Improvement Co. before the merge with Appleton, Tracy & Co. to form American Watch Co., of which he was president—1861–66.

KELLER, ISAAC & JOHN: Randolph, O., 1845–49 made watch springs with Co. slogan: "Anything made of iron, we can make." (*J.W.G.*)

KELLEY, ALLEN: (1791–1876). Sandwich, New Bedford, Hingham, Hanover, Nantucket, Provincetown, Mass., *ca.* 1810–38. G.F. at Winslow Croker House: Yarmouth Port marked "Sandwich"; another so marked in Sandwich, Mass. Shelf *ca.* 1810 "Provincetown"; P and S 8-day brass movt. in G. K. Smith Col. and "Nantucket." Mar. five times

with 10 children. (*Henry Kelly; G. K. Smith; J. E. Coleman*)

KELLY, JAMES H.: Pottsville, Pa. 1844–53 (tx. list) "Watchmaker" on overpasted label on a Forestville Mfg. Co. clock—42″ x 26″—label printed by Robert M. Palmer. Label further reads: "Yankee Clocks of every description, brass or wooden; 30-hr. or 8-day and Month Clocks." (*Amos Avery Col.*)

*KENDRICK & DAVIS Co.: Lebanon, N.H., 1874ff. Made the "Gem Key" for watches. Patents Sept. 1, 1874 and Aug. 12, 1880. Set in Author's Col.

*KENNARD, JOHN: (1782–1861) Newfields, N.H. Apt. at Portsmouth then to Nashua and Concord, N.H. and Newfields by 1812, making C. Kept store 1830–34 and with Newmarket Foundry. (*Hist.*)

*KENNISTON, J. L.: (1817–84), Manchester, N.H., 1835–60. American Watch Papers has one of his.

*KILLAM & Co.: Pawtucket, R.I., *ca.* 1939. Name on some banjo movts.; believed he made them.

KIMBALL, JACOB: Montpelier, Vt., *ca.* 1810. Made G.F.'s. One with white dial, arabic chapters with cherry case in Edwin Thomas Col.

KIMBERLY, ROSWELL: Ansonia, Conn., n/d. "Steeple type 22″ high shelf C. label reads 'Improved Eight Day Brass Clocks.' No printer's name. (*The Amos Averys*)

KIMG'S PRINT: New Ipswich Printer; not C. Labels for David Dutton, Mount Vernon, N.H., dated "March, 1836" in wood movt. L.G.'s. (*D. K. Packard*)

*KIMHAUSER: N.Y.C., *ca.* 1875. Small brass-cased watchman's tp. in leather case, 13 j. movt. so marked "looks American." 3 Patents: #7715, 11-30-1875; others; 1-25-1876; 12-5-1876; 6-26-1877. "Pos. predecessor of Newman watchman tp., same general type, but larger." (*Ray Walker Col.*)

KING, JOHN: Portsmouth, N.H., 1779. Adv. as "C. W. and J." (*C.S.P.*)

KING, ORMAND: Paterson, N.J. Dir., 1825–32. C. and W.

KIRBY, JOHN B.: New Haven, Conn. at 88 Chapel St. Dir., 1859–68.

KIRBY, SAMUEL H.: New Haven, Conn., at 834 Chapel St. Adv., 1885.

KIRTLAND, BROS. & Co.: N.Y.C., at 62 Fulton St. Adv., 1894.

KLINE, JACOB: Lieneck Twp. 1850 (Census). "W." (*J.W.G.*)

KLUMP, CHARLES M.: (?–1912), Phila. Partner of E. E. Dungan in the Mouse C. Development. (*C. O. Terwilliger*)

KNIGHT, ELIJAH: (1813–86) Hancock, N.H., 1834ff. With Stephen Collins Goffstown; 2 yrs. Nashua; one, Charlestown, Mass.; then Boston, Nashua again; out West 1841, then 12 yrs. Newmarket, N.H., then Concord, N.H. (*Hist.*) N.H. Mirror known.

KNOX, WILLIAM: Dover, N.H., 1841. W. (*C.S.P.*)

KRAUSE, JOHN SAMUEL: (1782–1815). Bethlehem, Pa. Apt. to John Geo. Weiss; to Lancaster, 1803; there mar. Maria Louisa Schropp. Later Bethelehem. 3 apts. were: Jedidiah Weiss; Charles F. Beckell; and John M. Hirsch. (*R.H.–J.W.G.*)

KRAUSE, SAMUEL: (1807–1904). Hanover Twp., Pa. *ca.* 1830. Made G.F.'s—63 in Lehigh Co. Inventor, farmer, store keeper, and miller at various locations. Retired 1882. Family made organs. (*R.H.–J.W.G.*)

KRAUSS (E) (KROUSE), JOHN J.: Allentown (Northampton) Pa., before 1835. The sold store there. 30-hr. G.F. known marked "Nathrampton." (*R.H.-J.W.G.*)

KRETMAN, ERNEST: Phila., 1311 Chester, last q. 19th Cent. Adv. card as W. and J. in Bir. Col.

KROEBER, FLORENCE (a woman?): N.Y.C. Dir., 1865–1912. Fascinating N.Y.C. C. production —from quantities extant, many of pleasantly unusual nature. Movts. prob. made in Conn., many to their own design. Full history not now known, despite research here, and by others. This is what is now available. There may be other "names" but so far there is (Dates from N.Y.C. Dirs.):

——(or F.): 1865–1912. Clock Co., F., at 360 Broadway, 1889–1900. Frederick J. Clock Co., at 360 Broadway, 1887. F. & Co. at 14 Maiden Lane, 1904–11 (dissolved, F. K. listed as "Mgr., 1911.")

——: resident addresses: 1865–171 Elm St., N.Y.C. 1866–1st Ave. at 52 St., N.Y.C. 1870–89–in N.J. 1889–316 W. 107 St. 1901–509 W. 142 St. 1904–207 W. 107 St. to 1911. 1912– "F." at 151 W. 80 St. (last entry Dirs.) Business addresses ("F." in business): 1865–70–25 John St. 1871–75–10 Courtlandt St. 1875–89–8 Courtlandt St.; then see above.

KOECKER, L. B.: Phila. 1889, oral surgeon; friend of Dr. L. Webster Fox, for whom he made a G.F. Now in Haverford, Pa. (*G. de Grandpre*)

KUMBEL, WM.: N.Y.C.–W. with 1793 London Hall mark on case; C.–G.F. type in Anthony Benis Col.

KUNSMAN, HENRY: Fredericksburg and Richmond, Va. n/d. (*Cutten*)

LANDER, T. D.: Newburg, N.Y., n/d. "C. & W." on a W. paper. (*Maurice Van Buren*)

LANE, FREDERICK A.: New Haven, Conn., *ca.* 1880. Two Patents on C.: #237,028 Jan. 25, 1881; and #436,583 Sept. 16, 1890. Also of Yale Clock Co. (*J.W.G.*)

LANE, MARK: Southington, Conn., before 1835. P & S with Mark Leavenworth 30-hr. wood wgt. movt. label reading, "Improved Clocks/ made by/–/Warranted equal to any manufacturer in the United States." Label has 1820 Census and Postal rates. Later was "Elizabethtown, N.J. 1835–37." There, not to be confused with Aaron Lane, last q. 18th Cent.

LANGDON, GEORGE: Whigville (Bristol), Conn., n/d. "Made C. at Jones Shop pos. with E. K. Jones, (*ca.* 1837) or for self–"Hist."

LAPP & FLEIRGHEIN: Chicago at 77 State St., *ca.* 1885. "Busiest House in America—Jeweler's Wholesale Supply Depot"; so says a bound, profusely ill. catalogue dated "1885." Shows C. by Waterbury, Seth Thomas, New Haven, and others: watches by Howard, American Waltham, Elgin, and others. (*Book & Catalogue Col. Dr. Robert Ravel*)

LATIMER, J. E.: Saybrook, Conn., at "Petty's Point," n/d. W. paper says "C. & W." (*Samuel Thorne*)

LATRUITE, JOHN P.: Alexandria, Va., 1807–12. Then Baltimore as S. 1814 at Alexandria shop on King St. 1821 mar. Barbara Moore. In first Wash., D.C. Dir., 1822 as W. and through 1834. (*Cutten*)

LAWRENCE, J. S.: Fair Haven, Conn., n/d. "C. & W. & rpr." on W. paper. (*M.M.A.*)

LEARNED, THOMAS: (1760–1819). Medford, Mass., 1790's. Son of Thomas, Bricklayer, of Cambridge. Mar. 1793 to Dorcus Bridges of Andover. Lived in Medford; bought house and lot 1783. G.F.'s extant. (*Dr. Charles Currier*)

LEARNED, WILLIAM B.: (?–ca. 1897). Boston. Wrote pamphlet pub. Chicago "The Watchmaker's and Machinist's Hand Book" as

"Late Supt. E. Howard & Co. Watch Factory." (*W. R. Prescott*)

*LEAVENWORTH, MARK: (1774–1849), Waterbury, Conn. Some of his own 30-hr. wood movt. shelf C. have labels reading "Warranted Equal to Any Manufactured in the State—Improved Clocks/sold by——" followed by "INVENTED & Sold by Samuel COOKE, Waterbury, Conn." (no records for Cooke). One James Babcock of New Haven printed some of the labels for him.

LEAVENWORTH, M.: Albany no exact dates. Several G.F. 30-hr. pull type wood movts. extant, one in Efroim Greenberg Col. Unsure if same or related to the one in Waterbury, Conn.

LEBEAU, J. B.: Virginia City, Mont., *ca.* 1864–90. W., J., and rpr. "Custodian" of the W. and Cs. of this gold strike country through the period of unrest to permanent settlement. Sign outside his shop in the reconstructed "City."

LE BOUTILLIER & CO.: Shepard, N.Y.C., 1880's. Name on dial of heavy but graceful French C. with marble case in Author's Col.

*LEIGH, DAVID: Pittstown, Pa. 3rd q. 19th Cent. "Adv. 1849." "Sold clock business to John A. Andre." (*R.H.–J.W.G.*)

LEIGHNER, CARL H.: Butler, Pa., *ca.* 1915. Shop, 209 So. Main St. W., C., J., D. and rpr. W. paper in Col. Efroim Greenberg, N.Y.C.

*LENHARD, GODFREY: York, Pa. Second half 18th Cent. "One of the earliest York C. Made G.F.'s before the Revolutionary War." (*R.H.–J.W.G.*)

LEONARD, CHARLES: (1826–73). Newburyport, Mass., *ca.* 1850. Son of Richard, bro. of John B. C. and W. with bro. and alone. (*Dr. Charles Currier*)

LEONARD, JACOB: Fredericksburg, Va., 1828. Adv. "start C. and W. on Main St. nearly opposite P.O. and repair would be by me." (*Cutten*)

*LESCHOT, LOUIS A.: (?–1838). Charlottesville, Va., 1830's. 2 wooden tenements next to Library, first occupied by him as W. & J. from Switzerland, who settled there by advice of Thomas Jefferson. Developed a substantial business. His widow Sophie later a success in dry goods to 1852. He was succeeded by Richard Matthews. (*Cutten; Gusta Jarman*)

LEVY, ABRAHAM: (?–1961). N.Y.C. and Brooklyn, 1905–61. Founder and entrepreneur of of the United Clock Co.

*LEWIS, BENJAMIN B.: Bristol, 1864–70 (tx.). Cal. Cs. of his own design were mfg. in the Manross Shop. Later, 1870–72, (tx.) listing in Bristol, "Benj. B. Lewis & Son." Sold Cal. patent to Welch, Spring & Co. They made them for a time. Label read "Benjamin B. Lewis's Perpetual Calendar/Patented Feb. 4, 1862 -9-10-'63; 6-2, '64; 7 Dec. 20, '68, Mfg. by Welch, Spring, & Co., Bristol, Conn., USA. This cal. never needs cleaning or rprs., and must NOT be oiled. Jewelers are requested to be particular not to change the length of the connecting rod."

LEWIS (LOUIS) & CATLIN: Litchfield, Conn., *ca.* 1809. G.F. with wood movt. in case by Ambrose Norton.

*LIDELL, THOMAS: Frederick, Md., *ca.* 1760. G.F. in Hist. so dated. Has face of man with moving eyes where usually is moon dial. At least two other G.F.'s extant. (*J.W.G.*)

"LINCOLN, A.": Name used by Illinois Watch Co., n/d. (*H.B.F.*)

LINDON, F. V. & SON: Brooklyn, N.Y., on Bond St. 1860–1918. Later, at 322 Livingston St. C., W., J., S. and rpr. (*Ed Lindon*)

LINIGER, JOHN: Woodsfield, Ohio, *ca.* 1860. W. paper says "C. and W." (*H.B.F. Col.*)

*LINNELL, KNOWLES: St. Albans, Ohio. *ca.* 1825. Had a clock factory there. He moved to Granville, Ohio, in 1828—the plant then becoming known as "Brace & French." (*J.W.G.*)

LITCHFIELD, CONN., Cabinet Makers (made some C. cases).

DAVID BULKLEY & GEORGE DEWEY: (2 doors W. of Court House), partners.

BULKLEY & COOKE: succeeded them (adv. July 25, 1839).

SILAS CHENEY: "Bought Cheney Homestead 1798—many yrs., only one in Litchfield County." d. 1820.

OLIVER CLARK & EBEN PLUMB, JR.: "Taken over shop late occ. by Mr. Ozias Lewis" (Adv. 1797).

AMBROSE NORTON: (1791–1865). Also C. case maker from *ca.* 1809ff.

LIVESEYS' YANKEE PRESSES: N.Y.C., at 74 Fulton St. Did print C. labels for F. C. Andrews of Bristol, Conn. Not C.

*LOCKE, JOHN: Cincinnati, Ohio, 1848. Inventor. Designed magnetic registering tp. with 'make & break' check. He called it "Rheo-ton"; in form of a glass tube, plus platinum contacts and mercury conductor. 1849, Congress appropriated $10,000 for a magnetic clock at National Observatory. (*J.W.G.*)

LOHEIDE MFG. CO.: St. Louis, Mo., *ca.* 1880. Made shelf C. under patent #883,886–a C. with slot-machine arrangement. The slot to receive coin fits $2.50 gold pieces. Black wood cases with metal trim. One, with 8-day pendulum movt. at Hagans Clock Manor Museum. (*Jo Hagans, Ray Walker*)

LONGMIRE, W. B.: Knox County, Tenn., *ca.* 1798. C., W., and J. (*Lynn George*)

LONG & PRICE: Cincinnati, Ohio, 1805. Adv. "Gives notice to the Public that they have commenced C. & W. making business at corner Main and Columbia Sts. (*J.W.G.*)

*LOOMIS, HENRY: Bristol, Conn., n/d. Not on tx. list. LG with this label extant, having also overpasted N.Y.C. firm name. Also a P & S good movt. 30-hr., extant.

LOVETT, WILLIAM: Boston on Bloomfield Lane, n/d. A miniature and portrait painter who also did C. tablets. (*L. E. Conlon*)

LOWERY, ALFRED: Bristol, n/d, no tx. list. An OG, 30-hr. brass wgt. movt. with label printed by Elihu Geer, Hartford (no street address). (*The Amos Averys*)

LOWERY, DAVID & ALFRED: Bristol, (Whigville Section), n/d. Thomas Lowery, the father, of "Red Stone Hill" built "the old red shop known later as Jones Shop (E. K. Jones) for a cloth mill. Succeeded by E. K. Jones, and George Langdon. (*Hist.*)

*LUSCOMB, SAMUEL: (?–1781). Salem, Mass. Reportedly made 2 tower Cs. for early Salem. One struck hours, but had no dial. Both later destroyed by fire. (*Arthur Sullivan–Charles Currier*)

LUSK, WILLIAM: Columbus, Ohio, *ca.* 1845. C. and W. (*J.W.G.*)

LUSK, U. S.: (?–1964). Fremont, Ohio, 20th Cent. W., J., and C. His masterpiece tp. in glass-sided case of solid black mahogany, 29" high; 8 j. movt. weight on left side; Graham dead-beat 'scape, mercury pendulum. Started 1924; finished, 1932. "Was outstanding craftsman." (*Van K. Belknap*)

LYMAN, C. A.: Palmer, Mass., *ca.* 1880. C. and W. Lithograph bus. card in Bir. Col.

LYMAN, F.: Bridgeport, Conn., 1880's. Rpr. and J. from adv. card in Bir. Col.

*LYMAN, THOMAS: (1770–?) Windsor, Conn., Pittsfield and later Marietta, Ohio, n/d. Apt. of Daniel Burnap. Fine G.F. extant with "Thos. Lyman, Pittsfield" on engr. brass dial. (*The Amos Averys*)

LYNN, ADAM: (1775–1836). Alexandria, Va., 1795–6, as Coryton & Lynn. His bro.-in-law on Nov. 1801 adv. added C. and W. to J. Also reportedly fought a duel. (*Cutten*)

McCARTY, T.: Litchfield, Conn., *ca.* 1800. Reportedly made G.F.'s. (*H. P. Davis*)

McGIBBON, JAMES: Boston, at Fish St., *ca.* 1810. Portrait painter who did clock tablets. In Dir. as "Painter-Gilder." (*Jim Conlon*)

*McINTYRE WATCH CO.: Kankakee, Ill., 1909–26, when dissolved. "Only 8 complete W.s made; 1 by C. DeLong; 7 of them extant. 6 master models as samples. 'Ultra high Quality'; machinery later stored in Chicago, then given to Mr. Samelius, Elgin School of W. Co. had 10 patents." (*J. E. Coleman*)

McIVER, COLIN: Alexandria, Va., *ca.* 1785. In Dawe & McIver. (*Cutten*)

McLEAN, HOMER: Williamsburg, Ohio, 1870. Listed in "Atlas" as "Mfr. of C. & W.; Surveyor, & Civil Eng." (*J.W.G.*)

McMARBLE, A.: Wilmington, Ohio, *ca.* 1880. "Made fine clock cases." (*J.W.G.*)

"McMILLAN PATENT": *ca.* 1905. Used by Vermont Clock Co. No further identification. (*W. C. Robinson; E. B. Burt; J. E. Coleman*)

*McNIESCH, JOHN: N.Y.C., at 94 Water St., *ca.* 1810. On W. paper. (*M.M.A. Col.*)

MAGNETIC WATCH CO.: Hinsdale, N.H., 1870. Adv. Godey's Lady's Book and Magazine "The Dollar Watch; with superior compass attachment, patented—Sole mfrs." (*C.S.P.*)

MALER, L. J.: n/p, n/d. Name stamped on rim and winding bbl. of wood movt., like Dutch, in G.F. (*G. H. Amidon Col.*)

MANISTEE WATCH CO.: Manistee, Mich. Estab. 1900. (*H. B. Fried*)

MANNING-BOWMAN: Meriden, Conn. 20th Cent. became a division of Parker Clock Co.

*MARANVILLE, GALUSHA: N.Y., 1861. Patent on Cal. C. from Hampton Corners, Wash. Co. N.Y. (*Albert L. Partridge*)

MARSH, OLIVER: Newark, N.J., *ca.* 1870. Took 3½ yrs to make 4-foot high marble pedestal double-dialed clock with 2 sets of pallets; very accurate solid bronze movt. now at Hagans Clock Manor Museum. To Binghampton, N.Y., 1880, where he owned and operated a store for C., W. and J. at retail. (*Orville Hagans*)

MARSHALL & CARD: Casenovia, N.Y., *ca.* 1864. C. (*J. E. Coleman*)

MARTIN, C. C.: Cleveland, Ohio, 1865. "Patent for 'Improved W.'" (*J.W.G.*)

MASON, MORRIS: Franconia Twp., Pa., 1799. (tx.) as C. (*R.H.–J.W.G.*)

MASSASOIT WATCH Co.: Boston, n/d, no definite data. W. so marked in Col. J. W. C. Might have been part of some estab. Co. as Waltham/Howard/Tremont/Palmer/Holmes/ or other. W. is full plate 18 size, silveroid case, open face, key wind, key set. (*J.W.G.*)

MATHEWS, HARRIET: (1807–82). Charlottesville, Va. Was b. Pt. Republic, dau. John Dunton. 1827, mar. Richard Mathews a C., W., and S. When he d. 1847, she continued the business, also administered his estate. Adv. 1850, "Their Agent B. Cromwell returned from N.Y.C. and Phila. with assortment of W., J. & S." Sold the business 1852. Another of the several women horologists. (*Gusta Jarman, Cutten*)

MATHEWS, RICHARD: (?–1847). Charlottesville, Va. Aw. 1826–47. Succeeded Louis Leschot *ca.* 1836. He mar. Harriet Dunton, 1827. "Following Leschot's practice, had all his W. made in Switzerland." Built brick bldg. on site of Leschot's wood tenement. Widow conducted the business till 1852. (*Cutten*)

MATHEWS, THOMAS: (?–1852). Charleston, Va., 1808 and later. "1st C. & W. there." On tx. list, 1812. Will dated 1852. (*Cutten*)

MATHEY, L. and A.: N.Y.C., at 119 Fulton St., *ca.* 1870. "Agents for H. L. Matile and Chas. E. Maylan—'Watches,' a small booklet "Time & Timekeepers," and brief sketch of the horological art, 20 pp., published 1877.

MEEK, BENJAMIN F.: (1816–1901). Frankfort, Ky. Apt. to J. Ayres as C., W., and "fishing reels." Estab. 1835 as "J. F. & S. F. Meek—skilled W. rprs." Also made at least 1 chronometer and 1 one regulator. Fine mechanic. (*J. E. Coleman, Lockwood Barr*)

MEGEAR, THOS. J.: Phila. "1799" engr. on back plate of G.F.

MEIER, FELIX: N.Y.C., *ca.* 1880. "Astra C." reported to have been maker of "The American National & Astronomical C., costing *ca.*

$30,000 to construct *ca.* 1867 18′ high, 7′ wide. On display at Worlds Fair 1893 Chicago, then 'lost.'"

MEIER, LOUIS: Detroit, *ca.* 1905. Reported to have made massive 13′ G.F., weighing 2,500 lbs. (*J. E. Coleman*)

MEILY (MILEY), EMANUEL: Lebanon, Pa., 1789–1810. Name on large C. Pos. a D. No exact data. (*R.H., J.W.G.*)

"MERCER": name used by New Jersey Watch Co., n/d. In J.W.G. Col.

MERMAD, JACCARD, ET CIE.: St. Louis, Mo., 1880s. Name on white dial of French marble shelf C. in Stuart Minton Col.

*MERRELL, A. (ANSEL): Vienna, Ohio. "Clock factory." Shelf C. in J. S. Fuchs Col. P. & S. with curly maple case in Col. Lee A. Stossell.

MERSHON, RALPH D.: Zanesville, Ohio, 1875 ff. "Famous as Electro Engineer. Inventor of a compound regulator for W. and used by E. Howard & Co." Grandson of G. A. Jones, son of R. S. (*J.W.G.*)

MERSHON, RALPH S.: Zanesville, Ohio, *ca.* 1850. W., J., and Engr. Mar. dau. of G. A. Jones. Had son Ralph, who succeeded him. (*J.W.G.*)

MEYLI, EMANUEL: Lebanon, Pa., *ca.* 1820. G.F. with white iron dial, center sweep second hand, also cal. hand. Moon dial in arched top. (*Robert Franks*)

MIDDLE, JAMES: Paterson, N.J. Dir.–1825–32. C., W. (*Mrs. Samuel Schwartz*)

MIKSCH, JOHN MATTHEW: (1792–1882). Bethlehem, Pa. Apt. of Jedidiah Weiss. Edw. F. Erwin successor at his d. (*R.H., J.W.G.*)

MILLER, REV. HARRY EDWIN: (1873–1947). Lebanon, Pa. "A Clergyman who made C Pastor of Salem United Brethren Church there." Reportedly made about 400 G.F. cases. (*G.K. Eckhardt, Robert Franks*)

*MILLER, RICHARD: N.Y.C. *ca.* 1710–20 G.F. at Colonial Williamsburg. (*John M. Graham*)

"MINUTE MAN": Name used by Dueber-Hampden W. Co. on "better W." #3550729 in Col. Henry B. Fried.

*MITCHELL, HINMAN & Co.: Bristol (tx.) 1828–30—as "traders"; 1831 as "C. Mfrs." Dealer in buttons, combs, cotton thread, etc. Also in N.Y.C. Dir.

*MITCHELL, GEORGE: (1774–1852). Bristol, Conn. Important entrepreneur. His name often seen on C. labels; with others, and alone; and "made for."

MIX, JAMES: Albany, N.Y., name engr. on movt. and case of pocket W., n/d.

MOIR, J. W.: N.Y.C., at 35 Hudson St. Name stamped on gold engr. W. Case maker or D. (*Henry B. Fried Col.*)

MOLLOY, GEORGE: Lowell, Mass., at 61 Market St., n/d. Labels of C. read: "The Best Clocks —etc." Also rpr. (*Amos Avery Col.*)

MONITOR CLOCK WORKS: Medina, N.Y. *ca.* 1910. 3 wheel brass wgt. shelf C. in Col. Henry Sayward.

MONTANDON, ALBERT: Lancaster, Pa. Only son of C.'s Henry Lewis and Hannah Montandon. Father d. 1802 and she continued business till 1810. To Baltimore, then Clarksburg, Va.; there by 1822 or before. After 1824 followed as C. by M. Barchett. (*Cutten*)

MOORE, R.: Nashua, N.H., at 8 Factory St. Dir. 1864 as W. (*F. M. Selchow*)

MORRILL, HARRISON O.:—N.H., *ca.* 1830. A N.H. mirror with his name on front plate, which strikes only 1 stroke on each hour; broken arch case of mahogany, flat pilasters. (*F. M. Selchow*)

*MORRIS, ABEL: (?–1800). Reading, Pa., 1774. "No tall C. known." A G.F., so marked, extant; inherited in family at his d. at Parkesburg, Pa.

MORRIS, SPENCER, & Co.: Litchfield, Conn. OG, 30 hr. wgt. as made pos. by Seth Thomas; no date, no data though this name on printed label. (*Floyd Thomas*)

MORRIS, ROBERT: (1734–1806). Phila. b. Liverpool, Eng. To Md. *ca.* 1747, soon to Phila. Worked with the Willing family, merchants, and became partner for 39 yrs. Financier for Revolutionary War. One of four men (Franklin, Jefferson, Pierre Caron de Beaumachais responsible for such war financing; all of them with a common interest in horology. A story about Morris: that when younger, he had learned well how to fix and repair watches. This skill allowed him when shipwrecked in Cuba to earn enough to get his crew and himself back to Phila. (See *Romance of Time*.)

*MORSE, H. and D. (HENRY and DLIJAH): Canton, Mass. Correct previous was as "Morris." G.F.s extant.

MORSE, MILES (MYLES): Plymouth Hollow, Conn., 1841 ff. Labels as on standard brass 30-hr. wgts. printed by American Office,

Printer, Waterbury, Conn.; 1 in Col. of Charles O'Neil.

MORSE, MOSES L.: (1781–1831), Keene, N.H., & Cambridgeport, Mass., 1804, 1809. Dated W. papers known. Adv. "Perpendicular, Horizontal, & Plain W." Adv. "Left Keene Nov. 4, 1805; to Sutton, Mass.; where he will mfr. W. (Wheelock & Morse) of a new and improved plan." This business continued later by Benjamin Comens. W. paper dated "1809" Cambridgeport, Mass. Did invent pin-making machine "first, U.S.A.," patent scales for weighing coins hydrostatically. Estab. a cutlery factory in Worcester, Mass., where he d. (*C.S.P.; Am. Watch Papers*)

MORSE, S. F. B.: used for his telegraph power source a wood movt. from a Conn. C. This now in Smiths. Inst.

MOSES, THOMAS: Sennett, N.Y., Shelf C. with label so marked.

MOTT BROTHERS: N.Y.C., at 7 Nassau St., *ca.* 1800, W. paper. (*Arthur Willis, Jr.*)

MOUNTAIN STATE ELECTRIC Co.: Wheeling, W. Va. Battery tp. 8⅞″ high, "no key" on dial. (*Charles O. Terwilliger*)

MOYER, SOLOMON: Allentown, Pa., 1887. Patent "Universal Clock" #369,462. "Universum C." Ill in *FT* and at Essex Inst. "Made by New Haven Clock Co." One also at American Museum of Time, Bristol. (*Shirley Morrell*)

MUHLENBERG, GEO. H.: Morgantown, Pa., *ca.* 1900. Prob. D. Seth Thomas cal. C. having special cal. mech. that swings out on hinges with his label. (*Robert Franks*)

MULLER, N.: N.Y.C., *ca.* 1856. Prolific maker of cast-iron fronts for shelf C.

MULLIKEN: very early C.-making Family of Distinction in Northeast Mass. John (1690– ?) was in Bradford, Mass., a blacksmith and pos. C. Two sons were clockmakers: *Samuel:* (1720–56) Bradford 1740–50, then Newburyport. Some excellent brass-dialed 8-day G.F.'s extant with both place names. *Nathaniel I:* (Aug. 8, 1722–Nov. 23, 1767), Bradford, Mass., 1749–50; then Lexington, Mass. In 1750, sold and made a G.F. for Deacon Stone. Met his dau. when C. delivered and mar. her June 6, 1751. Estab. C.-making in his shop at Lexington. Continued to make G.F.s till his d. It is now considered that Benjamin Willard began his C.-making at Lexington with Nathaniel

Mulliken I. There is the further belief that when Nathaniel II and his mother took over the C.-making that Willard may have stayed to help, pos. going back to Grafton on occasions, where he instructed his brothers. J. Ware Willard, in his book, agreed with this idea. *Nathaniel II:* (1752–77) was not long lived. He never mar. On April 19, 1775, the Mulliken home and C. shop were burned down by the British during their retreat back to Boston. It has been said that one British soldier was found dead on the Boston Road carrying a Mulliken C. movt. in his bag. After the shop was destroyed, Nathaniel II moved to Concord, Mass., and d. there.

Where the two Bradford C.-making Mullikens were apt. has not been fully estab. One place says that it was an "Uncle Jonathan" who, at Bradford, in 1742 mar. Martha Marsh and "there lived for a time where he worked at C.-making." No records have yet been found in Bradford, or surrounding area of the land ownership or deaths or church membership of either. Further, Benjamin Bagnall, Jr. (1715–?) mar. Anne Peaslee at Haverhill—across the Merrimack River from Bradford—in 1742. Taught by his father, he, too, was a fine maker of G.F.'s.

MULLIKEN, JOHN: (1754–?) Lexington, Mass. Son of Nathaniel I. Cabinetmaker who made excellent G.F. clock cases. Lived in the house across "the High Road," site of the Mulliken home and clock shop which the British burned on the retreat April 19, 1775. ("Scarcely a man is now alive where once the embattled Farmers stood, and fired the shot heard 'round the World.")

MULLIKEN, JOSEPH: (1765–1802), Concord, Mass., after 1789. 4th child of Nathaniel I. Pos. apt. to "Uncle Samuel." Mar. Hepziba Flint of Concord Dec. 23, 1790. Made good G.F.'s.

MUNGER, ASA: (1798–1851), Auburn, N.Y., *ca.* 1820–50. His labels printed by "Oliphant, Richard" 1823–29 and then "Henry" 1830 and later. (*Henry Sayward*)

NASH, COLEMAN: Cincinnati, Ohio, 1824. "W. from R.I." (*J.W.G.*)

NATIONAL CLOCK & MFG CO.: Chicago. 20th Cent. D. for Sessions, Ingraham, and pos. others. Large outlets through newspaper premium offers (*Life*—Feb. 5, 1951). (*A. L. Partridge*)

NATIONAL MAGNETIC CLOCK CO.: N.Y. and Chicago, early 1900s. Made battery tps., one in Janos Weinberger Col.

NATIONAL MFG. & IMPORT CO.: Chicago, at 324 Dearborn St. 1894 Adv.

NEGRIN, PAUL: Charlottesville, Va., 1820–23. W. and rpr. Last record, 1823. (*Cutten*)

NEWELL, E. E.: Bristol, 1896 ff. "After death of S. E. Root, his father-in-law continued the Root business for a few yrs." (*Hist.*)

NEWELL, GRANDETON & HART: Chester, Ohio. 1821–46 Founders. Cast first plow in the Western Reserve. Cast many clock bells, as for Riley Whiting (Winsted) & Ansel Merrell, Vienna, Ohio, *ca.* 1830. (*J.W.G.*)

NEW ENGLAND ELECTRIC CLOCK CO.: Bangor, Me., *ca.* 1900. Wall battery tp. 46″ high—pendulum impulsed at every cycle—"continuous action—no weights or springs." One in C. O. Terwilliger Col.

*NEW HAVEN CLOCK & WATCH CO.: 1959. "Out of the C. & W. business." (*Business Week*—June 5, 1965)

NEW HAVEN MARINE CLOCK CO.: New Haven, Conn. C. with double escape wheel like those of Chas. Kirke, in brass case at Marine Historical Assn., Mystic, Conn. (*Edwin Pugsley*)

NEWHOUSE, ADAM: Paterson, N.J. Dir., 1825–32 C. and W. (*Mrs. Samuel Schwartz*)

NEW LONDON WATCH CO.: New London, Conn., n/d. Name on dial of a "common pocket W." (*C. J. O'Neil Col.*)

*NEW JERSEY WATCH CO.: N.Y.C., at 116 John St. 1888. W. marked "Mercer" in J.W.G. Col.

*NEWMAN CLOCK CO.: Chicago, 1878 (org.) to 1900s made watchman tps.—pos. later to New Haven Clock Co.

NEWTON, I. L.: Portsmouth, N.H., 1806. Adv. in shop of Nathaniel S. Griffith, "having served apt. in London." (*C.S.P.*)

NEWARK CLOCK CO.: Newark, N.J., n/d. China plate (made in Germany) with 8 day spg. movt., also made in Germany. (*W. B. Woernley*)

"NEW COTTAGE TIME": n/p, 1877. "Patent March 13." A round top miniature tp. 9½″ high, wind hole at "2." Wood case with glass in door and 30-hr. spg. movt. Labeled on outside bottom of case. (*W. B. Woernley*)

OABIKE, CHARLES: Bristol, n/d. Standard 30-hr. wood movt. shelf C. (*Blie Tobias*)

OAKES, FREDERICK: Hartford, Conn., *ca.* 1804.

For a time, partner David Greenleaf, Jr.; on later W. paper "1828" at head of Ferry St. (*M.M.A.*)

OAKES, TILA: Ashby, Mass., after 1796. Did dial painting for husband, Alexander T. Willard and his bro. Philander for their wood movt. G.F.'s.

"O'CLOCK": Originally was "What of the clock?"; then, "of the Clock"; Shakespeare, in Henry IV said, "What's o'clock?" Now just "O'Clock."

"OGTO": name used by Parker Clock Co. on 30-hr. tps. (20th Cent.)

O G CLOCK CO., THE: n/p, n/d. Shelf C. measures 25¾" x 15¼" and label reading "American/Extra Bushed/Movement/Clocks /" followed by pictures of "many" factory buildings "8 day Striking/with Calendar/for sale only by/The O. G. Clock Co./" No place, no printers name on label. Front plate of spg.-driven movement has circle with star in center and "New Haven" around the top and "trade mark" around the bottom. (*Col. of C. S. Donahoo*)

OHIO WATCH CO.: Ohio, n/d. W. made in Switzerland like those of American design. (*H. B. Fried*)

OLIPHANT, RICHARD AND HENRY: Auburn, N.Y., 1823–30. Not C. Printers of labels of Munger clocks, to try to help in dating them. Both from 1823 till 1830 when Richard to Oswego, N.Y., to start a newspaper, selling printing businesses here to his bro. Henry. (*Henry Sayward*)

OLMSTEAD, NATHANIEL: (1785–1860). Farmington, then New Haven, Conn., early 1800s. B. E. Hartford, apt. to Daniel Burnap at Andover, Conn., mar. Burnap's niece, Phila., 1810 C. and G. W. paper M. M. A.—"& Son." n/d.

*ONE A MONTH CO.: Detroit at 11 Jefferson Ave., 1894. Adv. (*William Distin*)

ONE HAND CLOCK CORP.: Warren, Pa., after W. W. I to ca. 1935. Dial (3 sizes: 9", 10", 12" diameter) with single hand. 30-hr. spg. movt. made by Ansonia. Pos. some also by Warren Telechron Co., Ashland, Mass. Not much data available. All records destroyed after death of president, 1935. (*Royal Foote, Alfred Scott*)

ORBERTS, E. & CO.: Bristol. Label of shelf C. so marked. (*E.I.*)

OSBORN, SHELDON: Harwinton, Conn., ca. 1830,

L.G. with 30-hr. wood movt. Label printed by Joseph Hulburt, Hartford. (*Samuel Jennings*)

*OSBORNE & WILSON (THOMAS; JAMES): Birmingham, Eng., 1772. Adv. Osborne d. 1777(?) & Wilson alone at 11 Gt. Church St. till d. 1829.

OSGOOD, JOHN JR.: Haverhill, N.H., and Boston. Second q. 19th Cent. Only son to follow father in horology. One W. extant, his name on dial. Pos. mostly rpr. (*Charles Currier*)

OVAL CLOCK CO.: N.Y.C., at 35 Maiden Lane, ca. 1912. Sturdy elliptical, not oval wind-up alarm, with scene of International Exposition on dial of 1915. Pos. earlier. Movts. by New Haven. (*Ray Walker, H. B. Fried.*)

*OWEN, EDWARD: Birmingham, Eng., at 3 Weaver Row, Dir., 1816 dial maker for C., also pos. C.

"OXFORD": name used on shelf a/c tp. made by Gibralter Mfg. Co., Jersey City, N.J. "Model 124-D." (*Janos Weinberger Col.*)

PALMER, BACHELLER, & CO.: Boston, at 394 Washington St., last q. 19th Cent. Adv. card Birnbaum Col. as W. and J.

PALMER & HANKS: Cincinnati, Ohio. Unusual wall C. with skeletonized movt., extant 51" high, 17½" wide with plain glass; seconds pendulum. (*William B. Darby*)

*PALMER, DOLPHUS D.: (1839–1907), Waltham, Mass., ca. 1870. Estab. a school of W.-making at corner Spruce and Crescent Sts. Dir., 1882. "W. Mfr.—made ca. 40 W. movts. a month." In 1894 sold his interest to Eugene H. Swain, who stopped making movts., but continued the school successfully, specializing in W. rpr. "Thus, Palmer made ca. 4,800 movts." Also known as D. D. Palmer. (*J. E. Coleman*)

PALMER, ROBERT M.: (1826–62), Pottsville, Pa. Printer of labels, not C.

PALMER, SAMUEL AUGUSTUS: Monticello and Tallahassee, Fla., ca. 1850–90. G.F.'s extant.

PANET, PHILIP H.: Cincinnati, Ohio, at 27 Main St., 1830. "C. & W. maker from Switzerland." (*J.W.G.*)

*PARDEE, WILLIAM: Auburn, N.Y. "Patent" on lyre-like tp. with ladder movt. (*Ray McKinney Col.*)

*PARKE, SOLOMON: Phila. (pos. also "& Co.; Parke & Co.; & Son Family" etc.) From Newtown, Pa., 1782, to Phila. 1791 thru 1822. Considerable C. production reported, from various sources. Complete data not available.

PARKER, NOAH: Portsmouth, N.H., 1765. Adv. "an assortment of iron mongery, braziery, and cutlery wares—screw plates, clock maker's files, strip brass; clock bells; clock pins, etc." (*C.S.P.*)

PARKER, SAMUEL: Phila. *ca.* 1796 at Arch St. between 4th and 5th Sts. Brass founder, supplier of clock parts. Prob. no complete C.

PARKER, WILLIAM: Portsmouth, N. H., 1783–84. Adv. "C., W., & S." (*C.S.P.*)

PARKMAN, H. D.: N.Y.C., Hudson St., n/d. W. paper in Henry Fried Col.

*PARRY, JOHN J.: (1773–1835), Phila., 1794–1835. D. at various locations, with seemingly differing middle initials, but prob. the same man, incl. 30 and 38 S. 2nd St. (1824 Dir.). Nephew of David Rittenhouse, inherited his clock tools. G.F. by him at Century Club, N.Y.C. Was also at Trenton, N.J. (*Dr. Fordyce St. John*)

PARSONS, JOHN FITCH: Windsor, Conn., n/d. Cabinetmaker, joiner; not C. may have made G.F. cases, one of cherry with whalebone inlay. Osborne Bros. Birmingham (Eng.), dial. (*Ant, April, 1956*)

*PARSONS, SILAS: (1773–1859 or 1865), Swanset N.H., late 18th and 19th Cent. Son of Aaron. "Celebrated maker of Am. C. One was constructed as to play a regular psalm tune every Sunday, and secular tunes other days of week" (*Hist.*). One G.F. extant in Providence strikes every 4 hrs. (at 4, 8, at 12). In Col. Elisha Durfee. Made mostly G.F.'s, G.M.'s & Mass. Shelf. Examples in Ford Museum, Cols. Walter Roberts, John Walton, and Van Belknap.

*PARTRIDGE, HORACE & Co.: Boston, *ca.* 1868. In Bristol, Conn., bought out "Eureka Shop and Mfg. Co. Sales Agency in Boston." C. label reads: "Mfged by—Importers, Wholesalers, and Retailers of C., W. & J.; Fancy Goods, Yankee notions, Rogers and Bros. plated Ware and Silver Ware etc. at 51 Hanover St." (*A. L. Partridge*)

PATTERSON, JOHN: Alexandria, Va., n/d. From Pittsburgh; of Potter & Patterson, W. (*Cutten*)

*PATTON & JONES (ABRAHAM; SAMUEL G.): Phila. & Baltimore. Dir. 1804–14. G.F. on stairway at Mt. Vernon has movt. marked "Patton & Jones, Phila." Gen. George Washington (1732–99) purchased this C. for his nephew Augustine Washington. This authenticated C. shows earlier dates for the firm than those above. Also to note that Abraham Patton represented LESLIE & PRICE from Baltimore in 1795. Adv.

PAXTON, JOHN.: Danville, Va., 1814–62. W., C., J. & S. (*Cutten*)

PAYNE, J. B.: Terryville, Conn., n/d, 30-hr. brass OG shelf C. with figured frosted tablet in Col. of John A. Sinclair.

PEABODY, JOHN: Woodstock, Vt. 1808 Adv. (*D. Cooley*)

PEABODY, MOODY: Amherst N.H. 1810 Adv. "moved to Concord, N.H. & took shop of S. Foster."

PEARSON, CHARLES: Concord, N.H., n/d, W. paper in Ed Burt Col. (*C.S.P.*)

PEASE, ISAAC T. & Co.: Enfield, Conn., n/d (prob. 1830s). L.G. with standard 30-hr. wood movt. and label printed by P. Canfield reported by the Amos Averys.

*PEASLEY, ROBERT: BOSTON, 1735. Adv. brass-dialed G.F. in Col. Amos Avery.

PECK, S. & Co.: New Haven, Conn., *ca.* 1870. "Small gothic shelf C. label reading—in lower portion inside door." In Col. The Warren Stumpfs.

*PECK, TIMOTHY: Litchfield, Conn., 1789–92. Three yrs. at Middletown, Conn. G.F. with solid silver dial made 1790 as wedding present for John and Ruth Ranney White is now at Yale Gallery of Fine Arts. (*E. W. White*)

PENHALLOW, E. & B.: Portsmouth, N.H. Adv. 1798 "clock faces, brass kettles, time glasses, window glass etc." (*C.S.P.*)

PENNWOOD CO., THE: Pittsburgh, Pa., *ca.* 1940 ff. Makers of a/c tps. including 3 dialed type. Examples in author's Col. (*DeForest Galer*)

PELHAM & CO.: Cold Spring, N.Y., *ca.* 1870. 8-day shelf C. brass movt. stamped "N. Pomeroy, Bristol, Cn."—and label under bell gong "Sold to Robt. Jones, #1077—March 18, 1872." (*William Dilts Col.*)

PELHAM, W.: Peekskill Village, N.Y., *ca.* 1855, as W., C., J. & rpr. 1 of 3 on 1858 map of Dutchess County. (*Peter Pocaro*)

PERKINS & PORTER: Bristol, n/d. Large OG reported with this label. (*Dr. Howard R. Coats*)

*PERKINS, ROBINSON: (1766–1847), Jaffrey, N.H., *ca.* 1790–1826. Blacksmith, then C.; made G.F.'s with wood movts. with his name and "Jaffrey" on dial. *ca.* 1800 to Fitzwilliam, N.H. In trade with bro.-in-law 1826 till d. (*C.S.P.*)

PETERSON, HENRY, JR.: Alexandria, Va., 1787. Adv. as C. and W. and silver plate on "Fairfax St. opposite Coffee House, next door to Circulating Library—Lately from Phila." (*Cutten*)

PFALT, JOHN WILLIAM: Baltimore and Alexandria, Va., 1800–12. Various addresses as C., W., and math insts. maker. In Va., adv. 1805 "opened a shop and offered services as C. and W. and served time in Switzerland, afterwards in London & Paris." (*Cutten*)

*PHELPS & BARTHOLOMEW (ALBERT; A. H.): Ansonia, Conn., after 1880. Estab. 1881, Inc. 1886, mfr. C. movts. and C. parts. 1890, four-story savings bank property on E. side Main St. "Clocks of this Co. are very popular." (*Hist.*)

PHELPS & WAIT (J. W., E R.): Ravenna, Ohio, 1863. Rcd. patent on a W. (*J.W.G.*)

PHILADELPHIA (PHILA.): Has a long and fascinating C. and W. history. There were many able craftsmen; from Abel Cottey (aw. 1682) as pos. the first C. on these shores—this was the same year that William Penn arrived. The city was "layed out" by spring 1683 and "80 houses erected." By 1700, a "bell ringer was appointed to go around ye town with a small Bell in the night time to give notice of ye Time of night, and the weather, and—" In 1704, the town was divided into ten wards. "In 1736, Benjamin Franklin was appointed Clerk of the Assembly." "By 1743, the City had grown to a population (estimate) of nearly 20,000 people." The 1756 list of the city taxables (does not include all inhabitants) were 3 horologists: Chestnut Ward—Henry Flower, W. (1753–Adv., 1775); Lower Delaware Ward—John Wood, W. (1733–93); South Ward—Thomas Stretch, C. (?–1765). Many fine G.F.'s were here made, cases by the fine cabinetmakers of the city.

"PHIPPS": n/p, n/d. Other banjos reported with only this name. Standard wgt. driven 8-day tp. movt. Case usual size and tablets in throat and box; and with widely flaring side arms. Rumored previous purchase through Shreve, Crump and Low, Boston.

PHOENIX MANUFACTORY: N.Y.C., at 192 Pearl St. OG so labeled and after above name—

"William S. Sperry; Mfr. of Rosewood and Mahogany Pillar C. for the Foreign and Domestic Market etc." Movt. stamped "New Haven" with American Eagle with outstretched wings and "E. Pluribus Unum." (*Jerome Jackson*)

PIAGET, HENRY F.: N.Y.C., at 119 Fulton St., 1830ff. Came to U.S.A. after 13 yrs. apt. in Europe. W. Author of *The Watch, It's Construction, Merits and Effects; How to Choose it; and How to Use It*—1860. 3rd ed. 1877 renamed *The Watch, Handwork vs Machinery*. On title pg., "A W. of over 40 yrs. Experience." Worked in N.Y.C. over 50 yrs. "A highly finished duplex W." won him silver medal from Franklin Inst., Phila. and Mechanics Inst. N.Y.C.; a medal and diploma from American Inst., N.Y.C. One of his W. in James Arthur Col. (*Joseph Sternfeld*)

PIKE, B. & SONS: N.Y.C., 1795–1810. Name on brass sundial "Lat. 45," in Col. of John Walton. Also "made barometers."

PINKHAM & BRADFORD: Auburn, Me., 1835–65. C. case and furniture makers in 3 story bldg. on small river in East Auburn. Followed by Bradford & Conant. Flat OG in E. E. Runnells Col.

PITKIN, LEVI: Montpelier, Vt., n/d. Prob. not same as one in B.C.C. "Very active in early local History." Name on dial of a C. (*Dustin Cooley*)

PITKIN RICHARD, E.: Hartford, Conn. 1783–*ca.* 1830, "Factory—made some glass for clocks." (*Howard Sloane*)

PITTMAN, JOHN: Falmouth, Fredericksburg, and Alexandria, Va., pos. later Phila., 1792ff. Took care of clients across the river in Fredericksburg, but there (adv.) 1796. Alexandria in 1801. James Galt worked in same shop. Also pos. at Phila. Dir. 1818 as W. (*Cutten*)

PLACE, SAMUEL: (?–1800), Portsmouth, N.H., 1778. Adv. C., W., and J. D. at Dover, N.Y. (*C.S.P.*)

PLATO CLOCK Co.: N.Y.C.—name sometimes stamped on Plato tps.; prob. made by Ansonia. 4 basic models; 1st horizontal, others vertical. (*C. O. Terwilliger*)

PLATT BETTS, & Co.: Alliance, Ohio, *ca.* 1860. (*J.W.G.*)

*POMEROY: Hartford, Conn., *ca.* 1886–1900. Reported maker of Jig Saw C. cases, one with Seth Thomas movt. in author's Col.

POMEROY, JOSEPH: Hamilton, Ohio, ca. 1830. W. and J. formerly a partner of Gregg at Rossville, Ohio. (*J.W.G.*)

*POMEROY, NOAH: Bristol, aw. 1847–78. Add Wall regulator C.–8 day formerly was in restaurant in U.S. Senate, Washington, D.C. labeled "Eight Day Regulator/warranted a perfect timekeeper/made and sold by/—/also E Day and Thirty Hour Silent & Strike Levers." First legible rpr. date Nov. 13, 1869. (*Lewis Wilson*)

POND, JOHN: Portsmouth, N.H., 1809–11. C., W., and J. Adv. "shipment of Willard's elegant patent tps. and regulators." (*C.S.P.*)

POOLE BATTERY ELECTRIC TP: ca. 1934. Reported a Div. of Morse Chain Co., Ithaca, N.Y. 2 wall, 6 shelf (one with glass dome 10½" high) models. "Supposed to be one of the best battery timekeepers tho movts. complicated." (*P. DeMagnin; V. Grover; CT*)

PORTER, CARTER & CO.: Otis, Mass., n/d. L.G. shelf C. labeled: "Made & sold by Elisha Hotchkiss." (1820–40) "Cased & Sold by—" (*The Amos Averys*)

POTTER, "CAPT." JOHN: (1746–1818), Brookfield, Mass., last q. 18th cent. Lived whole life in Brookfield. A cherry cased G.F. with engr. brass dial in Dyar Col. (*Robert Hamilton*)

POTTER, JOHN: Alexandria, Va., before 1815. There apt. of John Adam, set up for self, partner for brief time with John Patterson, which ended 1815. Someone absconded with some of the partnership goods including all the W. and W. materials. To Norfolk, Va., 1816; on Church St. and 1818 adv. from 114 Main St. as C., W., and S. and for an apt. (*Cutten*)

POTTS, THOMAS: Phila. ca. 1770 and later. Supposed to be W. 1770 and pos. some connection with David Rittenjouse. Pos. later in Lancaster. (*J.W.G.*)

POWER, E. B.: N.Y.C., n/d. "Rcd. patent on Eureka Electric battery timepiece." "Electric Clocks"–by E. J. Wise. (*H. B. Fried*)

"PRAFF, R. F.": name used by U.S. Watch Co. #50,493 a 10 size g. hunting case 18k 15 j. key wind W. in C. A. Nathan Col.

*PRATT, DANIEL, JR.: (1797–1871), Reading, Mass. Add 1839 dated label 2 door, mahogany veneer 2-door shelf clock with standard 30-hr. wgt. movt., wood movt. with wood

dial with this beginning "Time Flies"—printed by J. Howe, 39 Merchants Row, Boston.

PRATT, N. JR.: East Haddam, Conn., n/d. "C. and W. maker" on a W. paper. (*Samuel Thorne*)

PRENTISS V. CLOCK IMPROVEMENT CO.: n/p, prob. N.Y.C. A 3 windowed cal. C. (day, mo., yr.) one above the other in base part of case. On movt.–2 patent dates in 1887 and 1890. Examples made by Gilbert Clock Co. at Winsted, Conn. Names also used were "Prentiss Calendar Clock Co.," "Prentiss Calendar & Time Co.," and "Prentiss Clock Co."

PRICE, ISAAC: (?–1798), Phila. "Also of Leslie & Price." Mentioned several times by George Washington in his household Account Book from 1793 to 1797.

PRICE, PHILIP: (?–1837) Chester Co., Pa. Not C.–Was Supt. West Town Boarding School, and later opened West Chester Boarding School for Girls. Mar. Racheal Kirk, 1784 at E. Nantmeal, Pa. D. West Chester. (*James E. Merrill*)

*PRICE, PHILIP, JR.: Phila. 1813–24 as C. Dir., 1825–49 as copper plate and type printer. Dir., after 1850 in tobacco, coal and R. E. Business. No record at Chester County, tho C. extant with his name.

PRICE, W. L.: Birmingham, Eng., ca. 1790 ff. Name found on some English dials with moon. Sold products to American makers. See "Dials," BAC-pg. 180.

PRINGLE, JOHN: N.Y.C. G.F. with this name on dial at N.Y. Historical Society.

PRITCHARD & MONSON: Bristol, n/d, not on tx. Extant wood movt. shelf C. with this name on label.

PROCTOR, G. F. & CO. (GEORGE): Beverly, Mass., ca. 1860. Ill. alarm with label reading: "Patent Aug. 7, 1860–Burglar and Fire Protective Clock–triple purpose–T.P.–a burglar and fire alarm;–and light a lamp at the moment alarm strikes." Earlier patent, Jan. 24, 1860 for "Lamp Lighting Device." Made by Seth Thomas, Plymouth Hollow with ST hands. (*Albert L. Partridge Col.*)

PROGRESSIVE MFG. CO.: Pana, Ill., 1887. Originally made foot warmers, novelties, and cal. C. 1 Patent to J. A. Shimp. (*R. F. Tschudy*)

PROGRESSIVE MFG. CO., THE: Pana, Christian Co., Ill., ca. 1880. Name on novelty shelf C. in Ray Walker Col.

PUTNEY, REUBEN: Plymouth, N.H., 1812. Adv. as W. and J. (*C.S.P.*)

*RAILROAD WATCH Co.: Albany N.Y., 1886. A 17 j. movt., open faced g.-filled case has engr. on back plate, "Cleveland, Ohio." (*J.W.G.*)

RALPH, S. W.: Mecca, Ohio, 1886. Rcd. patent on cal. C. (*J.W.G.*)

RAMAAL Co., G. W.: Chicago, *ca.* 1901. Made "Globe Chronometer Clocks" using movts. by Chelsea.

RANLET, CHARLES, JR.: Gilmanton, N.H., 1803. Adv. "co-partnership twixt Noah & Charles dissolved; C. R. continues in C. business as usual." (*C.S.P.*)

*RANLETT, SAMUEL: Monmouth, Me. On 3 different G.F.'s, this name reported by both Ray Walker and Ed Burt.

RANSOM, C. F.: Cleveland, Ohio, 1881. Rcd. patent on "night C." (*J.W.G.*)

*RANSOM, JASON B.: Athens, Vt., *ca.* 1840. (A small mountain town just outside Bellows Falls.) *L.G.*—30 hr. wood movt. owned by George H. Amidon. He was formerly at Holden, Mass. Then, "after a spring freshet after 1840 washed him out of business at Athens, to Saxtons River, Vt." (*The Dustin Cooleys*)

RAUCH, JAMES K.: Bethlehem, Pa., 1865–90. Apt. of Jedidiah Weiss, and acquired his business in 1865. (*R.H.-J.W.G.*)

READ, WATSON, & CHAMBERLAIN (Abner; Thomas; J. D.): Cincinnati, Ohio, 1811–12. Made and sold Watson's wood C. (*J.W.G.*)

REEVES, DAVID C.: Phila., at 54 North 4 St. Dir., 1830–35. (*J.E.C.*)

REEVESES & Co.: Youngtown, Tenn. Wood movt. shelf C. labeled so and under Eagle with Shield—Patent C. Invented by Eli Terry—etc. (No printer's name.) J. E. Coleman says there is no record on any Tenn. town by that name in the 1820s thru 1840s. Label similar to that in similar clock marked "Couch, Stowe & Co.—Rock Springs, Tenn." Pos. tax problems responsible. (*J.E.C.*)

REILEY (RILEY) JOHN: Phila. Dir. 1785–Dir. 1814. (*R.H.-J.W.G.*)

REILEY, WILLIAM: Newton, Pa., 1743. "Described as C.-maker." (*R.H.-J.W.G.*)

RELIANCE WATCH Co.: Chicago, Ill., 1880s. Movt. 29,437 engr. "C.W.C. Co.—Reliance" with star trade mark. On rim of case next to movt. "Pat'd Dec. 7, 1886." (*E. S. Tukey*)

REMPE, MFG. Co.: n/p, n/d. American wall battery, wall tp. 43″ high in Charles Terwilliger Col.

REVERE, PAUL: (1735–1818), Boston. Famous patriot and statesman. Helped Simon Willard with his clock business. Cast bells. Excellent engr., had a great part in estab. the American Brass Industry. One of his church bells, at Groveland, Mass., inscribed, "The Living to the Church I call, and to the Grave, I summon all." (*Revere*)

RICE & JOHNSON (G; Wm.): N.Y.C., at 106 Vesey St., 1840s. Wood movt. shelf C. with label reading: "(a spread eagle) mfgs. of Brass & Wood C. at Wholesale & Retail, with Patent spiral bells and warranted Accurate timekeepers."

RICHARDSON, FRANCIS: (1681–1737), Phila., *ca.* 1715–37. b. N.Y.C. and to Phila. 1690 as S., G., and C. 1736 adv. "Very neat clocks—made and sold and cleaned." *Bot* movts. from Peter Stretch. (*R.H.-J.W.G.*)

RICHARDSON, GEORGE E.: Nashua, N.H., at 35 Main St., 1866. Dir., as C. and W., J. & S. (*Fred M. Selchow*)

RICHARDSON, JOSEPH: (1706–70), Phila., 1733 ff. Son of Francis and with the family business. His 3 day books of 1733–40 at Penna. Hist. Soc. "Entries indicate C. making." (*R.H.-J.W.G.*)

RICHARDSON, JOSEPH, JR.: (1752–1831), Phila. Son of Joseph, bro. of Nathaniel, and in the family business. (*R.H.-J.W.G.*)

RICHARDSON, NATHANIEL: (1754–1827), Phila. Son of Joseph, bro. of Joseph Jr. and also in family business.

RIDGEWAY & ROCKWOOD: Keene, N.H., 1817. Adv. as W. & J., etc. (*C.S.P.*)

RIDGWAY, C. T.: Nashua, N.H., *ca.* 1830–95. With father, James, J. in Amherst, N.H. 1834 to Nashua. (*Hist.*)

RIDGWAY, JAMES: Keene, N.H., 1819. Adv. "Working for S. A. Gerould" and own store advs. 1817–24 as W. and J. and as R. and Rockwood. Later to Amherst, N.H. (*C.S.P.*)

*ROBERTS, T. M. (TITUS MERRIMAN): (1793–1856). Bristol. *L.G.* with label reading: "Mfg. by—for Henry Hart." (Canfield, Printer) Double Decker in Walter Robinson Col. reads, "Improved C.—Mfg. by—/for—"

*ROBIE, JOHN: Concord, N.H., before 1810. Adv. March 27 "sold to Samuel Foster, shop in Concord." Adv. Feb. 11, 1811 "taken the shop, formerly occupied by Mr. Jedidian Baldwin in Hanover, N.H. as C. and W."

ROBINSON & COLLINS: N.Y.C., ca. 1840. *OG* standard brass movt. wgt. with wood dial label reads: "Warranted Brass Clocks—made & sold by—"

"ROCHESTER": Trade name used for Cooper Card Time Recorder having S. Thomas movts., 1894 ff.

*ROCKFORD WATCH Co.: Rockford, Ill., 1873–1901 f. Also used trade name "Cosmos" in 1880s—17j.

*ROCKWELL, SAMUEL: (1722–93). Hampton, Va. Adv., 1752. Was previously at Providence, R.I. Later at Middletown, Conn. G.F.s. (*Cutten*)

ROCKWELL, THOS.: (?–1795), Norwalk, Conn., n/d. Estate Inv. shows he was a W.-maker and S. (*Lockwood Barr*)

ROEHRICH, JEAN LOUIS: N.Y.C. Mid-20th cent. C. and W.

ROGERS, EBENEZAR: (1763–1843). Norwich, Conn., n/d. C. and farmer. Left estate of over $18,000, including shares in Norwich Library. G.F.s. (*Vera Thorne*)

ROGERS, GEORGE W.: Concord, N.H., 1809–19. According to label in T. Chandler G.F., a cabinetmaker who made G.F. cases. (*C.S.P.*)

*ROGERS, JOHN: (1724–1815), Billerica, Mass. b. Boston. C. later at Newton, Mass. to 1800; d. there. (*E. B. Burt*)

ROOD & NORTON: Bristol, 1879. "—have been engaged in making movts. for a "globe clock" for a company in Canajoharie, N.Y." Each movt. is placed inside of a globe, the axis of the globe being placed at an angle to correspond with that part of the Earth. The globe revolves every 24 hrs., the hr. being shown on a dial. (*E.I.*)

ROOT, E. & S.: Bristol, n/d. (no tx.). Label in OG with 30 hr. wood movt. wgt. reading "Extra C.—made & sold by—" Elihu Geer, Printer (no address). In Col. John Hartigan.

ROOT, E. G.: Forestville, Conn., 1865. Mfr. marine and pend. c 7 tps. Had purchased machinery of Manross. In 1896, after his death, business continued by his son-in-law E. E. Newell. (*Hist.*)

*ROOT, SAMUEL EMERSON: (1820–96). Bristol. From 1846, alone in small part of the C. Boardman Shop making metal dials for C. 1851 had Edward Langdon as partner in

"spoon shop"—later moved to a shop at site of Dunbar factory. 1853, a new plant 3 stories at cor. Main and School Sts. (stood till 1903). Langdon & Root dissolved 1855; Root continued alone. 1859 rcd. Patent for use in small and fancy front tps. 1866 mfg. marine and pendulum movts.

"ROTO-CLOCK": made by *Lux*, ca. 1933. 2⅛ x 5" round horizontal with 1–12 hrs. indicated by pointer fixed on base as top revolved. [Fred Lux] "about 1 million made in mid-1930s by Lux Clock Co. as low priced novelty item—Case all metal, quiet resonant, could tell easily if running." Brass marine 30 hr. movt. horizontally mounted in base. "Not notoriously an accurate timekeeper." 3 in author's Col. Base used by Sam Barrington for Beer Bottle tp.

ROTARY PRESS: N.Y.C., at 321 Pearl St., 1841 ff. Printed labels for Clarke Gilbert & Co. of Winchester, Conn. (*Edythe Clark Col.*)

ROWELL, S.: Granville, Conn., n/d. "C & W" on W-paper at M.M.A.

RUSSELL, J. & Jos.: Boston, at Quaker Lane early 1800s. Printers of labels for Simon Willard for his early Roxbury C. & tps. They were like those of I. Thomas including prices for steeple (tower) C. from $300 to $900.

RUSSELL'S AMERICAN PRINTING HOUSE: N.Y.C., at 30 Centre St. ca. 1850. Printers of labels for Conn. Clock Co.

RYERSON, LUCAS: (1771–1855). Manchester Twp., N.J., n/d. C. and S. Celebrated in his time; specialty was G.F.s—many still in use. (*ANT., Oct. 1958*)

*SABER, GEORGE: Reading, Pa., ca. 1800. On dial of G.F. with 30-hr. brass wgt. movt. in Chippendale-styled walnut case. (Could this, repeated here, be mistaken again for "Faber?")

SADLER, W.: Manchester, N.H., n/d. W. paper in Ed Burt Col.

SAFFORD, HENRY: PUTNAM, O., 1812 and later. Adv. "Good W. Rpr." and warranted in Dirs. later. (*J.W.G.*)

SAGSMULLER, GEORGE N.: Rochester, N.Y., ca. 1875. Made C. Famous designer of scientific insts., as transits and levels; was for a time in partnership Bausch & Lomb. (*John Fielding Burns*)

SALEM CLOCK Co.: Hartford, Conn., n/d. No other data.

SANDS, C. V.: —, Conn., n/d C. & W., also G. & J. On W. paper, M.M.A.

SANDS, JACOB: Colebrook Twp. (no state), n/d. C. and W. On aged and tattered W. paper in Ephraim Greenberg Col.

SARGEANT, RALPH P.: Hartford, Conn., at Main St., n/d C. & W. On W. paper in M.M.A.

SARGEANT, THOS.: Springfield, Mass., n/d. W. paper says C. & W. In M.M.A. Col.

SARRATT, J. F.: (1879–?). Steubenville, Ohio. Patent on "Cosmochronatrobe." Example in James Arthur Col.; ill. back cover "Romance of Time."

SAYRE, CHARLES: East Town, Pa., n/d.

SCHAFFENBERGER, JOHANNES: Phila., ca. 1810. Name on a Pa. G.F. also with "Patton & Jones" (1804–14). (Amos Avery)

SCHMIDT, G. A.: Lawrence, Mass., at 204 Essex St., n/d. His sticker on back of Waterbury kitchen type shelf C. as "C.–expert Rpr.–W. & J." (Ray McKinney)

SCHNEIDER, JACOB: (?–1829). Reading, Pa., ca. 1788. b. Exeter Twp., Pa. "Was C., S., bookbinder, miller, teacher, etc." (R.H.-J.W.G.)

*SCHOLLENBERGER, JOHN: (1767–1840). Reading, Pa. (R.H.–J.W.G.)

*SCOTT, ANNE: Harrisburg, Pa., ca. 1850. Again reported as C.

SCOTT, JAMES: Cadiz, Ohio, 1819 ff. Son of Timothy W.; b. Yorkshire, Eng.; to Toronto, Canada; to Cadiz, Ohio, 1819, where he estab. a shop for W. rpr. and W. and C. where he was aw. till d. Held number of patents. At least 1 G.F. with his name extant. (J.W.G.)

SCOVIL, DAVID: Oswego, N.Y., ca. 1840. L.G. with this label. (Henry Sayward)

SEARS, RICHARD W.: Minneapolis, Minn., 1886. From Redwood, Minn. Organized R. W. Sears W. Co. for sales of W. He adv. Chicago Daily News for a W. Then secured one A. C. Roebuck of Gary, Ind. to join with him. At age 19, in 1883, he was appointed Station Agent on Minn. and St. Louis R.R. at North Redwood. An assignment of W.s arrived—no one claimed. "Distributors often shipt goods to smaller R.R. stations hoping that someone would buy for resale—these not addressed to any individual." Sears made enquiry among other station agents. Response being good, Sears paid $12 a W. and sold them at $14 (retailed then for $16). There was $2 profit on each. He ordered more W.s

and by 1886 was doing so well that he organized his W. Co., as above. (from "Born in a R.R. Station," R.R. Mag., Apr. 1958)

*SELF WINDING CLOCK CO.: N.Y.C. and Brooklyn 1888 ff. Specialized in C. and tps.

SEMA, J. K.: Canton, Pa., 1868. Patent #73127, "Improvement on cal. C." Unusual cal. in 30-hr. brass wgt. OG with Ansonia Brass Co. label in Louis Roumaine Col.

"SERVICE": Name on dial of small pocket non-j. pocket W. made by New Haven Clock Co. Full plate movt. stamped "Pat.–from 1910 to 1918." One in Author's Col.

SESSIONS CLOCK CO., THE: Forestville, Conn., 1903 ff. Successor to the Welch Clock Empire. Reorganized by William K. and Albert Sessions. (Dallas Webster)

SEWARD, JOSHUA: Boston, n/d. Pos. made only banjos and lyres. Dials so painted. One of them has name and "Boston" on lower tablet around pendulum opening. (E. C. Durfee)

SEXTON, NOAH: Paterson, N.J. Dir. 1824–33. C. and W. (Earl Dowd)

SEYMOUR, HALL & CO.: Unionville, Conn., n/d. Label reads, "Patent C. with brass bushings etc." (J. C. Blaker)

SEYMOUR, WILLIAMS & PORTER: Unionville, Conn., 1833–37. Also at Farmington, 8-day wood movt. shelf C. of "large Terry Type" with mahogany plates, count wheel 'twixt plates, fan fly at bot., compounded pulleys, seconds dial. (H. P. Davis–C. O. Terwilliger)

SHARP, SHEPARD: N.Y.C., at 12 Murray St., ca. 1880. Back label on 8-day brass Ingraham shelf C. (James E. Merrill)

SHAVER, MICHAEL: (1775–1859). Abington, Va. First a blacksmith, then C. and W. Mar. Letita Hill, 1807. In town politics; Elder, Presbyterian Church. (Cutten)

SHEARMAN, MARTIAL: Andover, Mass., n/d. Grandson of Robert; son of Thomas (Bristol, Conn., 1818). To here with brother William. Made metal movt. wags with dials of brass. (Charles Currier)

SHELDON CLOCK CORP.: Chicago, 1960s. Made a/c's. (R. S. Tschudy)

SHERATON, —: Pa., n/d. Good 8-day G.F. inlaid wild cherry case, inlay of curly and bird's eye maple. Case and hood trimmed in white and curly maple. (Harry P. Davis)

SHERBOURNE, JAMES: Paterson, N.J., ca. 1830. C. and W. (S. H. Gamp)

SHERMAN, JOSEPH: Lancaster, Pa., *ca.* 1830. On dial of a rather heavy shelf C. of Pa., with brass movt. (*Tony Sakowitz*)

SHOREY, EDWIN O.: Bluehill, Me., 1841. 19½" high OG with brass movt. mounted into backboard on iron plate. Label "1841." (*Thomas F. Burk*)

SHORT, JOHN: Alexandria, Va., *ca.* 1783–89. Then to Norfolk; later, Halifax, N.J. "Served his regular apt. in London." (*Cutten*)

SIBLEY, COL. TIMOTHY: Sutton, Mass., n/d. Cherry-cased "Willard type" wall C. in I. Sak Col. He was father of Asa, who was b. Sutton and prob. apt. there. (*Ruth Wallace Stegall*)

SIDNEY ADVERTISING CLOCK CO.: Sidney, N.Y., 1886. The product was large wall C.–69 x 27 at base with 19½" waist–with day of month only cal. on time dial. Three adv. cards at base changed every 5 minutes accompanied by a ringing bell. The movt. was brass 8-day spg., prob. made in Conn., and marked "Pat. July 20, 1886." (*A.J., Sept.* 1952)

SILLCOCKS & COOLEY: N.Y.C., at 4 Maiden Lane, *ca.* 1885. Adv. card in Bir. Col.

SILVER, DANIEL: Lawrence, Mass., at 533 Essex St. Sticker on door of S. Thomas 30-day gallery tp., twin spring powered, mounted on cast-iron frame. (*M. S. Burroughs*)

SILVER, M. A.: N.Y.C., at 193 Chatham St., 1840s. Standard 30-hr. wgt. OG with wood dial and decal tablet, with this overpasted label under which was William Johnson, N.Y.C. (*George Ponder*)

SIMNET, JOHN: Providence, R.I., 1769. Adv. from London and Dublin after 25 yrs., and not too complimentary remarks about his competitors. In 1770, to N.Y.C.

SIMON, OTTO: Detroit, Mich., 1900s. Name printed on dial of round tin alarm tp. at Ford Museum.

SIMONS BRO. & CO.: Phila., n/d. Mahogany-cased G.F. with this name on dial. (*M. W. Olsen*)

SIMPSON, ALEXANDER: Hagerstown, Md., 1799–1805. Alone till 1802, then 3-yr. partnership with A. Johnson, then to Cincinnati where he adv. C. and W. In 1810 also "made artificial teeth and set in an elegant manner." (*J.W.G.*)

SIMPSON, DANIEL: Burlington, Vt., 1841. Adv. "patent lever W.s from Liverpool." (*The Cooleys*)

SLAGELE, GEORGE WILBUR: (1859–1907). N.Y.C., 1878 ff. A C. in N.Y., also made cases at 2125 Lexington Ave., 1875–78. (*E. E. Runnells*)

SMALLWOOD, W. R.: Towanda, N.Y., 1890s. A 14-dialed tp. with 4½' pendulum; 235 lb. wgts. exhibited at Columbia Exposition, Chicago, 1893; now at Hallett Museum, Newport, N.H.

SMILEY, DAVID: (1800–73). Peterborough, N.H., n/d. W. and J. "Carried on this business for over 40 yrs. His great skill & mechanical ingenuity have given him great success." (*Hist.*)

SMITH & ROOT: N.Y.C., at 79 John St., n/d. OG so labeled. (*John E. Hartigan*)

SMITH & WILLSON: Keene, N.H., 1812. Adv. C. (*C.S.P.*)

SMITH, D. L.: n/p, *ca.* 1870. Patent on "Time Keeper Compass"–"to needle is attached a light paper disk so that instrument may be used directly to tell time of day by the shadow of vertical paper sun dial upon paper disk." (*M. T. Goodrich*)

SMITH, CAPT. ELISHA, JR.: (1769–1833). Sanbornton, N.H. Had a C. factory–pos. apt. to A. Hutchins.

*SMITH, ELISHA, Ill: (1795–1847). Sanbornton, N.H., n/d. Was apt. to Abel Hutchins; made C. Afterward, a machinist in Laconia, Pittsfield, Dover, and Manchester (all N.H.). d. Lowell, Mass. Several flat top G.F.s. Used various woods in same case.

SMITH, F. A.: Derry Depot, N.H., late 1800s. D. and rpr. in W.s; S. and J. Adv. card in Bir. Col.

SMITH, JAMES C.: Bristol, n/d. LG 28½" high 30-hr. wood movt. "with Improved Brass Bushings." (*Howard Alcorn*)

*SMITH, JOSEPH L.: N.Y.C., *ca.* 1841. May have been only agent–label on OG printed by John Black, 75 Fulton St., N.Y.C., and reads: "Improved Clocks–90 John St., cor. Gold." One label mentions "Clock Factory."

*SMITH, LUTHER: (1766–1839). Keene, N.H., n/d. An adv. read: "the brass founder. Was still making G.F.s as in former years." (*Hist.*)

SMITH, R.: Hartford, Conn., 1830s. Carved column. Transition shelf C. with 20-hr. wood movt. "Carving like acanthus, but reminds one of emaciated Chinese lettuce." (*Herbert Rand*)

SMITH, RICHARD RANSON: So. Parish, Woodstock, Vt., 1809. Adv. as W. (*John Moore*)

SMITH, S. B. & E.: Bristol, Dir. 1831–32. Mfrs. of looking glasses and glass for C.—not recorded as C. (*Howard Sloane*)

SMITH, SIMON: (1774–1826). Suffield, Conn. G.F. with name on dial. (*Edith C. Watts*)

SMITH, TUTTLE & BLAKESLEE: Oswego, N.Y. 30-hr. wood wgt. L.G. extant. (*Catherine Tobin*)

SNOW, BENJAMIN: Augusta, Me., last q. 18th Cent. G.F. extant with brass movt. and iron plates.

SNOW, JEREMIAH: Springfield, Mass., n/d. G.F. with name on dial. (*Stuart Havens*)

SNYDER, JOHN B.: Pottstown, Pa., 1860s. C. & W. W. paper extant. (*R.H.—J.W.G.*)

SOLAR WATCH CO.: N.Y.C., 1905. Standard 6 size W. marked "1863-Chicago" in H. B. Fried Col.

*SOLIDAY, SAMUEL: (1805–82). Doylestown, Pa., *ca.* 1828 to after 1837. Seat board of shelf C. 30″ high solid mahogany case, signed by him and dated "Feb. 21, 1837"—has brass 8-day movt. with solid brass plates, comp. wgts., pendulum on front plate. (*Richard Thomson*)

"SONNY LEEDS": Name on dial of non-j. pocket W. and "made in U.S.A. for A. Schulte, N.Y." In 1930s pos. New Haven made them. (*Dudley Ingraham*)

SOUTHERN CALENDAR CLOCK CO.: St. Louis, Mo., 1875–89 and pos. 1890s. Mostly mfg. by Seth Thomas, but examples by New Haven Clock Co. known. 2 dials: cal, day of month, only. Also Wm. L. Gilbert made some. (*J. E. Coleman*)

"SPARTUS": Tradename for a/c's currently available.

SPECIALE, MICHEAL & SON: N.Y.C., after 1900. Unusual octagonal drop wall tp. with an adapted S. Thomas movt. The map of the world is shown on dial with eastern hemisphere superimposed. Behind this, on a separate cal. hand passes in back, a simulated sun —a large brass star—attached to the hr. hand. "Patent C.-Makers" on printed label. (*Efroim Greenberg*)

SPELLIER, LOUIS: (1841–91). Doylestown, Pa., 1869, with Abraham Yeakel as a C. and W. shop. Was b. Germany. Made tower C. at Bucks County Court House—Lenepe Hall Towers. Also a 4-dial tower C. "exhibited in

Phila." 1876 invented a d/c galvanic battery tp. with electro escape, perfected further 1885 by devising method for make-break electric contacts. To Phila. where he d. (*George S. Hotchkiss*)

SPENCER, HOTCHKISS & CO.: Salem Bridge, Conn., *ca.* 1830. Famous as makers of 8-day brass wgt. movt. shelf Cs.

SPENCER, HOTCHKISS & WOOSTER: Naugatuck, Conn., *ca.* 1840. Three-decker shelf C. with 8-day brass wgt. movt. extant. (*Ernest Milligan*)

SPENCER, MORRIS, & CO.: Litchfield, Conn. No data, but reported as C.

SPENCER, T. W.: Circleville, Ohio, 1872. Patent on time lock. (*J.W.G.*)

SPERRY & GAYLORD: N.Y.C., at 75 Fulton St., n/d. W. in H. B. Fried Col.

SPIES, WILLIAM: Hanover, Pa., late 18th Cent. W. paper "1795" in H. B. Fried Col.

SPRATT, SAMUEL L.: Elkton, Md., before 1831. G.F. extant.

SQUIRE & LANDER: N.Y.C., at 97 Fulton St., 1857. Adv. in N.Y. *Times* as C. and W.—D.—J.

STANDARD ELECTRIC TIME CO.: Springfield, Mass.; formerly New Haven. From 1888 ff. In 1966, Pres. Frances Riggs Young and V.P. George L. Riggs presented a 70-yr.-old battery wall tp. to American Clock Museum, Bristol.

"STANDARD RAILROAD CLOCK, THE": Label in 8-day brass 8-day strap movt. of Cook & Jacques Terry & Co. Has rolling pinions. (*Ray Walker Col.*)

STANDARD TIME STAMP CO., THE: Binghamton, N.Y., 1899. Made a time stamp and card recorder. Absorbed by Bundy Mfr. Co. See I.B.M.

STANLEY, W. H.: New Haven, Conn. Not C. Printer of C. labels for Harry Thompson of Bristol, Conn.

"STARK, MOLLY": Name used by Dueber-Hampden Watch Co. in 20th Cent. for ladies' W.s. On back plate of stem wind movt.—"Canton, O.—#2492386." Gold case open face—"Hampden" on white dial, second hand at 6, vertical arabic chapters, graceful spade hands; in G. Longmire Col.

STARK, WILLIAM: Dayton, Ohio and Xenia, Ohio. Adv. C. and W. (*J.W.G.*)

*STARR, THEODORE BURR: (Aug. 6, 1837–May 9, 1907). N.Y.C. Famous for C. and W. and of

excellent reputation. G.F. at Princeton Club. b. New Rochelle, d. Plainfield, N.J. (*Theodore D. Starr*)

STEDMAN, O. F.: Ravene, Ohio, 1867. Patent on W.

STENNES, ELMER O. E.: Weymouth, Mass., mid-20th Cent. Fine reproductions of masterpiece American C.

STEVENS, THOMAS: Amherst, N.H., 1798. Adv "D." (*C.S.P.*)

STEVER & BRYANT: Bristol (Whigville), *ca.* 1840, (no tx.). "In J. Peck's Shop" In 1842, William B. Barnes worked for them on an early Conn. Marine type movt. Later the model was finished in Plainville in 1843. (*J. E. Coleman*)

STEWART, CHARLES G. & SON (GEO. L.): Charlestown, Va., 1847–49. C, W, and J. (*Cutten*)

STEWART, CHARLES G.: (?–1866). Charlestown, Va., n/d. S. who sold W. (*Cutten*)

*STILES, SAMUEL: Windsor, Conn. (Vt), n/d. G.F. in Guy Holt Col.

STOCKING, ABNER: Amber, N.Y. n/d. "Mfr. & Justice of the Peace" on overpasted label in L.G. (*Henry Sayward*)

STOKELL, I.: N.Y.C., *ca.* 1870–80. Oak-cased large "Regulator," long pendulum battery d/c powered tp. bearing this name on white dial. Located in New Haven R.R. Station, in Bristol, Conn. (*E.I.*)

*STOKELL, JOHN: N.Y.C., 1855. Made a 4-dialed tower tp. for Marble Collegiate Church on Fifth Ave. Ran 102 yrs. till replaced in 1957. (*Adolph Wenzell*)

STONE & MARSHALL: Cazenovia, N.Y., *ca.* 1850. C. (*J.E.C.*)

STONE, JASPER: Charlestown, *ca.* 1810. Dial of presentation banjo so marked. (*E. F. Mc-Keen*)

*STORRS, NATHAN: (1768–1839). Utica, N.Y. b. Mansfield, Conn., 1791. First Adv. "lately from N.Y." Northampton, Mass., 1792–94. Partner in Baldwin (Jedidiah) & Storrs. but by 1817 or later at Utica, N.Y. Pos. also at Northampton partner in Storrs & Cook (Benj.) with 1827–44 dates. "Storrs, Utica" on G.F. at M.M.A. Ill. #46–B.A.C. (*Charles A. Smart*)

STORRS, SHUBEL: (1778–1847), Utica, N.Y., 1803–47. Nephew of Nathan; "First C. in Utica." In Utica's Second Dir.; 1828 as W. (*Charles A. Smart*)

*STOWELL & SON: Charlestown, *ca.* 1840. Name on banjo.

*STRATTOM, CHARLES: Worcester & Holden, Mass., *ca.* 1831 thru 1840. Many of his C. labels carry printed year dates, as often did Daniel Pratt's. Product mostly wood movt. L.G.s. (*E. B. Burt*)

STREETER, GEO. L.: New Haven, Conn. at 266 Chapel St. Dir., 1868 as C. and W.

SWEENEY, J. C.: Houston, Tex., at 319 Main St., *ca.* 1890. His adv. card as C., W. and J. extant.

SWIFT, A. L.: Chicago, *ca.* 1890. Name on dials of 2-piece iron-cased C. resembling stoves of iron. Pos. use by some stove mfr. (*C. E. Durfee*)

SWING CLOCK MFG. CO.: Chicago, 1960s. Making a/c's. (*R. S. Tschudy*)

SYKES, WILLIAM: Beverly, Mass. Early 19th Cent. G.F.'s with white dials extant; one at Beverly Historical Society.

*TABER, ELNATHAN: (1768–1854). Roxbury, Mass., aw. 1790–1854. d. apt. to Simon Willard at age 16 "best." "Front plate of a banjo #629–Taber–July 16, 1803." (*Ed S. Jones*)

TACK, JEAN: Newark, N.J. at 215 Market St., *ca.* 1890 Two adv. cards in Bir. Col–"Watch work a specialty."

"TACOMA": Name used by New Haven Clock Co. for dash board tps. for autos and marked "Pat. 1920." Long stem, radium dial. (*Seward Baker*)

TANNEHILL, Z. B.: Pittsburg, Pa., *ca.* 1825. G.F.'s. (*D. H. Shaffer*)

TAPPAN, EBENEZER: (1761–1845). Manchester, Mass., n/d. Revolutionary War veteran; storekeeper; cabinet maker. Mar. Betsey Forster, 1790. Two sons Eben, Jr., and Isreal also both cabinetmakers. (*Charles Currier*)

TAPPAN, ISREAL: (1802–?). Manchester, Mass., early 1820s ff. Cabinet and C. case maker. (*Charles Currier*)

*TAPPAN, J. F.: Manchester, Mass., n/d. Son of Isreal. Prob. made C. cases only with his name thereon. 2 alarm banjos, and N.H. mirror tp. known. (*Charles Currier*)

TAYLOR, W. E.: N.Y.C., n/d. Ship's C. so marked on dial of brass round case in Rector's Office, Chapel, Governor's Island, N.Y. (*Otto Kerr*)

TEBBETS, GEO.: Newmarket, N.H., *ca.* 1830. Both on a N.H. mirror and banjo on M. H. (*Brightman Col.*)

"TELECHRON": Trade name used by Henry Warren, and now General Electric Co.; from 2 Greek words meaning "Time from a Distance."

*TERRY & ANDREWS: (Ralph & Theo.; F.C.) Bristol, 1842–1850. Label of theirs in Avery Col. marked "East Bristol."

*TERRY CLOCK Co.: At least 4 firms, all to do with S. B. Terry and his son, used this name:
1. Terryville–Organized 1852 or before.
2. Winsted–exact dates aw. not now known.
3. Waterbury–Dir., 1868 at South Main St.
4. Pittsfield, Mass.–1880 and later. (*J.W.G.*)

TERRY CLOCK Co.: Waterbury, Conn. Dir., 1868. (BAC) "Pos. such a firm existed." It did, example then in authors Col. Organized with cap. of $25M. Ambrose Upson, Pres. in Waterbury. When S. B. Terry d. 1876, to Pittsfield, Mass. 1880 and later. Factory was at corner West Main and South Willow Sts. "To be noted Jan. 11, 1886, Jno S. Kingsbury gave quit claim deed to Estate of S. B. Terry." One of the sons at Pittsfield got a C. patent, assigned to Co. Rumor in Waterbury that C. were made there that carried "Henry Terry" name on some labels. Of this there is no record except that H. T. was an employee. To tx. extant a/c fire in Waterbury in 1880. 6"-high round top black iron-cased C. bears this Waterbury label. Several sizes 1 and 8-day C. and tps. (*J. L. Reeves*)

TERRY DOWNS & Co.: (R. E. George) Bristol, *ca.* 1855. Cast-iron octagonal case with painted metal dial so labeled in E. F. Tukey Col.

TERRY, FAIRBANKS & Co.: Chesterville, Conn., n/d. Steeple shelf C. so labeled. (*Ed Burt*)

TERRY, HENRY: (1801–77). Plymouth, Conn. Son and apt of Eli. In E. Terry & Sons. 1818–24. E. Terry & Son, or Henry Terry, 1825–36. To woolen business 1836. Then later, pos. reentry into C. business or use of his name allowed in 1850s and in Terry C. Co., Waterbury. Authored in 1853–*American C.-making–Early History and Present Extent.* 30-hr. wood movt. shelf C. in Clinton McGlamery Col. reads: "Patent Cs.–[picture of Eagle]–Invented by Eli Terry–Made and Sold at Plymouth, Conn. by ——" There was also: TERRY, HENRY & Co., Plymouth, Conn. On some labels no exact dates.

*TERRY, SAMUEL: (1774–1853). Plymouth, then Bristol, Conn., 1818–35. Bro. of Eli–called "The Clockmaker's Clockmaker." In 1831 Bristol Dir. of Business "Mfr. of Patent 30-hr. Wood C. with various patterns of fancy cases, as well as 8-day, Church, Steeple C.–also a Brass Founder." (*E.I.*)

*TERRY, SILAS BURNHAM: Plymouth, Conn. (*BAC*). "No Plymouth Labels known." There are many on his fine C.'s.

TERRY, SOLON M.: Waterbury, Conn. Dir., 1868 and later. Son of Silas B. Residing with Father on Main St. (*J.W.G.*)

"TERRY, THOMAS & HOADLEY": Greystone, Conn., *ca.* 1808. (This is just north of Waterbury.) Here, Eli Terry, b. Apr. 13, 1772, established a factory to mass produce some "4,000 wood movt. hang-ups with dial and hands *ca.* 1806 for the porters of Waterbury." An extant label read: "Cs.–made & sold by Eli Terry, for Levi, G., & E. Porter –" There has been some speculation if the above 3 names ever appeared together on these or other C. dials, even though so listed in Moore. This was entirely Terry's enterprise. He employed fine craftsmen; among them Seth Thomas (b. Aug. 18, 1785) and Silas Hoadley (b. 1786). In 1808, Terry was age 34; Thomas 21, and Hoadley, 20. No C. has actually been seen by or reported to our knowledge with these three names on the same C. dial. Terry, completing this venture in 1809–10, did sell this plant to Thomas & Hoadley. He returned to Plymouth, where, at another location, established a new plant where the successful Pillar & Scroll shelf C. came into being after 1814. Thomas & Hoadley continued together to make 30-hr. wood movt. G.F.'s till 1813. Then Thomas sold to Hoadley his Greystone interests and went to Plymouth Hollow. There he established the Seth Thomas C. business. Hoadley continued at Greystone, later being named Hoadleyville, till 1849, when he retired with a fortune, a success in C. making.

TERRY, WILLIAM A.: (1828–1917). Bristol, *ca.* 1870. Son of Samuel Steele Terry. Invented a cal. C. and Pat. Jan. 25, 1870 "self-adjusting for leap years." First made by Atkins Clock Co., then later sold rights to Ansonia, and they made some.

TEWKESBURY, THOMAS: Meredith, N.H., 1819. Adv. "Commenced C., W., and J." (*C.S.P.*)

THAYER, H. C.: Kennebunkport, Me. *ca.* 1835–

L.G., wood movt. so labeled *(John LaFlamm)*

THOMA (J. A.) & COTTELL: Piqua, Ohio, 1930. Of the One Hand Clock Co. *(J.W.G.)*

*THOMAS, SETH Co.: Thomaston, Conn. models 1883–1914+. W. 1–13 ¾ plate 18s, except #5. 3–key wind numbers 35001-718200. 5– full plate 25s. 10–11 thicker models. 12–13 Then "Century." 18 large #950.000 P. *(H. B. Fried)*

*THOMAS, SETH & SONS Co.: Plymouth, Conn. and N.Y.C., 1866–79. Organized in 1866; became part of Seth Thomas Co. in 1879.

*THOMAS, SETH: (1785–1859). 1849 subscribed to $15,000 of stock to build the Naugatuck R.R. (Opened to Winsted in Sept., 1849. Now, 1967, largely abandoned.)

THOMASON, J. A.: Salem, Va. name on 18s Elgin W. in H.B. Fried Col.

THOMSON, HARRY: Bristol, n/d. Brass 1-day wgt. OG labeled: "Patent Brass Clocks, made & sold by—" Label printed by W. H. Stanley, New Haven.

THOMPSON, WILLIAM: Paterson, N.J. Dir., 1830 with Geo. Hilton, C. and W. *(Oscar Hockenson)*

THRASHER CLOCK Co.: Manchester, Conn., *ca.* 1910. "No exact date." *(E.I.)*

THRASHER, SAMUEL POWERS: New Haven, Conn., *ca.* 1890. 16 patents on electric impulsed self-winding 3-dial jumper C. used in Thrasher Time System. *(J.E.C.)*

THRASHER TIME SYSTEM, INC., THE: New Haven, Conn., 1904. Adv. office and building; electric impulsed pendulum C., also running secondary C. (Slave tps.) using Thrasher Patents. C. show 3-dial jumper, rather than hands over dials. Installed in new $300M New Haven YMCA." *(J. E. Coleman)*

TIFFANY, D. B.: Xenia, Ohio, 1888. Patent on alarm C. case. *(J.W.G.)*

TIFFANY ELECTRIC MFG. Co.: Buffalo, N.Y., 1900s. Battery tps., some having Geo. Tiffany on dials. Several in C. O. Terwilliger Col. "Thrust given to torsion pendulum at every half-cycle; thrust ending at end of cycle. Largest—13¼″ to top glass dome; middle size—12¼″.

*TIFFANY, GEORGE: Buffalo, N.Y., 1900s. Rcd. Patent 1904 for Battery tp. He was a part of Tiffany Electric Mfg. Co. and Tiffany Never Wind Clock Co.

*TIFFANY NEVER WIND CLOCK Co.: Buffalo,

N.Y., 1900s. Battery tps., one with "Cloister" on dial and inside "Cloister Mfg. Co., Buffalo." Another by "Niagara Mfg. Co., Buffalo." *(C. O. Terwilliger)*

TODD, HENRY: Concord, N.H., 1819. Adv., 1822, as W. and J. *(C.S.P.)*

*TOLFORD, JOSHUA: Gilmanton, N.H., 1794 (adv.) G.F. in F. M. Selchow Col.

"TORY CLOCK": G.F.'s made pre-Revolutionary War still having original lead wgts. when lead was essential for making bullets. Sometimes referred to.

TOWEL, HENRY: (1788–1867). Haverhill, N.H., 1805–32 and later. A dated W. paper "1832"–"J. and W. Property of drugstore for many yrs." *(Charles Currier)*

TOWER & FRISBIE: New Hartford, Conn., 1840s, OG so labeled. *(Glen Roundy)*

TRACY, WILLIAM: Phila., at 1 Adams St. Dir., 1844 and later. C. *(R.H.–J.W.G.)*

TRENCHARD, RICHARD: Salem, Mass. Name on brass-dialed G.F. *(Arthur Sullivan)*

TROTTER, JEREMIAH: N.Y.C., *ca.* 1820–30. Then to Cincinnati to *ca.* 1850. *(J.W.G.)*

TWIN-FACED CLOCK Co.: N.Y.C., late 1920s. Made double-opposed dialed a/c's, one in author's Col.

TYLER, DAVID, III: (1790–1862). Sandusky, Ohio, 1833ff. From Hector, N.Y. and lived there a yr. while making C. To Clarksburg, Ohio, and built there a shop where he made most everything which required the use of tools. Also mus. insts. *(Hist.)* *(J.W.G.)*

UNION CLOCK Co.: Chicago, *ca.* 1940. Simple cased a/c non-self-start tps. in brass cased frying pan cases with handles. No marking on motorboard in back labeled "Mfr. by—. *(Ephraim Greenberg)*

UNION CLOCK MFG. Co.: Bristol, 1843–45 (tx.) OG 1-day brass wgt. movt. with separate alarm bell; label reading, "—For the Foreign & Domestic Market; Warranted;" etc.

UNION WATCH Co.: N.Y.C., n/d. W's. stamped "Boston" are 17 j., key wind. Example in James Arthur Col. *(The Curator)*

UNITED CLOCK Co.: Brooklyn, N.Y., at 379 De Kalb Ave., 1905ff. Founder was Abraham Levy; Pres. till d. 1961. Makers of unique and decorative tp. as well as staple C. and tps. Inc. 1931. Pres. now—Dr. Harold Levy; Sec.—Donald Levy. "A/c's made with motors made by them." A Division of United Metal Goods Mfg. Co.

UNITED METAL GOODS MFG. CO.: Brooklyn, N.Y., *ca.* 1905ff. Incorporated 1931, The United Clock Co., one of the associated Co's.

*UNITED STATES WATCH CO.: Marion, N.J. 1863–72ff. Among names used for W's. was "R. F. Pratt."

*UPSON BROS., MARION: Bristol, Conn., *ca.* 1850. Some movts. made by Brewster & Ingrahams (1844–52). Some dials made by E. G. Goodwin (1852–55). E extant C. is 16″ high pearl inlay iron-cased Bee Hive with 8-day spg. movt.; with label reading: "Plain & Ornamental Inlaid Pearl & Ivory 8- & 1-day brass C. & Marine tps.; Mfr. and sold by—" (E. C. Durfee). Another—8-day brass spg. movt. "Cottage Type" case—in Col. of William S. Woernley.

VAN CAMP, J. G.: N.Y.C., at 839 Broadway, *ca.* 1885. Adv. card Bir. Col. as "C., W. and J."

"VANTAGE": Name used for W.'s by Hamilton Watch Co.'s Vantage Products Div. at E. Petersburg, Pa., 1962ff. (*Robert Gunder*)

*VERMONT CLOCK CO.: Fairhaven, Vt. 1910–21 "Ship's bell striker in round turned brass case like Chelsea, but bell on top of case; hammer shaft is vertical, extending through hole near top of case so that hammer is inside of the bell, striking horizontally. Movt. is 3 plate, like Chelsea, except that rack and snail mechanism is between front and middle plates and escape is on round bridge behind back plate, covered with a round cap with watch crystal set in so that escape is visible through the crystal. Lever escape, 7 j., "good workmanship throughout. 'MacMillan Patent' is only wording on dial." (*J. E. Coleman*) "No other identification of MacMillan Patent." (*W. C. Robinson*)

VIALLE, ALEXANDER: Baltimore, Md., *ca.* 1815. Name on brass dial G.F. with "case similar to later clocks of Benj. Willard."

VOTTI, G.: Phila. 1880s. Wall tp. extant in Van Belknap Col. Winds at "12"—3 patents rcd. by him.

VUILLE (VIALLE) ALEXANDER: Baltimore, Md., 1766. Adv. "Cases have characteristics of some of those of Benjamin Willard's G.F.'s." (*C. E. Durfee*)

WADSWORTH, SAM'L.: Keene, N.H., 1875. Glass-domed model of battery tp. 22½″ high with electricity conducted by piece of silver at bottom tip of pendulum running through small alabaster cup of mercury. "Of superb workmanship" in C. O. Terwilliger Co.

WALKER, JAMES: Fredericksburg, Va., 1791. Adv. aw. till *ca.* 1810. (*Cutten*)

WALKER, J. E.: Zanesville, Ohio, 1822. Adv. "late from Baltimore." C., W. and S. (*J.W.G.*)

WALLACE: Name on battery tps.; some in banjo cases 32″ high, also Round Top Shelf tps. 12″ high. Two in C. O. Terwilliger Col.

WALTHAM CLOCK CO.: Waltham, Mass. Was a Co. separate from that purchased in 1911. Made high-quality products. Ceased *ca.* 1930, or later.

WALTHAM WATCH CO.: "In 1957, shut down plant making W.'s. Product now solely imports." (*Business Week*—June 5, 1962.)

WARD, GEORGE B.: Hillsboro, N.H. W. movt. #6522 "is prob. Model 57 of American Watch Co." (*F. M. Selchow Col.*)

WARD, RICHARD: Salem Bridge, Conn. 1829ff. Shelf C. with 8-day brass strike movt., no comp. pulleys, second hand on dial, flat top case with full side columns 29″ high, labeled "Eight Day, Repeating, Brass Clocks, made by—" printer: Baldwin & Peck, New Haven. Rcd. patent 1829—"Self moving Clock for winding up." (*W. C. Robinson*)

WARD, W. D.: Springfield, Ill., n/d. "C.-maker." (*R. D. Tschudy*)

WARNER, ASEPH: Solesbury Twp., Pa., 1783. G.F. so dated extant. (*R.H.—J.W.G.*)

WARREN CLOCK CO.: Ashland, Mass. 1912 Org. ff.

WARREN, HENRY ELLIS: (1874–?). Ashland, Mass. "Father of Electric Time." Graduate M.I.T., 1894. In 1907, mar. and moved to Ashland, there to experiment with tps. driven by electricity. Organized Warren Clock Co. in 1912 to make and sell an accurate battery-operated tp. First factory was his country barn. Continued experimenting and in 1916 made his synchronous, self-starting a/c tp. First attempt, plugged into current, failed in accuracy by as much as 15 min. a day, gaining or losing. Convinced his tp. was right, but that a/c cycles were not at 60, he invented and built a master tp. with second pendulum plus 1 of his a/c tps. to correlate power cycles at the power house. First demonstration at Boston successful on Oct. 23, 1916, showed the a/c cycles then not at standard. Named his a/c's "Telechron" ("Time from a distance"). In 1917, the General Electric Co. reportedly acquired a half interest in the Warren Clock Co. Name was changed to Warren Telechron Co. in 1926 with a factory located on Homer Ave., Ashland, Mass. Became Telechron, Inc. in 1946. In 1951, merged with G.E. as Telechron Dept. of G.E. In 1955, became General Electric Co.—Clock & Timer Dept. Products continue to be made. (*Edwin Pease-Louis Babb*)

WARREN ONE HAND CLOCK CO.: Warren, Pa., 1918. See One Hand Clock Co.

WARRINER, CHAUNCEY: Washington, D.C., on Penn. Ave., n/d. W. paper. (*Efroim Greenberg*)

*WARRINGTON, SAMUEL W.: Phila. Dir. 1822–55. "C. and W.-maker."

WASHINGTON STREET WATCH CO.: Chicago, Ill., 1872–74. W.'s made by Illinois W. Co. and sold mostly for Montgomery-Ward. (*Joseph Dean*)

WASHINGTON WATCH CO.: See Illinois Watch Co.

WATERBURY, CONN. "Old tx., including those of C.-makers destroyed by fire in 1880." (*J. L. Reeves*)

WATERBURY CLOCK CO.: Waterbury, N.Y., 1880s–1890s. A N.C. assembly plant location. "Vernon" labeled Waterbury kitchen C.—on back of back board—one of several seen by J. C. Folger.

*WATER, GEORGE F.: (?–1846). Keene, N.H., n/d. C., W., J. and store for J. on W. paper. (*George Scammon*)

WEINBERGER, JANOS: N.Y.C., 1946ff. apt. Europe to N.Y.C., 1939. Described as "golden touch on rpr."

WEISS, JOHN GEORGE: (1758–1811), Bethlehem, Pa., 1795–1811. Gunsmith who made locks and nails. Turned to C.-making ca. 1795. This name engr. on W. in J. W. G. Col.

WELBY CLOCK CO.: Elgin, Ill., 20th Cent. (*R. F. Tschudy*)

WELCH & GRAY: Bristol, 1830s (no tx.). Purchase books indicate clockmaking and assembling. These at American Museum of Time, Bristol, Conn. (*Shirley Morrell*)

*WELCH, ELISHA N.: (Feb. 7, 1809–Aug. 2, 1887 at Forestville) Bristol, from ca. 1850, became one of the largest and successful mfrs. of Am. C. and W. Many enterprises. Became first Pres. of Bristol Brass and C. Co.

1850 and actually was then started at C.-making. 1854 absorbed the Manross Clock businesses at Forestville, Conn., then in 1855, those of J. C. Brown; in 1856, Frederick S. Otis, thus combining the Cs. of John Birge, Elisha Manross, Irenus Atkins, Jonathan Clark Brown, and others, becoming 1864–1903 E. N. Welch Mfg. Co. In 1868 Welch, Spring & Co. was organized separately but combined in 1884. This firm made also Lewis Cal. C.'s. "Eureka" was one trade name used on 8-day alarm, striking hrs. C.'s. In 1903 became The Sessions Clock Co.

WELCH, H. M. & CO.: (Harmanus) Plainville, Conn., ca. 1840. Bro. of Elisha. To Plainville early 1830s, owning a lumber yard on Farmington Ave. Then owner general store on West Main St. Also a founder of Plainville Mfr. Co.—knit underwear. Mfg. C. ca. 1840, steeple shelf C. so labeled. E. Greer printer at 26 State St. (1838–47). Has brass spg. lyre type movt. like Terry & Andrews. Moved to New Haven in the latter 1840s. (*E.I.*)

WELCH, JOHN: Fincastle, Va., 1823. Adv. for an apt. for C. and W. reading "a boy of respectable conventions and sober habits, from 13 to 16 yrs. of age would be taken." (*Cutten*)

WELCH, VINE: (1735–?). Norwich, Conn. b. Norwich. Cherry-cased G.F. with heavy wood movt. extant.

*WELLS STEAM PRESS: Hartford, Conn., at 26 State St. Printers of C. labels for J. C. Brown & others.

*WELTON, ISAAC: Bristol, ca. 1830 (no tx.). Made G.F.'s 8-day brass movts. 1 in Hartford with unique case with cast glass columns. Also 3 decker shelf C. so labeled in Wesley Hallet Col.

WENTZ, HILARY: (1800–32), Phila. n/d. Son of C.-maker. Col. John Wentz (*R.H., J.W.G.*)

WESTCLOX: La Salle, Ill. 1895 organized as Western Clock Mfg. Co. After purchase by W. Mattiessen in 1895 reorganized the Co. and introduced American "Vertical Lever Watches" for the pocket. In 1910, Big Ben alarm tps. introduced. Baby Bens in 1915. Battery powered tps. from 1921; a/c electrics from 1930. In 1930, became part of General Time Corp. Wrist W.'s from 1936 as well as timers. Now one of the largest producers of American tps. Approx. dates of various models:

Baby Ben models:
Original 2 front-legged nickel cased—1915–27 1 A & 3 A, 1927–35. 61 N, 1935–39. 61 R, 1939–49. 61 V, 1949–56. 61 Y, 1956–64. Oval-faced, 1964 ff.

Big Ben models:
Original 2 front-legged nickel cased—1910–27. RD, 1927 ff. 69C, 1939 ff. 48d, 1939 ff. New oval form, 1964 ff.

WESTERN CLOCK MFG. CO.: La Salle, Ill., 1895–1930. See Westclox, now part of General Time Corp.

WESTERN CLOCK TOWER MANUFACTORY: Iowa City, Iowa, 1899. Formed by Joseph Barborks as D. in tower C. (*J. E. Coleman*)

WESTERN WATCH CO.: Chicago, 1880. Organized and f. Machinery sold to Illinois Watch Co.

WHITING, WILLIAM & CO.: Buffalo, N.Y., n/d. Label in shelf C. at American Museum of Time, Bristol, reads: "Riley Whiting Winchester, Conn., cased and sold by—."

WHITTEMORE, THOMAS: (1774–1845). Pembroke, N.H. 1800 ff. made maple cases for G.F.'s (*C.S.P.*) He made cases, may have purchased movts. Legally changed name 1829 to "Happy Thomas." Whittier, John Greenleaf, Haverhill, Mass. in one of his famous poems:—(John A. Sinclair) "With warning Hand I mark Time's rapid Flight."

WHITTLE, JOHN: Hopkinton, N.H. 1845 Adv. as C., W. and J. (*C.S.P.*)

WILBOUR, JOB (not Wilbur): Newport, R.I., 1853–63. C. and W. Ancestor of Hamilton Pease, horologist.

WILCOX, ALVIN: New Haven, Conn., at 63 Chapel St., n/d. "W.-maker" on W. paper at M.M.A.

WILKES, S. C. & CO.: Birmingham, Eng., after 1800. English dial maker—name cast in iron plate.

WILLARD & FRICK (J.L., F.A.) MFR. CO., THE: Rochester, N.Y. 1894. Organized to market the Cooper Card Time Recorder with trade name "Rochester." The time printing mechanism powered by S. Thomas movts. See I.B.M. (*Arthur Willex*)

*WILLARD & NOLAN (Aaron, Spencer): Boston, *ca.* 1806. Dials. On Nov. 15, 1806, adv. "Partnership Dissolved" and underneath adv. NEW CO. Partnership, Nolan & Curtis formed."

WILLARD, BENJAMIN: (1743–1803). Lexington, Grafton, Roxbury; *ca.* 1764–1800. Son of Benjamin Sr. and Sarah Brooks Willard of Concord, Mass. Oldest of the 4 C.-making bros. Now considered probable that early training as C. was with Nathaniel Mulliken at Lexington, *ca.* 1764–65 to *ca.* 1767 or later. Several of his fine brass-dialed G.F.'s have dials engr. "Lexington" and bear striking similarity to those of Nathaniel Mulliken. "It is difficult to believe that he would engr. 'Lexington' on a G.F. which he would have made in either Grafton or Roxbury, and if so, he must have been coached by Mulliken, Sr." (*A.L.P.*) In his book J. Ware Willard said that after Nathaniel 1's death, Willard may have stayed on and helped Nathaniel II, still young, with C.-making. He also commented on the similarity of the G.F.'s of both. Benjamin is also credited with instructing his 3 bros. in the art of C.-making. In 1771, he adv. "Clocks may still be had from the Factory at Lexington." Then, for a time he seemed to be elsewhere for in 1783 he adv. "After 8 years absence—" At Grafton, then Roxbury. d. at Baltimore. Excellent G.F.'s extant made by him.

WILLARD, J. L.: Rochester, N.Y., 1894. With F. A. Frick was Willard & Frick Mfg. Co., marketing the first time card recorder. See I.B.M.

WILLARD, SIMON & SONS: Boston, *ca.* 1828. And later, name used by Simon Jr. (*A. L. Partridge*)

*WILLARD, SIMON: (Apr. 3, 1754–Aug. 30, 1849). "A Volunteer from Grafton on the Lexington alarm. Rcd. a patent from U.S. Govt. for his improved tp. Appointed in 1791 to take care of the Church Clock—had charge of it for many yrs." (Hist. First Church in Roxbury, Mass.) Aaron Willard & Elnathan Taber also belonged to this Church (Howard Wilbur). Patent 1819 for "Alarm Clock" and signed by Pres. Monroe. "There is an alarm wheel with teeth like the pallet wheel—with small pallets on which the hammer is attached and reaching thru the clock plates on the other side—when let off—it strikes on the top of the case and makes a noise like some one rapping on the door—it will wake you much more quickly than to strike a bell in the usual way." Found on one of his labels inside a G.F.:—"Gentlemen will receive satisfactory evidence that it is much less expensive to purchase new than old and second-hand."

WILLEY, STEPHEN: Dover, N.H., 1830. Dir. as C. and W. (*C.S.P.*)

*WILLIAMS ORTON & PRESTONS: Farmington, Conn. Prestons is plural—label says, "Improved C. with Brass Bushings." (*Nelson Booth*)

WILLIAMS, J.: Alexandria, Va., 1795. adv. "From London, W. & C.—opened shop." (*Cutten*)

WILLIAMS, JEHU: (1793–1845). Lynchburg, Va., 1815–45. Partner with John Victor as S. As early as 1814 they were adv. as C.'s G.F. at Raleigh Tavern Williamsburg. Several owned in Lynchburg. (*Lockwood Barr*)

WILLIAMS, NATHANIEL: Dighton & Taunton, Mass. After Revolutionary War in which played active part. Also G.F. dial marked "N.W. Portsmouth, R.I." (*Theodore Waterbury*)

WILLIAMS, WILLIAM A.: (1787–1846). Alexandria, Va., 1809. Adv. formerly in Washington. Back 1835 till d. Mar. Catherine Ward in 1820. (*Cutten*)

*WILSON & OSBORNE: Birmingham, Eng., ca. 1772–1815. Makers of clock dials which were furnished to many American C.s. Often on G.F.'s only name on entire C. But not maker of the C. (*J.W.G.*)

WILSON, ANDREW DEXTER: (1854–1927). Providence, R.I., n/d. Made some banjos.

WINKLEY, JOHN: (?–1813). Durham, N.H., before 1813. C. (*C.S.P.*)

WINSTON, ALANSON: Bristol, n/d (no tx.). Standard 30-hr. wood movt. OG labeled "Extra C's. Warranted Good." (*Carlyle Alexander*)

WOLF & DURRINGER'S CLOCK HOUSE: Louisville, Ky., at 5th and Market Sts., n/d. Dealers overpasted label in one Terry Clock Co., Waterbury, Conn.

*WOOD, BERT FRANCIS: (1870–1952). Winchester, N.H. Had brass pieces from the old bell in town after the building was destroyed by fire—a Paul Revere bell—also made G.F.'s and banjos. Also designed and built automatic wheel cutter now in Selchow Col.

WOODRUFF, ISAAC B.: Winsted, Conn. 1883. Rcd. patent for alarm C. with rocking Liberty Bell mounted on the top of square metal case. Also used with black marblized wood cases. (*W. D. Butler*)

WOODWARD, ISAAC: (1789–1862). Amherst, N.H., n/d. C.

*WOOLSON, THOMAS, JR.: (1777–1837). Amherst, N.H., 1812. Built town C. Mfr. of machine cards 1813 and C. and W.-making business. Then to Claremont, N.H., where he was iron founder and stove maker, cards for carding wool. Made several tower C.'s. (*Hist.*)

*WRIGHT, CHARLES CUSHING: (1796–1854). Utica, N.Y., ca. 1815. Apt. to John Osborne at Utica, then to Homer, N.Y., 1816, then 1818 to Savannah, Ga. Burned out in big 1820 fire. To Charleston, S.C., as engr. 1824 to N.Y.C.

YALE, CHARLES M.: New Haven, Conn., 1865. Dir.—"Clock factory h.—10 Academy St." (No entry in business section.)

*YALE CLOCK CO., THE: New Haven, Conn., 1881, ca. 1885. 1st adv. "Mfrs. of 'The Yale Gem'—the smallest and most reliable Clock in the World"; "Other specialties in Clocks." Adv. 1882, "F. A. Lane's Patented Improvements in Clocks." Adv. 1883, plus 2 ills. of tps. "Novelties in Clocks." N.Y.C. office at 52 Maiden Lane; S. F. office at 528 Market St. Adv. 1884, "Novelties—Special Work Taken and Contracts made for supplying small brass work etc." Adv. (last) 1885—same as 1884. "F. A. Lane Sec. of Co.;—h.1312 State." In 1882 Dir. (*Helen Worobec, N. H. Library, J.W.G.*)

YATES, EURASTUS W.: Butternuts, N.Y., ca. first half 19th Cent. Also "ran hotel; made ox-bows; no reference as C. (*Galen*) Extant is a mirror shelf C. 28″ high with Torrington-type 30-hr. wood movt. (11¾ x 3¼ x 4¾″) label with spread eagle starts "Patent etc."

YEAKEL, ABRAHAM: Doylestown, Pa., from 1869. From Germany. Later to Perkasis, Pa., as C., W., J. and rpr. (*George Hotchkiss*)

*YOUNG, JESSE M.: Candia Village, N.H., before 1870. W. paper extant. Town officer, 1870; Tax Col. 1880–84. (*Robert Kline*)

YOUNG, L.: Bridgeport, Conn., n/d. "W.-maker & J." on W. paper at M.M.A.

*YOUNG, SAMUEL: Charlestown, Va. 1811. Adv. as C. and W. (*Cutten*)

*YOUNGS, ISAAC: (1793–1865). New Lebanon, N.Y., "1840" on G.F. Ill. ANT. Oct. 1957.

ZAUMSEIL, C.: Brown County, Ohio, 1859. Adv. "W.-maker from Germany." (*J.W.G.*)

ZILLIKEN, WM.: Pittsburgh, Pa., ca. 1850. Pos. C.-maker.